Is Jesus God?

What the Bible Says

Lyle Dockendorf

Is Jesus God? What the Bible Says
Copyright © 2012, 2024 by Lyle Dockendorf

Published in the United States of America

Library of Congress Control Number: 2024905563
ISBN Paperback: 979-8-89091-664-8
ISBN eBook: 979-8-89091-665-5

All rights reserved. No part of this publication may be reproduced, stored in a retrieval system or transmitted in any way by any means, electronic, mechanical, photocopy, recording or otherwise without the prior permission of the author except as provided by USA copyright law.

The opinions expressed by the author are not necessarily those of ReadersMagnet, LLC.

ReadersMagnet, LLC
10620 Treena Street, Suite 230 | San Diego, California, 92131 USA
1.619. 354. 2643 | www.readersmagnet.com

Book design copyright © 2024 by ReadersMagnet, LLC. All rights reserved

Book cover designed by Lyle Dockendorf

Table of Contents

Preface	1

Part 1 Premise — **11**
1. The Premise — 13

Part 2 Evidence: Jesus Is Not God — **25**
2. Overview: What the Bible Says about Jesus Not Being God — 27
3. God: Old and New Testament — 30
4. Jesus is a Person Separate from God — 39
5. All the Power is in the Father's Hands — 48
6. Jesus' Roles Are Inconsistent with Being God — 58
7. Jesus' Post-Resurrection Roles — 67
8. Refuting the Apologists' Claims: Part 1 — 70
9. Refuting the Apologists' Claims: Part 2 — 87
10. Negative Inferences — 95
11. Jesus Himself Indicates that He Isn't God — 104
12. Bible Inerrancy? — 107
13. Summary — 118

Part 3 Evidence: Jesus is Divine — **123**
14. Exploring Christ's Divinity — 125
15. Pre-existence — 128
16. Divinity — 137
17. Lordship — 148
18. Metaphors and Descriptors — 152
19. Who, Then, Is Jesus? — 155

Part 4 The History of the Dogma — **165**
20. The Historical Perspective — 167
21. Early Church History — 168
22. The Politics of the Establishment of the Trinity — 180
23. Athanasius' Discourse Against the Arians — 197
24. Historical Conclusion — 202

Part 5 Conclusion — **207**
25. Conclusion — 209

Notes, Bibliography and Scripture Index — **225**
Notes — 227
Bibliography — 234
Scripture Index — 237

Except as noted, the Scripture quotations contained herein are from the New Revised Standard Version Bible, copyright © 1989 by the division of Christian Education of the National Council of the Churches of Christ in the U.S.A., 475 Riverside Drive, New York, NY 10115-0050. Used by permission. All rights reserved

Some verses of Scripture are taken from the HOLY BIBLE, NEW INTERNATIONAL VERSION® Copyright © 1973, 1978, 1984 by International Bible Society. Used by permission of Zondervan Publishing House. All rights reserved. The "NIV" and "New International Version" trademarks are registered in the United States Patent and Trademark Office by International Bible Society. Use of other trademark requires the permission of International Bible Society.

Some verses of Scripture texts used in this work are taken from the Revised New Testament of the New American Bible, Copyright © 1986 by the Confraternity of Christian Doctrine (CCD), Washington, D.C. All rights reserved.

Preface

"What is truth?" Pilate asked Jesus during his trial.

Part of the answer to that question was standing before him: Jesus—the way, the truth and the life [John 14:6].

For me, honesty and an understanding of the truth have always been driving principles in my life. For example, in the present wrangling of American politics, I am constantly bothered—even outraged—by the half-truth rhetoric, innuendos, and even out-right lies that emerge from the candidates, their parties and supporters, and the media. Rarely do I hear a voice that provides the multiple sides of an issue in a dispassionate way so that I can make a genuine value judgment based on my other principles.

So it is with religion. Rodney Stark, in his defense against those who warp Christian belief because they cannot find (or actually prefer to ignore) historical evidence, says:

> Worse yet, rather than dismissing the entire historical undertaking as impossible, these same people use their distain for evidence as a license to propose all manner of politicized historical fantasies or appealing fictions on the grounds that these are just as 'true' as any other account. This is absurd nonsense. Reality exists and history actually occurs. The historian's task is to try to discover as accurately as possible what took place. Of course, we can never possess absolute truth, but that still must be the ideal goal that directs historical scholarship. The search for truth and the advance of human knowledge are inseparable: comprehension and civilization are one.[1]

Equally, Stark's statement should be applicable to religious dogma. I often find that an individual believer adheres so strongly to a particular belief or set of beliefs that dialogue about tenets is virtually impossible. Many of these beliefs are "inherited." That is, our culture, religious denomination, and our parents (and relatives) have imprinted upon us their own particular beliefs, often as unquestioned doctrine, and it becomes so strongly embedded that the painful surgery of the biopsy—the true examination of the validity of the belief, with the potential for radical surgery—the removal of that belief, is avoided and evaded, often for a lifetime.

But faith can be tragically misleading. Consider the basic religions of the world: Christianity, Islam, Buddhism, Hinduism, animism, atheism, and all the rest. Then also consider all the individual sects and offshoots of those religions. At least 95% of all people must be wrong in one or more important doctrinal aspects of belief.

God has blessed me with a drive to uncover the truth despite the pain. I grew up Catholic, and attended Catholic schools for twelve years. Because I grew up in the pre-Vatican II days, that older Catholicism seemed largely ritualistic—following the rules and attempting to avoid the guilt. Fortunately for me, Vatican II came along in my teen years, and truly turned the Catholic Church toward emphasizing the love of God. As a result, it fostered the first revolution in my life when a friend convinced me that I was still worthy to receive Communion even though I hadn't gone to Confession in the previous week. That was the first time I threw off a shackle of my old culture.

Since then, I have become aware of many questionable beliefs and practices that my religion espoused. Most of these doubts were instigated by well-meaning and proselytizing acquaintances of other Christian faiths, and some resulted from reading about the checkered history of the Catholic Church. But, like the political arguments I had become familiar with, I suspected that the truth lay somewhere in between. And so I was led on a path to resolve what that truth was. In a way, I was emulating the early Jewish Christian converts in Beroea who "welcomed the message very eagerly and examined the scriptures every day to see whether these things were so." [Acts 17:11]

Like mathematics, one must begin with a foundation—axioms and postulates as they were. I certainly grew up with a strong Christian bias. But I even questioned that. However, between the revelations of Saint Paul and the arguments of C. S. Lewis, I became convinced that I wasn't wrong in staying with Christianity. Jesus was an amazing man who was reported to say and do amazing things. And he said and did some odd things as well ("foolishness to the Greeks"). To paraphrase Lewis, either he was the Son of God or a lunatic. Those gospel and epistle writers of the First Century didn't just write stories that they had imagined. They were so convinced of their truth that most of them died as a result of their preaching and defense of that truth. After Pentecost they didn't run away. They declared that the actual Son of God had come down to earth, and allowed himself to die an excruciating and degrading death. But more radically, they claimed that he was also the first person to rise from the dead, not as if asleep, but in a glorified body. Since their beliefs didn't provide any earthly or temporal gains (wealth, power, status), I find them to be convincing witnesses to the truth of their story.

Yet how was the truth of Christianity passed on? And was it passed on reliably? Here, the early Church is intimately entwined with the information that was passed down. Multiple authors wrote multiple letters and documents in the first century after Jesus' death. Some of these written records could be traced back to the earliest times and so were well established; it was relatively easy to reach agreement that they represented the truth. But other documents were not. Early Church Fathers—those who would later be claimed as the true defenders of the faith—identified beliefs that ran contrary to what they perceived as the truth, and declared them heresies. Documents that supported these heresies were disregarded, and in some cases condemned. Thus, in an atmosphere of bias, disagreement and politics, as well as a drive for the truth, the main Church began to claim a particular set of writings that were to be considered the basis for truth: a Canon. Still, this Canon did not truly begin to solidify until the Fourth Century.

Thus, the New Testament came about. And it was strongly tied to the Jewish writings, which we term the Old Testament. This New Testament, then, became the foundation for Christian belief. And for most Christian religions it is the sole source of teachings and beliefs: *Sola Scriptura*, or "Scripture Alone." In contrast, for the Catholic Church Scripture is not sufficient. Instead, along with the Canon, they put an equal weighting onto "Tradition," the practices and writings that were passed down from the original Apostles and their immediate successors, plus what is called the Magisterium, the rulings of the Church. These three are considered equal.

Because of the care with which the New Testament was assembled, I basically put my anchor of belief in the "bulk" of the New Testament. Yet, there are two facts that strongly color what exactly I believe. The first is that these original documents were often argued about before their inclusion. Politics and power played a major role in regard to some of the books in a way that is not easily traceable. Secondly, what we have for texts are copies of copies of copies. In the process of copying, mistakes were made in transcription, and deliberate exclusions, additions, and combining took place. Those are the copies we have, and biblical scholars have done their best to try to figure out what the originals said. The results are some of the best translations we have. But they are not perfect. And we don't know which passages are original and which are not. Furthermore, unless we believe that the political body that determined the Canon was infallible, we don't know if any of the books actually contain theological errors.

What this means for my anchor in the New Testament is that I have confidence in the truth of what the spirit of the writings contain, and I firmly believe those tenets that are supported in multiple books—especially those whose authenticity are unquestioned. However, I do not have confidence in the accuracy of statements that only appear in one or two places. That is, I do not believe the New Testament is inerrant, except in its spirit. Certainly, the New Testament has its obvious contradictions. For example, the Synoptic Gospels claim Jesus died on the feast of the Passover; John's Gospel claims he died on the day before. Mark said the cock crowed the first time at Peter's first denial of Jesus; the other Evangelists state that happened only after his third denial. Although these do not affect any theological conclusions, they do point out that some words are incorrect. And we don't always know which ones!

In a similar vein, verses taken by themselves may not be trustworthy. In many cases, the context is important. Two examples are Old Testament prophecies that are applied to Jesus, and yet were clearly meant for a distinct historical person of the time; or a quote from someone (other than Jesus) in the Gospels or Acts that people might assume is a true literal statement. As it says in one of Shakespeare's plays "The devil can quote scripture for his purpose," and this is indeed what happens during Jesus' temptation in the desert.

Thus, I seek corroboration by multiple authors before I feel confident about any particular spiritual teaching. And I look skeptically at those beliefs which don't have that corroboration. I don't believe a faith or religion should be so reliant on rare or unique declarations. As for Tradition, I am more comfortable with those traditions established in the earliest times, when theological disagreements were settled amongst the Apostles and their first successors. As time progressed, belief became diluted with culture, and also became influenced by power and fear. In particular, the transformation in the Fourth Century Church resulting from Constantine's establishment of Christianity as the dominant faith was heavily tainted with power, wealth and politics.

From this I have concluded that Tradition (or new dogma) can never supersede "confident" Scripture. That is, if the Tradition claims a tenet of belief that is contrary to what can be found in various places of Scripture, then something is wrong with that Tradition.

This postulate is consistent with Origen, the great Christian scholar of the Third Century. His claim is to let the Bible speak for itself, since it is inspired by God. But he resists basing theology on single texts, where he describes that "the persistent tendency of heresy, whether ancient or contemporary, is to lay hold upon a few impressive texts and to wrench some rigid and erroneous interpretation from them. ... He wanted the whole Bible to speak, because he knew that what the Bible taught in its entirety are the central Christian truths of catholic Christianity."[2]

To some extent, the postulate also is supported by some modern Christian theologians. For example, the question and answer in Father Ray Brown's book <u>Responses to 101 Questions on the Bible</u> is illustrative:

Q. 14. I can see the need for some information supplied by scholars, but I don't see why we should be told that we are dependent on human interpretation of the word of God. Why such human intermediaries?

Every word in the Bible was written down by a human being, and so human attempts to understand the bible are perfectly appropriate aids. The use of human intermediaries is, in my judgment, intrinsic to the Judeo-Christian conception of God's actions.

Part of the problem involved in this type of question may be the recognition that scholars change their mind, and therefore, there is an uncertainty about the opinions one finds in notes and commentaries. That is part of the human condition. What one needs to avoid, however, is the idea that older views were safe and modern views are changeable. Older interpretations of the Bible were scholarly opinions of previous centuries; modern views are scholarly opinions of this century—neither has a privileged or unchangeable status. The reader should be responsible only for seeking out the best scholarship available. If there are better ideas in the 21st century, or the 22nd, let the readers of that future period worry about them. And if you object, "Were my ancestors in Christianity misinformed when they read the Bible with the views of their time?", the answer is that presumably they did the best they could with the information then available, and therefore fulfilled all their responsibilities. If we do as well with the information available to us, we can stand before the throne of God without guilt.[3]

To be fair to Father Brown, in his answer to the very next question, he defends Church dogma and doctrine from personal interpretation:

> The type of private interpretation that the Catholic Church distrusts involves doctrinal statements based on interpretations of the Bible that deny what has been taught in the creeds or in the official pronouncements of the church.[4]

Brown says that he personally has never encountered any contradictions with Church doctrine, but admits that if someone pointed out a real conflict, he could be wrong. Yet he would demand that "scholarly reasons be brought forward to show who is right and who is wrong."[5]

There are many beliefs which are ambiguously represented in the Scriptures. Is faith alone sufficient for salvation; or must our faith be manifested by our actions? When we accept Christ as our Lord and Savior are we saved for all time, unable to lose our salvation; or can we fall back? Support for each side can be abundantly found in the Scriptures. Nevertheless, these don't fall under the definition of dogma.

However, there is one article of faith, something which had its foundation developed in the Fourth Century, which is an accepted and well-known dogma: Jesus is God and co-equal with the Father. But this doctrine is not supported by Scripture. As uncomfortable as it is to say, it is actually contradicted by Scripture. There are over 250 passages and verses in the Bible which are inconsistent with this dogmatic teaching! And the purpose of this book is to address this doctrine and the many details of why it is incompatible with the Bible.

I first became aware of this potential error in Church teaching nearly 40 years ago. Since that time, I have read the New Testament much more carefully, seeking for a clarification of this issue, and looking at the precise words that were used. I sought to understand the reasons behind the Church's dogma, and how it might dovetail—or be contradicted by—other Scripture. However, each year that I studied, the stronger the body of proof against this dogma became, especially as I began to see both more obvious contrary evidence and just as importantly, more options in the interpretation or translation of the writings used to support the dogma. These alternatives significantly diminish their supportive power.

To test my own doubts, I still had to come up with another postulate. It is true that theologians and apologists have covered aspects of this dogmatic ground many times before. Perhaps there was hidden meaning present in these Scriptures that only the "Elite" could interpret! But let's test this assumption. The Gospels, Acts, and Letters were all written by common men inspired by an uncommon source. In the cases of the Gospels, and perhaps Acts, there were oral stories told from person to person which probably made their way into these written accounts. But when all these documents were written, were they expected to be read by the local elite who would then "translate" the story or letter into the people's common language? Or would they be read out loud, verbatim?

The answer is pretty obvious. These stories and letters must have been written so that the common man could understand them. As William Barclay emphasizes about St. Paul's letters:

> It was his [St. Paul's] aim to warn *every man* and to teach *every man*, and so to present *every man* mature in Christ Jesus. Against a salvation possible for only a limited intellectual minority, Paul presents a gospel which is for every man, however simple and unlettered or however wise and learned he may be.[6]

Therefore, for the most part, the writers must have been straightforward in their meaning and language (my postulate). That isn't to say that there sometimes wouldn't be local understanding of words or metaphors, nor even deeper meanings. But the main messages of these writings were intended to be accessible to the common man of that culture and time. Taking into account the culture of the time, when a simple explanation is justified by the readings, it seems that that interpretation is to be preferred.

Does this invalidate the need for exegesis, the deeper understanding of the background, history, culture and language that these words might be influenced by? Of course not! It's important to understand such things as that Matthew was written for a Hebrew audience and Jesus' sacrifice of himself was an emulation of the sacrifice of the Passover lamb. Or even that the Greek *logos* in the prologue of John's Gospel refers to something that doesn't directly mean the "Son." But in most cases this exegesis should supplement our understanding of the Scripture and not be the basis of that understanding.

(And indeed there are deeper meanings that we can access—especially with the help of the Holy Spirit—as we intertwine these inspirational words with our own particular experiences and circumstances. Of such is the manifestation of the Holy Spirit in our lives, such that we are led individually on a path closer to God. Sometimes these insights are more universal and good for devotional reading. But usually they do not apply to theology.)

Thus, as I encountered these many contrary passages, they began to speak much more loudly than the mere handful of passages that apologists cited to support the dogma. And as I looked more deeply into those special dogma-supporting passages, I came to realize that all of them either contained errors of translation, could be translated or understood in an alternative way, or for which other ancient, reliable sources—that were not chosen—had alternative words; and these different possible translations no longer sustained the dogmatic view. Simply stated, they were neither many nor conclusive. On the other hand, there were numerous passages that were directly contrary to the dogma, and which were clear and unambiguous. This book is my attempt to unveil all these relevant passages and put forth the "scholarly reasons" why the dogma should be questioned.

Interestingly, I discussed my concerns with a dozen people who were more knowledgeable than I was in theology, including Catholic priests, deacons and theologians (including a seminary professor), an Eastern Orthodox priest, a Protestant minister, and lay people. To some, the reaction was a quick dismissal—how could I possibly believe that! Others cited the standard "support" verses that I had cited as faulty. Still others claimed that metaphors were proof enough. One Catholic essentially implied that in the Church teaching, Tradition supersedes Scripture. With the single exception of one who brought up a minor and rebuttable point, no others came close to addressing any of the key passages which I had found. No one refuted my arguments. Instead they clung to the dogmatic teaching—some claiming that it was just a matter of faith.

Faith is not only a difficult thing to measure. It is also very difficult to understand. I firmly believe that the Holy Spirit can work through each of us, and I have even more confidence that it can work more powerfully through its collective body, the Church. Must this mean that everything the Church declares as inspired is actually inspired? Protestants would definitely say "no" to this, since they felt—justifiably—that serious errors had crept into the Catholic Church. Father Raymond Brown has written something very interesting that relates to this:

> First, in Catholicism dogma expresses divine revelation as interpreted by the teaching church. Therefore, it is perfectly possible to claim that the Bible, historically-critically considered, does not offer sufficient proof for a doctrine and still think the dogma must be accepted as infallibly taught because of church tradition. Sometimes such an approach has been dismissed as fideism {*author's note: fideism is belief that is based solely on faith*}. It would be fideism if one held that the church teaching was to be maintained even though the biblical evidence denied the dogma, or if there was no intelligible argument for a position of the church which goes beyond the biblical evidence.[7]

In my careful research, what I have discovered is that the biblical evidence apparently does indeed <u>deny</u> the dogma. I am now convinced that the evidence against that dogma is so powerful that I believe that the Church is almost certainly wrong (God does work *very* mysteriously at times, and He is not averse to throwing in a bit of confusion now and then. After all, we are reminded in Isaiah 55:9, "For as the heavens are higher than the earth, so are my ways higher than your ways and my thought than your thoughts."). But since I feel that God has insistently placed this truth within my understanding, I cannot remain silent about it. Indeed, just as Martin Luther defended his theses in saying he was "overcome by the Scriptures," so have I been overcome by what is written in the Bible. I have spent hours in prayer, especially trying to understand how this error could have continued so long; why God would allow it to go on. Perhaps this is the greatest source of any doubt that I have! But, as I have just written, God sometimes works very mysteriously, and it isn't always for us to understand why.

I am not trying to tear down the Church. In fact, I wish that I could just forget about it and get on with living the Gospel message. The friction has really been so very painful for me, that it would be far easier to stop my challenge of this dogma. I have no pride in this matter. My refusal to acquiesce to Church authority is not because I don't respect it, but because I believe there is a higher authority that I must first respect. I feel that it is God's will for me and that I have no choice.

I expect that there will be *ad hominem* attacks because I am only a layman with no formal theological background. How can this layman know more than the greatest theologians of the world? But my claim isn't based on some esoteric knowledge I possess. Rather it is almost entirely based on what the Bible and history tell us, organized in a fashion to be clear and convincing. The facts need to be argued, not the credentials.

And so I trust in God that this treatise will bring about something positive rather than division. I hope that it brings peace, and even joy, to those who have been discomforted by the inconsistencies between what they often encounter in their Scripture reading and the dogma they have been told to believe. I also hope that there may be an acceptance of what the Scriptures actually say about this "mystery," and that that revelation can perhaps bring more unity of understanding—and humility—among the various Christian churches and sects. God only knows what His ultimate plan is!

This revised edition contains only a few corrections and additions (yes, more supporting verses), and was necessitated because of a need to change publishers.

Finally, a word about translations. For the vast majority of the Bible verses quoted in this book I have used the HarperCollins Study Bible, the New Revised Standard Version (NRSV). Unfortunately, Bibles may be colored by their translators' biases. So I felt that it was absolutely essential to rely on a source that provided one of the best literal translations. The NRSV is derived from the Revised Standard Version, but which introduces changes "warranted on the basis of accuracy, clarity, euphony, and current English usage. Within the constraints set by the original texts and by the mandates of the Division [of Education and Ministry of the National Councils of Churches of Christ], the Committee has followed the maxim, 'As literal as possible, as free as necessary.' As a consequence, the New Revised Standard Version (NRSV) remains essentially a literal translation."[8] When comparing Commentaries' quotations of more literal meanings of specific verses, other than the use of inclusive language, I have found the NRSV to be excellent. Even if the given translation is not literal, such as with Philippians 2:6 or Luke 19:44, the study notes reference the more literal meaning. When an apparent conflict arises with regard to a reader's experience of certain verses, I urge that reader to investigate further into the more literal translations.

Part 1

The Premise

Chapter 1
The Premise

Introduction

Who can fathom the mind of God? Who understands His ways? Who can define "eternity," "all-powerful," "all-knowing," "omnipresent," or "divinity?" Yet church history is filled with theologians who have wrestled with these questions—and provided potential answers. Many of these answers were the result of applied logic coupled with what was known through ancient writings. But does this "logic" always serve believers well when we consider the true mystery of God? And has this logic been consistent with God's own revelation about Himself?

For centuries, most Christian churches have held as doctrine that there is one God, who exists as three divine persons: the Father, the Son and the Holy Spirit. This is the "mystery" of the Holy Trinity, in which these persons are considered co-equal and co-eternal within that Trinity. The doctrine is stated elaborately in the Athanasian Creed (probably developed in the Fifth Century), a creed that the Roman Catholics church and many Protestant denominations claim as essential religious truth. The first part of the Creed reads:

> Whosoever will be saved, before all things it is necessary that he hold the Catholic Faith. Which Faith except everyone do keep whole and undefiled, without doubt he shall perish everlastingly. And the Catholic Faith is this, that we worship one God in Trinity and Trinity in Unity. Neither confounding the Persons, nor dividing the Substance. For there is one Person of the Father, another of the Son, and another of the Holy Ghost. But the Godhead of the Father, of the Son and of the Holy Ghost is all One, the Glory Equal, the Majesty Co-Eternal. Such as the Father is, such is the Son, and such is the Holy Ghost. The Father Uncreate, the Son Uncreate, and the Holy Ghost Uncreate. The Father Incomprehensible, the Son Incomprehensible, and the Holy Ghost Incomprehensible. The Father Eternal, the Son Eternal, and the Holy Ghost Eternal and yet they are not Three Eternals but One Eternal. As also there are not Three Uncreated, nor Three Incomprehensibles, but One Uncreated, and One Uncomprehensible. So likewise the Father is Almighty, the Son Almighty, and the Holy Ghost Almighty. And yet they are not Three Almighties but One Almighty.

So the Father is God, the Son is God, and the Holy Ghost is God. And yet they are not Three Gods, but One God. So likewise the Father is Lord, the Son Lord, and the Holy Ghost Lord. And yet not Three Lords but One Lord. For, like as we are compelled by the Christian verity to acknowledge every Person by Himself to be God and Lord, so are we forbidden by the Catholic Religion to say, there be Three Gods or Three Lords. The Father is made of none, neither created, nor begotten. The Son is of the Father alone; not made, nor created, but begotten. The Holy Ghost is of the Father, and of the Son neither made, nor created, nor begotten, but proceeding.

So there is One Father, not Three Fathers; one Son, not Three Sons; One Holy Ghost, not Three Holy Ghosts. And in this Trinity none is afore or after Other, None is greater or less than Another, but the whole Three Persons are Co-eternal together, and Co-equal. So that in all things, as is aforesaid, the Unity in Trinity, and the Trinity in Unity, is to be worshipped. He therefore that will be saved, must thus think of the Trinity.[1]

This essentially defines what is meant when the terms "Trinity" or "Holy Trinity," emphasizing the capitalization, are used. This teaching as doctrine has a foundation that goes back to the Fourth Century, and has developed a longstanding tradition of development and ecclesiastical support. By human reasoning it is totally incomprehensible and self-contradictory. Thus, it is simply termed a "mystery" that Christians are to believe on faith.

As believers, we have assumed that this theological teaching is rooted in our primary source of information about God—the Bible. But what if a tradition or teaching contradicts what is in the Bible? Should we not question that teaching before we question the Bible? Certainly, we find frequent references to the Father, the Son and the Holy Spirit in the New Testament. But surprisingly, if we look diligently into the Bible to understand the Trinitarian relationship, we find only a single passage that names the Father, Son and Holy Spirit in a single verse, Matthew 28:19 (note that 1 John 5:7 is considered a very late add-on, and is not considered legitimate), and absolutely nothing that would support a co-equal status of either the Son or the Holy Spirit to God the Father.

Furthermore, if we uncover what the Bible says about the relationship of Jesus to God, we find a very significant number of passages which contradict the basic tenet of Jesus being God, and hence challenge that God can be a Trinity of three equal persons.

For example, during Peter's first speech on the day of Pentecost, he declares a substantially different view of the relationship between God and Jesus:

> This Jesus God raised up, and of that all of us are witnesses. Being therefore exalted at the right hand of God and having received from the Father the promise of the Holy Spirit, he has poured out this that you both see and hear . . . Therefore, let the entire house of Israel know with certainty that God has made him both Lord and Messiah (the Christ)... [Acts 2:32, 33, 36]

Paul similarly tells us in Philippians:

> Therefore God also highly exalted him and gave him the name that is above every name, so that at the name of Jesus every knee shall bend, in heaven and on earth and under the earth, and every tongue shall confess that Jesus Christ is Lord, to the glory of God the Father. [Phil. 2:9-11]

Even Jesus himself describes what is to happen after his death. During his Passion, when he appears before the Sanhedrin, he is asked if he is the Messiah:

> Again the high priest asked him, "Are you the Messiah, the Son of the Blessed One?" Jesus said "I am; and you will see the Son of Man seated at the right hand of the Power and coming with the clouds of heaven." [Mark 14:61-62]

If Jesus, the Son of God, was raised from the dead <u>by</u> God, exalted <u>by</u> God above all others, and then elevated <u>by</u> God to his own right hand, how can Jesus be God? Furthermore, St. Paul writes in First Corinthians:

> When all things are subjected to him [Jesus], then the Son himself will also be subjected to the one who put all things in subjection under him, so that God may be all in all. [1 Cor. 15:28]

This passage proclaims that the Son is also subject to the Father (at the end of the world). These four passages strongly indicate that Jesus is not God. If, in fact, these were the only four statements which gave that indication, we might find ourselves doubting that this evidence is sufficient to overturn the established doctrine. However, they are just a small subset of over 250 passages that support not only Jesus not being God, but also that <u>only</u> the Father is definitively and unambiguously called "God" as the Supreme Being of the universe. If Jesus is subordinate to the Father, how can we even consider him to be equal to God, the Father? Our Christian churches may have taught us that Jesus holds a throne in heaven as part of a Trinity of three equal persons, but the vast majority of relevant New Testament passages declares something radically different. They actually teach that God is completely separate from Jesus, and that Jesus, the Son of God, is subordinate to the Father.

Yet just as there is overwhelming evidence that Jesus is not God, there is also substantial evidence that Jesus is divine: he shares attributes of God, he pre-existed creation, and he has powers that only the God of the Old Testament had. These multiple passages either declare or imply a divine status for Jesus. Prominent among them are John 1:1 and Philippians 2:6:

> In the beginning was the Word; and the Word was with God, and the Word was God. [John 1:1]

> Christ Jesus, who though he was in the form of God ... [Phil. 2:6]

Although the first verse of John is often taken as positive proof of Jesus being God (ignoring all other passages to the contrary), it will later be shown that it is actually a mistranslation to say the Word—implied to be Jesus—is "God." Instead, it is better translated to mean a "God-likeness" for the Son. Both the John and Philippians passages require further elaboration since they are used frequently by the Church in support of its doctrine. But they do provide strong implications that Jesus is more than a man—to the point that many wrongly say these passages declare that Jesus is God.

Thus, we reach a point of apparent contradiction, a contradiction that early theologians wrestled with. How can Jesus, the Son of God, be God, and at the same time be subject to and subordinate to God, who is Father? And if Jesus is divine, how can he not be God?

The key to these questions rests with the answer to another question: must "divinity" be equated with "deity?" Already we may recognize that the Church has opted to answer "yes," to conclude simply that the Son of God is God, while basically ignoring the passages that declare his subordination. But if we really believe that the word of God in the Scriptures provides us with truth, we should feel very uncomfortable about blatantly ignoring a huge part of those

Scriptures that tell us that Jesus is not God.

In Part 2 we will explore the myriad of passages that declare Jesus' separateness from the being referred to as God and Jesus' subordination to Him, while in Part 3 we will explore those passages that imply or declare his divinity or Godhead. The purpose of this book is to explore the truth—what the Bible actually says about the relationship of Jesus to God—and contrast it with what religions have told us to believe, along with the passages they use to support that view. (This book will be different than most other books involving the divinity of Jesus, in that it will specifically address most of the Scriptural claims made by its opponents. That is, it looks at the evidence of <u>both</u> sides.) But we can only discover the truth if we earnestly seek it with an open mind, while submitting everything to the final test of God's word.

Now let's try to understand this apparent conundrum more deeply by exploring potential answers to the question, "must 'divinity' be equated with 'deity?'"

<u>Divinity?</u>

The New Testament does include quite a number of references from which one could infer that Jesus has a divine nature: "The Word was God" (John 1:1), he is the only begotten Son of God, he existed before creation, he participated in creation, the fullness of deity exists in him bodily, he does things (e.g. miracles and forgiving sins) which reveal the power of God, and many more. Since these statements are usually cited to make the claim that Jesus is God, they need to be explored—and addressed—in much more detail. This will be done both in Part 3, and in Part 2, Chapters 8 and 9, titled *Refuting the Apologists' Claims, Parts 1 and 2*. Indeed, the Son of God has so many attributes of divinity, that we should consider him divine.

But what do we really know about what divinity means? In 1884, Edwin Abbott wrote an insightful book called <u>Flatland</u> which gives us some hints about our ignorance. The residents of the Flatland world live in only two dimensions—essentially a large sheet of paper. Their visions and experiences are consistent with their world: they see things as points and line segments, there is only muted depth perception, and their movements are considerably constricted, at least to our way of thinking. Into this world intrudes a being from the third dimension. When his "body" intersects the Flatland plane, he suddenly appears out of nowhere to the Flatland residents. He can be in two places at once. He can easily see where each resident is, and can arbitrarily intrude wherever he wants. If he so desires, he can even see inside any resident. Even though Flatlanders cannot understand this third dimension, they are aware of something awesome in their presence. Is this God?

Even "The Wizard of Oz" has similar elements. Dorothy's Kansas is a black-and-white world. But when she enters Oz, everything is splashed with color. In a sense, a new dimension of color has been added to her perception which she didn't have before. If we could suddenly see infrared, ultraviolet, microwaves and X-rays, we would probably experience something similar.

Perhaps the supernatural is very much like this. God probably exists in a fourth or fifth dimension—or even something beyond that! Just as Flatlanders can't imagine the depth of what it means to be in a third dimension and a pre-Oz Dorothy couldn't have imagined what it would be like to see in color, can we dare to imagine what God's "universe" is like? Perhaps by analogy we can guess some of His powers (e.g. He can see anywhere inside us and reads our thoughts, just as though these thoughts exist in another dimension), but our attempts are feeble. We cannot have more than an inkling of what it means.

Also, we are already convinced that God exists outside time. As part of creation, he decreed the laws of physics which are all time based. He knows our future, and He can even change it; He is not bound by time. But who can even imagine what being outside time means? When we die and "go to heaven" we will inherit eternal life. Will we also then enter a realm where there is no time? To those restricted by time will we look as if we ourselves had no beginning and no end?

Simply put, it is impossible for humans to really understand the divine universe.

Theology is a risky enterprise! How can we truly surmise what God is all about through our own reason? Yet we have experienced two thousand years of theologians trying to uncover the truths of God. What are some means that are used to try to accomplish this task?

A first avenue is God's direct revelation to us, and this is primarily recorded in the Scriptures. Even here caution is necessary, first because translations do not always do justice to the meaning that the writer intended, and second because through the course of copying, these writings may have also been miscopied and even tampered with. But within this body of writing certain truths become quite evident. These will be explored in considerable detail, since they should provide the foundation and true test of any conclusions made about the nature of the Son of God.

A second avenue is more social. There are many who are able to take the biblical truths and extend them to our present circumstances. Sermons and homilies, as well as spiritual readings, all can bring to life how we should live and ultimately grow closer to God. We ourselves can also be enriched by our exposure to the Bible and other writings. For example, except in the case of hypocrisy, Jesus was non-judgmental. We can learn from his example and try to emulate it. For Jesus is the image of God.

A third avenue is more personal. We also are gifted by the Holy Spirit with insights and motivations that reveal God's love and plan. This is attested within the New Testament itself. Jesus believed that his original mission was solely to the Jewish people [Matt. 15:24]. The early church followed this direction, but then radically changed when it was directly revealed to Peter (Acts 10) and Paul (Acts 13:16, 46-48) that the Gospel should also be made available to the gentiles. This revelation to the Church has a direct scriptural foundation, being recorded in the book of Acts.

In a similar vein, we can all get to know God better as His Spirit acts through us as individuals. For example, in my own prayer time I have had analogies revealed to me. One of these involved understanding how we ourselves might share in—that is, inherit—some aspect of the kingdom of God. As one born in America, I get to share in the bounty of the country—the free beauty of its scenic parks, the roads, the bridges, the culture, etc. All these come as being a citizen of the United States. In God's kingdom, we will co-inherit and share in the bounty and beauty of heaven, with our leader, Jesus, providing the richest culture we can imagine. I better realize what lays in the future for me because of what I already have! However, it is important to realize that insights such as these generally may not be a 100% infusion of the Spirit into us. We bring our own culture, history and bias: God speaks to one personally, and generalizations to others are often inappropriate.

So these second and third avenues of knowing God may bring us closer to understanding His nature and loving Him, but they cannot stand as universal reliable witnesses for all believers. They are either too anecdotal or personal to have general applicability. They should not be used as the basis for theological belief.

Models, Analogies and Archetypes

A fourth avenue that is often a standard device of theologians is the "model." In trying to describe God they use symbols, analogies and logic. These models can often get us closer to understanding our limitations, and are useful insofar as they illuminate. For example, we know that God must exist outside of time and that He must exist beyond our restrictive three dimensions, so the "Flatland" analogy can provide some potential insight. But can anyone truly fathom what existing in four or more dimensions and outside-time means?

Analogies also go only so far, especially in the realm of the supernatural. Of course, the ancient writers also faced this limitation. Some were quite honest in admitting their ignorance. St. Paul tells us:

> What no eye has seen, nor ear heard, nor the human heart conceived, what God has prepared for those who love him. [1 Cor. 2:9]

St. John also has this to say:

> Beloved, we are God's children now; what we will be has not yet been revealed. What we do know is this; when he is revealed, we will be like him, for we will see him as he is. [1 John 3:2]

St. John in his Gospel also struggles with a similar concept when he refers to the Son as the "Word," or "*logos*." This expression had a much deeper meaning to the Greeks for whom John was writing, indicating something akin to God's will as action.

One important requirement of any model is that it is consistent with known facts. For example, Einstein's Theory of Relativity was essentially a model that could explain certain phenomena, and predicted other, yet-unobserved ones. One prediction was that gravity could bend light. This phenomenon was later observed, which gave substantial credence to Einstein's theory. In theology, most of the "facts' we possess are the Scriptures. Thus, any valid theological claim must be consistent with the written word of God.

There is credible evidence in Genesis that the Father and Son provide the archetype for humanity. It begins:

> Then God said, "Let us make humankind [man] in our image, according to our likeness..." So God created humankind [man] in

his image, in the image of God he created them; male and female he created them. [Gen. 1:26-27]

But note that God doesn't create man and woman at the same time. Adam comes first. When God creates animals to provide company for Adam, these are unable to provide appropriate companionship. God then puts Adam to sleep, removes a rib, fashions a woman from the rib, and then presents the woman to Adam [Gen. 2:21-22].

Thus, the woman isn't created from the dust like everything else, but is actually begotten from the original man. As we see from Patriarchal leadership, and indeed the male dominance predominant in the Old Testament, the woman is never considered equal to the man; she is to be obedient and dependent. So this pattern may describe the Father and the Son. The Son is begotten from the Father, but still remains subservient and unequal. In a real sense, he likely shares a part or even all of the "substance" with the Father, but does not have His fullness.

These "models," analogies and archetypes might help us surmise what God is truly like, but these models are only that—they are not necessarily the truth. And care must be taken to not declare them as truth. All else is speculation—but the danger is that speculation can become doctrine. And it seems that the Church of the Fourth Century has done exactly that, especially since that doctrine is not consistent with the Scriptures.

For lack of a better word, let us call God's "universe" a "divine" universe. And so the inhabitants might be called "divine" as well. Just as we presently live in a material universe delineated by three (supposed) infinite dimensions of space and a restricted unidirectional dimension of time, God's supernatural universe exceeds our own. It might not even be bounded! And as St. Paul has hinted, eternal life with God will involve entering some part of that universe.

To an extent, we already admit to a multi-level divine universe, although we call it "supernatural." Even St. Paul admits that there are "many gods and many lords" in heaven and on earth (1 Cor. 8:5). Most agree that angels and demons (fallen angels) exist in the supernatural realm—yet their regions of habitation are not equal. Were they created in time and exist only in time? The angels serve God, so they must be in His presence. But no one would call them co-equal with God just because they inhabit at least part of that divine universe. Thus, we recognize that there are different levels in the supernatural realm. This means that instead of assuming that a divine nature implies being God, we need to accept that divinity is an attribute of God rather than a definition. There are different levels of divinity, and God is at the highest level.

The Son of God exists within God's universe, and may even exist within the fullness that God enjoys. We cannot know except through God's own revelation, and there the Bible only sheds a dim light. As part of God's universe, Jesus shares in God's divinity. Yet the Scriptures are clear that he is subordinate. The Son is divine, but he exists at a level below the Father, who is God alone.

We already have a model for the divine universe in our own material world. Various living species rank in a kind of order of advanced capability from plant to animal, and animals rank from single cell organisms to a being capable of thinking and loving. There are clearly levels in the natural world. Why must it be different in a supernatural world?

God loves analogies! This shift in paradigm regarding divinity is further illustrated through the analogy of the human family—as exemplified by St. Paul in his writings (as "sexist" as this might seem in modern times). Within that family, the family members are not equal (except, of course, in the eyes of God). The father has the control; he assumes responsibility, he makes the decisions, and he holds the power. The son is subservient; he is expected to obey and give honor to the father. Discipline by the father onto the son is an expectation. The son is clearly not equal to the father, although both are human. To emphasize this point even further, the Salvation History of the Old Testament continuously follows families, especially fathers and sons. But the father is always superior—except at the risk of a son's insubordination and ultimate destruction, such as what happened with David and Absalom. In our own restricted world there are clearly different levels of power and ability. And we see in the Bible these exact roles being followed by God, the Father, and Jesus, the Son.

Taking this analogy one step further might also provide an important insight. God loves his only begotten Son more than we can imagine. However, although the Patriarchs may have died and left their favorite sons their inheritance, God will never die. But he wants his Son to have everything He has. The only way He can do that is to now share them with His Son, giving him what he can, and sharing what He can. For example, God had been Lord alone, and now He has elevated His Son to be lord, and share in that lordship with Him. He grants His Son His own prerogatives, so that now the

Son possesses the powers of God. Yet all these gifts and powers depend on God continuing to provide them.

This analogy makes sense more powerfully in the following way. A king may have a son, the prince. The prince has very little power of his own; he derives whatever respect that he has because he is the king's son. All power belongs to the king alone. However, the king may set up his son as his representative, or lord, in a district. To the subjects in that district, the prince acts as the king, and has the full power of the king—except that he himself is subject to the king. When the subjects see the prince, they are seeing the image of the king, and fully consider the prince their lord. The prince, even though of noble birth, is still not the king, and the king and the prince certainly are not equal. So the Son of God has been granted lordship on earth by God, but he is not the true king nor is he God. Yet to those on earth he appears to have all of God's power.

That leaves us with trying to understand the true nature of Jesus (as much as our minds can fathom it!). Perhaps the following may be a reasonable attempt. When we think of things divine, we rightly interpret them as things belonging to the nature of God. However, we also are prone to extend our definition so that when we speak of the divine, we are actually speaking *about* God. This doesn't have to necessarily follow. The difference is subtle but important. Mankind has the divine attributes of free will, creativity, and the capacity to love, yet we do not refer to humanity as God. In a manner of speaking, humans are like "gods" for these reasons.

Although fully human, Jesus possesses the complete array of divine attributes—as far as humans can tell. These are the results of two actions of the Father. First, he "begot" Jesus before time began. And secondly, he bequeathed power to his son voluntarily. Jesus, as the only begotten Son of the Father possesses the divine attributes, but not in the total fullness that God himself possesses.

The writers of the New Testament are very adamant in their declaration that Jesus is the "Son of God," which to them is quite distinct from being God. However, this title is not a denial of Jesus' divinity. This distinction is frequently the theme of many of their theological teachings and helps us in our understanding of the true nature of Jesus Christ.

With different levels of divinity, Jesus is divine but not God. God <u>allows</u> Jesus to participate in creation and the continuing salvation story, but it is not something that Jesus could do of his own intrinsic power. That is also why Jesus continually submits himself to the will of the Father. His Father is his God.

At this point, some readers may be tempted to reject the possibilities presented so far, declaring that this is a heretical viewpoint. Many church goers will declare that this is Arianism and the issue has been already decided—case closed! Indeed, in a sense, it is a form of Arianism (but read Chapter 22 for a better exposition about the Arian controversy). However, what has just been written about the subordination of the Son to God while possessing a divine status is entirely consistent with the Bible. If the reader truly believes that the Bible is the basis for truth, then ignoring or disregarding what is actually written there shows a great lack of respect for that book. In fact, it means that the reader has more faith in his church than in the word of God that provides the foundational information for that church. But if the reader instead attempts to view what the Bible says in light of the paradigm being suggested, he or she may gain a much fuller understanding of our God, and of His Son.

> If we receive human testimony, the testimony of God is greater
> [1 John 5:9]

Clarification

There is an added dimension of theological thought that I am choosing not to directly address in this book, and that involves the details of the nature of the Holy Spirit. There can be no dispute about the existence of the Holy Spirit, but the biblical evidence is much more vague about its nature than what is presented about the Son. Although it appears most often as a power of God, at times it does appear in a form that can be described as a person. Certainly, no direct evidence links it as being equal to the Father—a fact which should be taken as a strong negative inference that it is not. But, in short, to discuss the deity or divinity or even personality of the Holy Spirit would involve far too much speculation.

Thus, when the subject of Trinitarians or Trinitarian belief is raised in this book, it is primarily aimed at the compound belief expressed in the Athanasian Creed—that God is a Trinity of three co-eternal and co-equal "persons." But the primary belief of interest in this book involves whether Jesus is co-equal with the Father. If this part of the Athanasian Creed is not true, then the Trinitarian belief is not true.

Part 2

Evidence:

Jesus is Not God

Chapter 2

Overview: What the Bible Says about Jesus Not Being God

When we think of God, we think of the Supreme Being of the universe. In the first millennium of church history this view was expanded to state that there is one God in three persons—the Trinity. However, the Bible appears to say something entirely different: there is only one God, who is Yahweh and Father; Jesus Christ is <u>not</u> God, but the Son of God, who derives his power and glory from the Father—which makes him subordinate to the Father.

The Bible is filled with evidence for the above declaration. All we have to do is look for it! Unfortunately, our Trinitarian paradigm has masked the majority of those passages. Our pastors and ministers seemingly never address them: our liturgies may contain a few of the passages, but "larger" issues are instead brought forward in our sermons and homilies, because our doctrine has already decided the issue for us. Religious talk radio ridicules "deviant" objections, clinging to a few "tried-and-true" passages presumed to prove Jesus is God. And even the few references by theologians to these passages either provide a convoluted re-interpretation which is contrary to the passage's simple meaning or they wave their hands and say the pro-doctrine evidence "wins." Overall, we are intimidated into not questioning the real meaning of these important passages.

The purpose of Part 2 is to cite, and interpret, those passages which haven't been given their due consideration. For the most part, the interpretation will be extremely straightforward: the words can generally be taken at their face value! Of course, if we did this with only a handful of selected passages, we would be treading on very dangerous ground. Standard exegesis requires understanding far beyond that of an English translation with a Western view point. The New Testament was written by Israelite Jews living in a Mediterranean culture dominated by the pagan Roman empire. For the most part, it was written in Greek by Aramaic people for whom Greek was a second language. And the culture within it was written was flavored by a combination of Jewish, Greek and lesser philosophies.

But the proofs presented here will not depend on a few select passages. Instead, the theme of Jesus as the subordinate Son of God pervades every New Testament book. Surely, some of the passages could be re-interpreted with a deeper understanding and application of the historical culture within which they were written. But there is such a preponderance of the evidence, that if we reject it, then we must reject any hope of an ordinary individual reading the Bible and being able to reach the truth. We are forced to deny an assumed divine inspiration, since God would be playing tricks on us in only allowing the elite to be privy to his intended meanings.

That is absurd! The New Testament was written for the common man to hear and understand. The Gospels are the "good news" for the masses. Paul's epistles were expected to be read to the congregation, and copied so that his message could reach others. Thus, we will rarely err if we take the writings of the New Testament at face value. But we can more easily err if we hang our theology on just a few passages. Trinitarian theologians would agree with that, but that's what Trinitarians have done.

Preview

Part 2 has been laid out so as to categorize the different types of evidence supporting the position that Jesus is not God. Within the chapters numerous passages will be quoted along with related references that highlight the chapter's theme. Just as multiple witnesses are brought before a court to uncover the truth, it is hoped that these multiple passages, from multiple New Testament authors, will provide convincing evidence. The divinity of Jesus will not ordinarily be addressed in these chapters. His divinity is examined in Part 3. But realize again that the premise of Part 2 is that Jesus— even though he may be divine—is not God, nor an equal person in a Trinity which comprises God.

The general layout for this section is as follows:

- The God of both the Old Testament and of the New is depicted as a single personality, either as Yahweh or the Father, who is also the God of Jesus.
- The New Testament consistently references separately the Father and the Son, and frequently provides a context of superiority of the Father over the Son. Jesus is the son, he is an heir, he was sent by the Father, and he is always obedient to the Father.
- It is equally clear that the Father holds all the power, both before and after the resurrection. Jesus' power is derived from

the Father, the Father alone raised Jesus from the dead, God conferred on Jesus a Lordship, and the Son now "sits" in heaven at the right hand of the Father—a place of inferiority to the Father.
- Jesus possesses multiple roles which are inconsistent with being God, including being mediator between man and God and the high priest of God. He also acts as teacher, advocate, and Messiah. The Son is referenced as the wisdom, word, image, and power of God, all of which imply an issuing out from God, rather than being the integral person.
- In the end times, the Son will hand over everything he has been given and be subject to the Father.
- There are several negative inferences as well. If Jesus is God, why don't any of the New Testament authors directly say so? And can God sin?

None of these by themselves should be considered conclusive. However, when taken together (and these comprise over 250 passages), they provide an overwhelming body of evidence that avers that Jesus is not God in the way God has revealed himself, nor in the way expressed as a Trinity of three equal persons.

Chapter 3

God: Old and New Testament

God is the Supreme Being of the universe. Certainly, the exact nature of God is a mystery, since our finite minds can never fully grasp His reality. We can only hope to use our weak language to make pathetic approximations of His nature. Fortunately, we have been given revelations about Him in the Bible, and these must guide our thinking—and our faith.

Jewish scripture—the Old Testament—is adamant is saying there is only one God, whose name is Yahweh. This Jewish view, in opposition to the polytheistic nations surrounding Israel, created the basis for their monotheistic religion, and very much separated Israel from its neighbors. However, in the first millennium of the Common Era, the Church significantly modified this view to account for the entry into the world of the Son of God and the work of the Holy Spirit. The Church expanded the definition to state that this one God is three persons—the Trinity. This view became doctrine for most Christian churches.

However, there is a major dilemma, for the writings of the New Testament never contradict or even contraindicate the original Jewish view! In fact, the New Testament books are consistent with the Old Testament on this matter. That is, together they say that there is only one God, who is Yahweh and Father; and Jesus Christ is <u>not</u> God, but God's Messiah and the Son of God, who derives his power and glory from the Father—which makes him subordinate to the Father. Since a biblical view is essential to our understanding, we need to first explore what the Bible says about "one" God.

One God

Both the Old and New Testaments strongly testify to the existence of only <u>one</u> God. However, this one God is also identified as only a <u>single</u> person. In the Old Testament, that God is written with the name designated by our English approximation to the four Hebrew letters used: YHWH (Hebrew did not include the vowels). Standard English uses either the name Yahweh or Jehovah. Unfortunately, most of our Bibles (including the New Revised Standard Version, NRSV) obscure that <u>single</u>, personal name by substituting a much more impersonal "the LORD" (using all capital letters) for the

Hebrew "YHWH" in their text. What else can we make of the following?

> I am the LORD {YHWH} your God, who brought you out of the land of Egypt [Ex. 20:2]
>
> God said to Moses: "I AM WHO I AM." [Ex. 3:14]
>
> Hear O Israel: the LORD {YHWH} is our God, the LORD {YHWH} alone. [Deut. 6:4]
>
> For who is God except the LORD {YHWH}. [Ps. 18:31]

When God speaks to the people in the Old Testament, he universally speaks in the first person <u>singular,</u> as in the Exodus 3:14 quote. If he really is composed of three persons, might he not have revealed himself in a totally different way?

Some may claim that there is the use of plural forms for God in at least two ways. The first is during the creation of man and after his fall:

> Then God said, "Let us make humankind in our own image, according to our likeness." [Gen. 1:26]
>
> Then the LORD {YHWH} God said, "See the man has become like one of us, knowing good and evil." [Gen. 3:22]

Of course, this does not have to mean that God is a Dyad or a Trinity. The pre-existent, non-God Son could certainly be the one addressed, or there may in fact be more "sons of God" (as alluded to in Genesis 6:2) or other beings not of this earth whom God created outside our world's creation (e.g. similar to angels, which also aren't mentioned in the Creation story).

The second way comes in the common use of "*Elohim*" for God. The word is a plural form, but was also frequently interpreted in a singular sense—especially for the monotheistic Hebrews.

The Old Testament also sets a clear distinction between Yahweh, God, and his Anointed One, who is to rule God's Davidic kingdom. The Messianic Psalms give ample reference to a person distinct from Yahweh, such as when God says:

> "I have set my king on Zion, my holy hill." I will tell of the decree of

the LORD {YHWH}: He said to me, "You are my son; today I have begotten you." [Ps. 2:6-7]

The Book of Daniel also provides a distinct separation between God, who is described as "the Ancient One" (or more accurately "the Ancient of Days") and another individual who will be given God-like powers:

> As I watched, thrones were set in place, and the Ancient One took his throne, his clothing was white as snow, and the hair of his head was like pure wool; his throne was fiery flames, and its wheels were burning fire. [Dan.7:9]

> As I watched in the night visions, I saw one like a human being coming with the clouds of heaven, and he came to the Ancient One and was presented before him. To him was given dominion and glory and kingship, that all peoples, nations and languages should serve him. His dominion is an everlasting dominion that shall not pass away, and his kingship is one that shall never be destroyed. [Dan. 7:13-14]

Here we see not only a distinction between the "one like a human being," which we can easily identify as Jesus, but also that this individual is <u>given</u> glory and kingship from God.

In the New Testament, except in the Book of Revelation, God is universally addressed as the Father, and there is usually a strong differentiation between God and Jesus. As Christians, we have too often become complacent about using terms like "God the Father" and "God the Son," as if these were first, middle and last names. So we have adapted to the interpretation that when we see "God the Father" or "God our Father," we don't think that the actual meaning is "God." We should understand, too, that the original Greek used no punctuation. Thus, translators of the Bible are biasing their interpretations when they use "God the Father" rather than "God, the Father." We see another bias in the use of the name "Jesus Christ." "Christ" is one of the few (*Petros* = Peter is another) words that survives from the Greek; it means "Messiah." Thus, a better translation for today is "Jesus, the Messiah." Then Paul's greetings, such as that in Romans 1:7 would read: "Grace to you and peace from God, our Father, and Jesus, Lord and Messiah." In fact, if these two changes were consistently used, Christians would be far more inclined to view the Father alone as God. As a last note on nomenclature, in contrast to the frequent phrase "God the Father," there isn't a single, unquestionable biblical reference to Jesus as "God the Son."

In fact, while there are several Bible references that indicate that Jesus is God-like, there really are none that clearly indicate that Jesus is God (although a few ambiguous, and potentially misinterpreted passages in the New Testament, such as John 1:1, have been used to support that viewpoint). The very opposite is true! God is equated with the Father, as in many references such as the following:

> There is . . . one Lord, one faith, one baptism, one God and Father of all, who is above all and through all and in all. [Eph. 4:4-6]
>
> And this is eternal life: that they may know you, the only true God, and Jesus Christ whom you have sent. [John 17:3]
>
> For there is one God; there is also one mediator between God and humankind, Christ Jesus, himself human, who gave himself a ransom for all. [1 Tim. 2:5]
>
> Yet for us there is one God, the Father, from whom are all things and for whom we exist, and one Lord, Jesus Christ, through whom are all things and through
> whom we exist. [1 Cor. 8:6]
>
> for as all die in Adam, so all will be made alive in Christ. But each in his own order: Christ the first fruits, then at his coming those who belong to Christ. Then comes the end when he hands over the kingdom to God the Father... [1 Cor. 15:22-24]

These passages just cited highlight that there is one God, who is <u>not</u> referred to as three persons, or even two persons, but as <u>one</u> person--the Father.

Obviously, these verses vigorously challenge the current theology which doesn't differentiate Jesus from God. Thus, <u>any theology that holds that Jesus is God must also be able to address the passages just quoted</u>. The author has yet to encounter a rebuttal against these passages. Instead, apologists make non-related claims, citing a handful of passages. However, a later chapter will challenge the validity of the interpretation of those few passages frequently referenced that purport to support the theology that Jesus is God. Too often the arguments have only been in favor of those passages that appear to support the traditional view without ever addressing these conflicting passages.

The Father is the God of Jesus

The extension of the single personhood of God is evident in additional New Testament passages which clearly indicate that the Father is also the God of Jesus:

> Blessed be the God and Father of our Lord Jesus Christ, who has blessed us in Christ with every spiritual blessing in the heavenly places, ... [Eph. 1:3]

> I pray that the God of our Lord Jesus Christ, the Father of glory, may give you a spirit of wisdom and revelation as you come to know him. [Eph. 1:17]

> ... so that together you may with one voice glorify the God and Father of our Lord Jesus Christ. [Rom. 15:6]

> Blessed be the God and Father of our Lord Jesus Christ, the Father of mercies and the God of all consolations. [2 Cor. 1:3]

> The God and Father of the Lord Jesus (blessed be he forever!) knows that I do not lie. [2 Cor. 11:31]

> In our prayers for you, we always thank God, the Father of our Lord Jesus Christ... [Col. 1:3]

> Blessed be the God and Father of our Lord Jesus Christ! [1 Peter 1:3]

> To him who loves us and freed us from our sins by his blood, and made us to be a kingdom, priests serving his God and Father, to him be glory and dominion forever and ever. Amen. [Rev. 1:6]

> "I [Jesus] will write on you the name of my God, and the name of the city of my God, the new Jerusalem that comes down from my God out of heaven, and my own new name." [Rev. 3:12]

Even the Old Testament makes a similar declaration, although it does not specifically use the title "Father." In the famous passage from Micah 5, which cites that the Messiah is to be born in Bethlehem (the same message that is passed on to Herod when the Magi asks where to find the newborn "king of the Jews," and which Matthew 2:6 references as prophecy), Yahweh is called Jesus' God:

> But you, O Bethlehem of Ephrathah, who are one of the little clans of Judah, from you shall come forth for me one who is to rule in Israel, whose origin is from of old, from ancient days. Therefore, he shall give them up until the time when she who is in labor has brought forth; then the rest of his kindred shall return to the people of Israel. And he [the Messiah = Jesus] shall stand and feed his flock in the strength of the LORD, in the majesty of the name of the LORD {YHWH} his God. [Mic. 5:2-4]

Simply put: if the Father is Jesus' God, how can anyone extrapolate to a position in which Jesus is equal to the Father? But it is not just those who write about that relationship in a descriptive way that provides evidence. In the Gospels, Jesus also makes clear that God is someone else:

> Now during those days he went out to the mountain to pray; and he spent the night in prayer to God. [Luke 6:12]

> "I thank you, Father, Lord of heaven and earth ..." [Luke 10:21]

> At that time Jesus said, "I thank you, Father, Lord of heaven and earth, ..." [Matt. 11:25]

> "How can you believe when you accept glory from one another and do not seek the glory that comes from the one who alone is God?" [John 5:44]

> "It is my Father who glorifies me, he of whom you say 'He is our God.'" [John 8:54]

> "Do not let your hearts be troubled. Believe in God, believe also in me." [John 14:1]

> "And this is eternal life that they may know you, the only true God, and Jesus Christ whom you have sent." [John 17:3]

Here we have some of the most definitive declarations to be found in the entire Bible! Jesus is praying to his Father, his God, and plainly states a distinct separation as well as his role. His Father is the "only true God." This reference is singular as well. When apologetics are discussed later, it becomes paramount for supporters of the Trinity to be able to address these particular passages.

Jesus' temptation by Satan in the desert provides another reference to God as separate. Satan requests Jesus to jump from a height to show that God will send his angels to rescue him. Jesus' reply is:

> "Again it is written, 'Do not put the Lord your God to the test.'" [Matt. 4: 7; also Luke 4:12]

Jesus is clearly not talking about himself when he referenced "the Lord your God." He knows that there is Another who is greater, who is his God, too.

There is one particular verse that ties both the Old and New Testaments together in their affirmation of only one God who is Yahweh. It occurs when Jesus exclaims from the cross:

> "My God, my God, why have you forsaken me?" [Mark 15:34]

A reasonable discussion can be made as to whether Jesus is drawing attention to the parallels between his own suffering and what is recorded of an unknown person in Psalm 22 or if he is truly calling out to his Father. It is likely to be both. What is important is that Psalm 22 is clearly addressed to Yahweh, for this name appears in verses 8 and 19 of that Psalm as the one addressed. Furthermore, the prayer is also addressed to the tormented's God:

> On you I was cast from my birth, and since my mother bore me you have been my God. [Ps. 22:10]

Mark is making sure that the reader understands that Jesus is fulfilling a prophecy when he calls out to his God in his agony.

There is another interesting verse for which the context is important:

> Jesus said to her, "Do not hold on to me, because I have not yet ascended to the Father. But go to my brothers, and say to them, 'I am ascending to my Father and your Father, to my God and your

God.' " [John 20:17]

This last quotation, from Jesus himself to Mary Magdalene, occurred *after* his resurrection. Even in a "glorified" state, he distinctly separated himself from being God. Some apologists will claim that those previously cited quotations from Jesus in declaring only the Father is God result from Jesus' limitations as a human. That is, because he is still a man, he is unaware of his Godhead. This *could* be true, although it is highly unlikely based on his demonstrated knowledge of supernatural things. But the statement by Jesus after his resurrection to Mary Magdalene points to his complete awareness of being different than God.

Rather than ever writing that Jesus is God (the apparent declaration of "the Word was God" in John 1:1, is a mistranslation and will be discussed later), the New Testament writers—Jesus' apostles and disciples—provide a clear delineation between God, who is the Father, and the Lord, who is Jesus. And this is the collective testimony of several writers and not just one or two:

> But I want you to understand that Christ is the head of every man, and the husband is the head of his wife, and God is the head of Christ. [1 Cor. 11:3]

> ... and you belong to Christ, and Christ belongs to God. [1 Cor. 3:23]

> For Christ did not enter a sanctuary made by human hands, a mere copy of the true one; but he entered into heaven itself, now to appear in the presence of God on our behalf. [Heb. 9:24]

> James, a servant of God and of the Lord Jesus Christ. [James 1:1]

> ... Jesus Christ, who has gone into heaven and is at the right hand of God, with angels and authorities and powers made subject to him. [1 Peter 3:21-22]

> ... to the only God, our Savior, through Jesus Christ our Lord, be glory, majesty, power and authority, before all time and now and forever. Amen. [Jude 25]

> And we know that the Son of God has come and has given us understanding so that we may know him who is true, and we are in

> him who is true, in his Son Jesus Christ [1 John 5:20]

There is also a quote by Jesus in the Gospels that is relevant; it cites Psalm 110:1. Who else but Jesus could be referenced by the second "Lord?"

> For David himself says in the book of Psalms: "The Lord (YHWH) said to my Lord, 'Sit at my right hand until I make your enemies your footstool." David thus calls him Lord; so how can he be his son? [Luke 20:42-44; also Matt. 22:43-45, Mark 12:36-37]

These writers of the New Testament knew Jesus the best and were fully infused with the wisdom, power and inspiration of the Holy Spirit. Yet, they did not believe Jesus was God in the full sense, the Yahweh of the Old Testament. How can we know better?

Chapter 4

Jesus is a Person Separate from God

In the previous chapter, evidence was presented which stated that God is an entity separate from Jesus. In this chapter we will further explore how this separation is demonstrated, both in the way Jesus is described and how the Son of God is really subservient to God, the Father.

<u>The Son of God</u>

The most obvious evidence indicating that Jesus is different from being God is the fact that Jesus is, instead, the <u>Son</u> of God. The occurrence of this title in New Testament passages is overwhelming, although the Gospels themselves use the reference sparingly, such as in Matthew 26:63-64 and Luke 4:41 and 22:70. Perhaps the most powerful reference is what the angel says to Mary at the Annunciation:

> "And now you will conceive in your womb and bear a son, and you will name him Jesus. He will be great, and will be called the Son of the Most High, ... therefore the child to be born will be holy; he will be called the Son of God." [Luke 1:31-32, 35]

Nearly as strong is God's own testimony that occurs both at Jesus' baptism and at the transfiguration:

> And a voice came from heaven, "You are my son, the beloved; with you I am well pleased." [Luke 3:22; also Matt. 3:17 and Mark 1:11]

> ...and from the cloud a voice said, "This is my son, the beloved; with him I am well pleased. Listen to him." [Matt. 17:5; also Mark 9:7 and Luke 9:35]

The obvious interpretation of these passages should be that if someone is the son of another person, then they cannot be that person! Simply put, how can the "Son of the Most High" be the "Most High?" But apologists find no inconsistencies here in claiming a Trinity of one God. Rather than discuss this now, the intricacies of this topic shall be covered later.

This raises a very important question. Was Jesus autonomous? That is, did Jesus have his own free will, so that he could choose his own earthly destiny? In relation to the Trinitarian definition, how is a "person" actually defined? Usually, Trinitarians obscure any answer to this question, just as the Athanasian Creed evades understanding. But unless we can accept some reasonable definition of divine personhood, our acceptance of that Creed is fideism. If we are to believe in the redemptive work of the Son, we have to accept that Jesus was an autonomous being, with a will that was totally separate, although totally in concert with, the Father. He must be considered a separate person from the Father, who is God.

Although we will later return to the topic of Jesus being the Son of God, it is important to emphasize the multiple number of New Testament references to this title (although some are a little indirect (e.g. "God's son"). Just to cite a few of the direct ones: Romans 1:4, 2 Corinthians 1:19, Galatians 2:20, and 1 John 4:15. And finally, two strong examples:

> For several days he [Paul] was with the disciples in Damascus, and immediately he began to proclaim Jesus in the synagogues, saying, "He is the Son of God." [Acts 9:20]

> Whenever the unclean spirits saw him, they fell down before him and shouted, "You are the Son of God!" [Mark 3:11]

We certainly find numerous analogies in the Bible, and one of the most important is that of the family. It is in the Old Testament where Israel is an unfaithful wife. We see it in the reference of Christ being the groom and the Church being his bride (Eph. 5:25; Rev. 21:9). We see it in God being referenced as "our Father" (e.g. Matthew 6:9-13—the "Our Father" prayer). A common reference to believers is "children of God." Why, then, can we not claim the most obvious reason for the name "Son of God," that Jesus really is God's Son?

But from a more important familial and biblical perspective, the father is always considered superior to the son. This is most obvious when the children are minors, in which case they are considered little better than slaves. The father holds all the power. Consistent with this hierarchy, the New Testament also makes it clear that Jesus, the Son, derives his power from God. Thus, the analogy is complete with regard to the superiority of the Father. And if the Father is superior, they cannot be equal.

We see this theme of family brought up when Jesus is told that his family is waiting outside. But Jesus replies in a somewhat cryptic manner, essentially saying that those who do his Father's will are his relatives [Matt. 12:48-50]. With God as his Father, Jesus extends to his followers inclusion into this holy family. But they will do so on a plane that Jesus possesses—as direct relatives. There is another startling role of Jesus that is consistent with him being the Son of God—but separate from God. He is an heir! If Jesus is already God, then he already possesses all things by full right of being God. However, if he is an heir, then there is the strong implication that he indeed does not possess them by right, but by the will of the Father.

> ... but you have received a spirit of adoption. When we cry, "Abba, Father!" it is that very Spirit bearing witness with our spirit that we are children of God, and if children, then heirs, heirs of God and joint heirs with Christ—if, in fact, we suffer with him so that we may also be glorified with him. [Rom. 8:15-17]

> Long ago God spoke to our ancestors in many and various ways by the prophets, but in these last days he has spoken to us by a Son whom he appointed heir of all things, through whom he also created the worlds. [Heb. 1:1-2]

The passage from Romans is particularly telling. Here Jesus is essentially included not with God but with Christians, who all stand together to gain what God is offering through an inheritance. Of course, talking about an inheritance seems odd, because generally the inheritance results from a person dying. Since God will not die, then what must be referenced is more a share of what is owned by God. In a sense, believers will become co-owners of something mostly unknown, but something that Jesus now possesses as he sits at the right hand of God. Yet we do know that it will include the gift of eternal life.

Within that same theme we encounter a passage in Romans which is enigmatic if Jesus is God, but makes sense if he is not:

> For those whom he [God] foreknew he also predestined to be conformed to the image of his Son, in order that he might be the firstborn within a large family. [Rom. 8:29]

Here Jesus is completely associated with the human family. As a "firstborn," he takes on a very special role consistent with the previous verses we considered (Romans 8:15-17), amplifying their meaning in a larger context which implies Jesus' preexistence, but on a scale that separates Jesus from God as persons. This point is somewhat repeated in another of Paul's epistles:

> Just as we have borne the image of the man of dust [Adam], we will also bear the image of the man of heaven [Jesus].
> [1 Cor. 15:49]

One mystery that must be dealt with if the Son is equal to the Father is how power is divided between them. If they are equal, then the Son should be able to be independent of the Father with regard to power and authority. However, once again the New Testament is quite clear that the Son totally derives his power and authority from the Father.

God, the Father, Sent Jesus

One specific indication that the Father is superior to the Son is represented in the plethora of passages that say the Son was sent—by God, the Father. There is really nothing indicating that this was a cooperative decision in the sense that both the Father and Son jointly determined that it was propitious for the salvation of mankind.

In all, there are at least 30 New Testament passages which declare in one way or another that the Son was sent. John's gospel contains twenty-three of these references. Some are overt in declaring that God, the Father, sent the Son:

> [Jesus said:] "If God were your Father, you would love me, for I came from God and now I am here. I did not come on my own, but he sent me." [John 8:42]

> "And this is eternal life, that they may know you, the only true God, and Jesus Christ whom you have sent." [John 17:3]

> "This is the work of God, that you believe in him whom he has sent." [John 6:29]

John the Baptist gives testimony that Jesus is sent by God. He says:

> He who God has sent speaks the words of God, for he gives the Spirit without measure. [John 3:34]

Other overt references from John include 3:17, 6:44, 6:57, 12:49, 17:18, and 20:21. However, most others verses from John are passive:

> "... I am going to him who sent me." [John 7:33]

> "... because they do not know him who sent me." [John 15:21]

Other such references from John include 7:28-29, 8:26, 8:29, 9:4, 11:42, 12:45, 13:20, 16:5, 17:8, 17:21, 17:23, and 17:25. There is even another passage besides 8:42 in which Jesus says he comes from God; the verses in context indicate the sense of being sent, rather than being an actual part of God:

> "For the Father himself loves you, because you have loved me and have believed that I came from God. I came from the Father and have come into the world;" [John 16:27-28]

References from other sources may be subtle, but just as obvious upon simple reflection:

> "Whoever welcomes you welcomes me, and whoever welcomes me welcomes the one who sent me." [Matt. 10:40]

> "I must proclaim the good news of the kingdom of God to the other cities also; for I was sent for this purpose." [Luke 4:43]

> For God has done what the law, weakened by the flesh could not do; by sending his own Son in the likeness of sinful flesh ... [Rom. 8:3]

> God sent his Son, born of a woman, ... [Gal. 4:4]

> God sent his only Son into the world so that we might live through him. In this is love, not that we loved God, but that he loved us and sent his Son to be the atoning sacrifice for our sins. [1 John 4:9-10]

Five other verses echo the same idea: Matt. 15:24, Mark 10:45,

Luke 9:48 and 10:16, and 1 John 4:14.

Saint Paul echoes this same idea in being redeemed by the Father's act of sending Jesus:

> ... all have sinned and fall short of the glory of God; they are now justified by his grace as a gift, through the redemption that is in Christ Jesus, whom God put forward as a sacrifice of atonement by his blood, effective through faith. [Rom. 3:23-25]

Verse 8:32 of Romans echoes the same idea.

Jesus Obeys the Higher Authority

Jesus always follows the Father's will. Most Christians see this as an act of human submission to God, but miss the contradiction if Jesus is God. For then Jesus would more likely talk about "our" will rather than the "Father's" will. But when we see this in the context of Jesus not being God it makes complete sense. Once again, the New Testament provides multiple references:

> He [Jesus] said to them, "Why were you searching for me? Did you not know that I must be in my Father's house?" [Luke 2:49]

> "Abba, Father, for you all things are possible; remove this cup from me; yet not what I want, but what you want." [Mark 14:36; also Matt. 26:39, 42, 44 and Luke 22:42]

> "I do as the Father has commanded me ..." [John 14:31]

> Although he was a Son, he learned obedience through what he suffered... [Heb. 5:8]

> Consequently, when he [Christ] came into the world he said, "... Then I said 'See, God, I have come to do your will, O God.'" [Heb. 10:5, 7]

> ... he humbled himself and became obedient to the point of death—even death on a cross. [Phil. 2:8]

Simple Separation in the New Testament

Too often it is easy to miss the subtle indications of the language that presents Jesus, the Son, as separate from God, the Father. It may occur as simply as when God is referred to as "Father" alone, such as:

> We always give thanks to God for all of you and mention in our prayers constantly, remembering before our God and Father your work and labor ... [1 Thes. 1:2]

> Religion that is pure and undefiled before God, the Father, is this ... [James 1:27]

Often, the separation is even greater, and the New Testament is filled with such separation. The first type falls under the heading of "greetings." Here St. Paul regularly provides examples:

> Grace to you and peace from God our Father and the Lord Jesus Christ. [Rom. 1:7]

The exact (or nearly exact same) words are repeated at the beginning of all fourteen of Paul's epistles except Colossians (omitting "and the Lord Jesus Christ") and Hebrews (no greeting at all): 1 Corinthians 1:3; 2 Corinthians 1:2; Galatians 1:3; Ephesians 1:2; Philippians 1:2; 1 Thessalonians 1:1; 2 Thessalonians 1:2; 1 Timothy 1:2; 2 Timothy 1:2; Titus 1:4; Philemon 3. James' greeting is different, but provides the same separation:

> James, a servant of God our Father and of the Lord Jesus Christ. [James 1:1]

And even John has a like greeting in his second epistle:

> Grace, mercy and peace will be with us from God the Father and from Jesus Christ, the Father's Son, in truth and love. [2 John 3]

These greetings all sound alike in wishing a peace from God, the Father, and Jesus. Yet Trinitarians ignore the obvious absence of the Holy Spirit. If these authors believed that the Holy Spirit was God, or even a person intimately connected with God, they surely would have included him in their greetings. It is quite certain that they did not conceive of God as a Trinity of three co-equal persons.

A similar separation is observed every time "God," "God the Father" or "God our Father" is found with "the Son," "Jesus," "our Lord Jesus Christ," etc. This occurs in Romans 5:1 and 16:27; 1 Corinthians 1:9 and 15:57; 2 Corinthians 3:4, 5:18, 13:13; Galatians 1:15; Ephesians 3:21, 5:5, 5:20, 6:23; 1 Thessalonians 1:3, 3:11, 3:14; 2 Thessalonians 1:1, 1:12, 2:16; 1 Timothy 1:1, 6:13; 2 Timothy 4:1; 1 Peter 1:2, 2:5; 2 Peter 1:2; Jude 1. It is implied in Luke 2:52 and in the following:

> The child [Jesus] grew and became strong, filled with wisdom; and the favor of God was upon him. [Luke 2:40]

The book of Revelation gives a somewhat different perspective in using the word "lamb" for Jesus, but the separation is still strongly evident in such passages as:

> Salvation belongs to our God who is seated on the throne, and to the Lamb. [Rev. 7:10]

and six others: Revelation 11:15, 12:10, 21:22, 21:23, 22:1 and 22:3.

Every time we read "God" in a passage which also independently references the "Son" or Jesus, we are also witnessing another occurrence of how the Son is not God, for why would the authors create such an odd construction? Prominent among such passages is John 3:16:

> "For God so loved the world that he gave his only Son, so that everyone who believes in him may not perish, but may have eternal life." [John 3:16]

Of course, there are many other such passages stating the two separately, among them:

> "For it is on him [Jesus] that God the Father has set his seal." [John 6:27]

> "... but now you are trying to kill me [Jesus] who has told you the truth that I heard from God." [John 8:40]

> Martha said to Jesus "... I know God will give you whatever you

> ask of him." [John 11:21-22]

> ... as I testified to both Jews and Greeks about repentance toward God and faith toward our Lord Jesus. [Acts 20:21]

Sometimes this separation is expressed more strongly. Consider first the following passages when Jesus is being tempted by Satan in the desert:

> "Again it is written, 'Do not put the Lord your God to the test.'" [Matt. 4:7; see also Luke 4:8]

> "Worship the Lord your God and serve only him." [Matt. 4:10; see also Luke 4:12]

And also consider:

> For God, whom I serve with my spirit by announcing the gospel of his Son ... [Rom. 1:9]

> ... and live in love, as Christ loved us and gave himself up for us, a fragrant offering and sacrifice to God. [Eph. 5:2]

> ... do everything in the name of the Lord Jesus, giving thanks to God the Father through him. [Col. 3:17]

In summary, it is quite obvious that the New Testament writers were determined to show a distinct difference between God, whom they knew as "Father," and Jesus, whom they came to know as the Son of God. They understood the Father as the God revealed in the Old Testament, Yahweh, and they believed that Jesus, as Messiah, was both sent by that God and was being fully obedient to that God. And through his sonship, Jesus was also an heir to all that God possessed—not in the sense of possession after death, but in fully sharing God's life. In all this, God is clearly superior to the Son.

Chapter 5

All the Power is in the Father's Hands

In the previous chapter we saw how the New Testament authors drew a clear distinction between God, the Father, and his Son, Jesus. Through that familial designation, the patriarchal Jewish society would understand that the Father "stood" above the Son and had control over him.

However, this superiority involves far more than rank, for the New Testament writers were also quite clear that the Son was essentially powerless without the Father—that he was dependent on the Father as the source of his own power. The theme of this dependency also runs consistently through the entire New Testament, from his early public life, to Jesus being raised from the dead by God, and even after the Son joins his Father in heaven. As such, the Son could never be considered equal to the Father!

God Raised Jesus from the Dead

Two related expressions (or their equivalent) that are repeated throughout the New Testament are that "God raised Jesus" or that "Jesus was raised" from the dead. (The Easter hymn that declares that Jesus raised himself by his own power is bad theology!) This is not only a clear declaration of separation, but also that the power of resurrection resided with the Father and not the Son. This testimony is repeated at least 29 times in at least twelve of the New Testament books. This can be expressed in the passive voice as simply as Jesus being raised:

> He [Jesus] is not here; for he has been raised, as he said. [Matt. 28:6]
>
> ... he was raised on the third day. [1 Cor. 15:4]

The statements can also be expressed in a more active voice, and become even more emphatic, such as:

> But God raised him [Jesus] up, having freed him from death... [Acts 2:24]

> ... we testified of God that he raised Christ. [1 Cor. 15:15]

> Now may the God of peace, who brought back from the dead our Lord Jesus ... [Heb. 13:20]

> Through him you have come to trust in God, who raised him [Jesus] from the dead and gave him glory ... [1 Peter 1:21]

This last verse foreshadows even greater evidence that the Son is subordinate, for there is the added revelation that God has given Jesus glory—after the resurrection. Twenty- four other similar verses are: Matt. 20:19; Mark 16:6; Luke 9:22; Acts 2:32, 3:15, 4:10, 5:30, 10:40, 13:30, 13:33, 13:37, 17:31; Romans 4:24, 6:4, 6:9, 7:4, 8:11; 1 Corinthians 6:14; 2 Corinthians 4:14, 5:15; Galatians 1:1; Colossians 2:12; 2 Timothy 2:8; 1 Peter 3:18. One further verse that implies the power of God in raising Jesus is:

> In the days of his flesh, Jesus offered up prayers and supplications, with loud cries and tears, to the one who was able to save him from death, and he was heard because of his reverent submission. [Heb. 5:7]

But perhaps the strongest relevant verse attests to what St. Paul declares as a true article of faith:

> ... because if you confess with your lips that Jesus is Lord and believe in your heart that God raised him from the dead, you will be saved. [Rom. 10:9]

Are we commanded to believe that Jesus is God? Are we commanded to believe that Jesus raised himself? The explicit and implicit meanings are clear, and they do not support the Church's theology.

There are only two passages that indicate Jesus would raise himself up. Both occur in John's gospel. The first happens immediately after Jesus chases the money changers from the Jerusalem Temple:

> Jesus answered them, "Destroy this temple, and in three days I will raise it up." The Jews then said, "This temple has been under construction for forty-six years, and you will raise it up in three days?" But he was speaking of the temple of his body. After he

> was raised from the dead, his disciples remembered that he had said this; and they believed the scripture and the word that Jesus had spoken. [John 2:19-22]

Here is referenced one of many apparent contradictions that we encounter in a careful reading of the Bible and comparison of other verses. We will see later that John in his gospel and epistles is the New Testament writer who makes the most numerous claims relating to the divinity of Jesus, and we will discuss that in more detail. But first we need to be concerned that all the other writers make the claim either that "Jesus was raised" or "God raised Jesus," and ask if we should base our decisions on this single passage or of many. Even John, here, uses the phrase "after he was raised from the dead." Certainly in John's passage there is the inference that Jesus' quote refers to his own body, but note that we are basing this on the evangelist's interpretation. And if he truly believed that Jesus had raised himself, why didn't he change that subsequent phrase to "after he raised himself from the dead"? We have a contradiction within the passage itself! Also, in context, Jesus' statement is in direct reference to an actual Jerusalem temple. He may, in fact, be referring to his second coming, in which a new temple will already have been built—and recently destroyed by the enemies in Armageddon. John's inference could be incorrect.

The second passage of interest, which occurs immediately after Jesus' "I am the good shepherd" speech is:

> "For this reason the Father loves me, because I lay my life down in order to take it up again. No one takes it from me, but I lay it down of my own accord. I have power to lay it down, and I have power to take it up again. I have received this command from my Father." [John 10:17-18]

Verse 17 is quite curious! Does the Father love Jesus primarily because Jesus will sacrifice himself—with the knowledge that he will be raised from the dead? Note that this verse by itself does not imply Jesus will raise himself; only that he will receive life back again. Does verse 18 indicate that Jesus will take up his life again because the Father has commanded him to? Is this a conferring on the Son by the Father of an extraordinary power? If so, then the Father is still, strictly speaking, raising Jesus from the dead. Furthermore, this passage may take on the more simple meaning that Jesus can choose his own fate, and that he will be sacrificing through a free choice.

Here we are faced with double meanings.

Jesus' Power Is Derived Entirely from the Father

Saying that Jesus was sent by the Father and that he was raised from the dead by the Father are relatively weak statements of subordination. However, there are many other New Testament passages which make it quite clear that the Son totally derives his power and authority from the Father; these clearly indicate that the Father is the source of Jesus' power and that the Father is greater. We can see it hinted at already in Jesus' statement at the Last Supper:

"... because the Father is greater than I." [John 14:28]

But other verses are much stronger in their indication of where the power originates. Typical verses which highlight the source of Jesus' power are:

"All authority in heaven and earth has been given to me." [Matt. 28:17]

"He will be great and will be called the Son of the Most High, and the Lord God will give to him the throne of his ancestor David." [Luke 1:32]

"The Father loves the Son and has placed all things in his hands." [John 3:35]

"... the Son can do nothing on his own, but only what he sees the Father doing..." [John 5:19]

"... even as I also received authority from my Father." [Rev. 2:28]

Other verses echoing the same idea are Matthew 11:27, Luke 10:22, John 5:30, John 6:39, John 8:28, John 13:3, John 15:16, and John 17:2. There are certain other verses that follow with a similar theme, but point out somewhat different aspects of the Father's "gifts" to His Son, Jesus:

"You are those who have stood by me in my trials; and I confer on you, just as my Father has conferred on me, a kingdom."

[Luke 22:28-29]

"The Father judges no one but has given all judgment to the Son, so that all may honor the Son just as they honor the Father." [John 5:22]

For he [Jesus] received honor and glory from God the Father ... [2 Peter 1:17]

The Messiah is a frequent theme within the Old Testament, particularly in Isaiah. In many instances he cites the "suffering servant." In chapter 53 he makes a telling observation about this servant for whom "it was the will of the LORD {YHWH} to crush him with pain" [Is. 53:10]:

Therefore I [God] will allot him a portion with the great, and he shall divide the spoil with the strong; because he poured out himself to death, and was numbered with the transgressors. [Is. 53:12]

Thus, even in the Old Testament we find evidence that Jesus the Messiah will be gifted by God because of what he does. If the Son were God he would already have these.

Perhaps one of the most interesting illustrations of Jesus' relationship with the Father is described in the fifteenth chapter of John's Gospel. In verses 1 – 11 Jesus describes how he is the vine, we are the branches, and the Father is the vinegrower. In this analogy, the Son is totally a conduit for the Father's actions. The growing of fruit is surely a cooperative effort between the Father and the Son, but as the vinegrower, the Father holds total control over both the branches and the vine.

The dichotomy is strengthened in that the branches—the disciples—are directly a physical part of the vine. They are connected to and are of the same nature as the vine. Note, however, that the vine is not directly connected to the vinegrower. These are of different natures. In this analogy, Jesus could have been the vinegrower who prunes the branches of the vine, which would now be interpreted as his church. This kind of separation would have been appropriate if Jesus was God.

A final lesson we receive from these passages is how Jesus follows up the analogy. Jesus describes how his disciples are to abide in him, just as he abides in the Father—revealing a hierarchy with the disciples' dependency on him and his dependency upon the Father.

Jesus Is at God's Right Hand

Perhaps one of the strongest biblical distinctions that show not only the separation of the Son from God but also his subordination is the fact that the Son, in heaven, is seated at the right hand of God, the Father. During Jesus' times the act of being at the right hand of someone in power meant a position of prestige and also power, since one would be considered to have full access to the main person in power (e.g. the king) and also his trust. But this position and power was solely derived from the one in power, and did not exist on its own.

This position was well understood by the followers of Jesus, who saw him as being a likely ruler of some kind of future kingdom. It went so far that the mother of James and John asked for this position for her sons next to Jesus. But Jesus responds that he doesn't have the power to grant that! Who else holds that power, except the Father?

> [The mother of James and John said:] "Declare that these sons of mine will sit, one at your right hand and one at your left in your kingdom." [Jesus answered:] "... to sit at my right hand and at my left, this is not mine to grant, but it is for those for whom it has been prepared by my Father." [Matt. 20:21, 23]

The same story is told in Mark 10:35-40, although in that version it is James and John themselves who ask for this favor. Obviously, because the apostles then became angry with the "Sons of Thunder," this request was considered both bold and arrogant.

It is clear from numerous passages that Jesus was honored with this position next to God in heaven:

> "And you will see the Son of Man seated at the right hand of the Power, ..." [Mark 14:62; also Matt. 26:64 and Luke 22:69]

> So then the Lord Jesus, after he had spoken to them, was taken up into heaven and sat down at the right hand of God. [Mark 16:19]

> [Peter said:] "This Jesus God raised up, and all of us are witnesses. Being therefore exalted at the right hand of God, ..."

> [Acts 2:32-33]

> It is Christ Jesus, who died, yes, who was raised, who is at the right hand of God. [Rom. 8:34]

> So if you have been raised with Christ, seek the things that are above, where Christ is, seated at the right hand of God. [Col. 3:1]

> ... we have such a high priest, one who is seated at the right hand of the throne of the Majesty in the heavens, ... [Heb. 8:1]

Two other passages that repeat the same message are Acts 7:55-56 and Ephesians 1:20. A final relevant passage comes from 1 Peter:

> ... Jesus Christ, who has gone into heaven and is at the right hand of God, with angels, authorities, and powers made subject to him. [1 Pet. 3:21-22]

This last passage (as well as Acts 2:33, just cited) highlights another related theme that is important in understanding that the Son did not assume this position on his own, but was given it by the Father. Once again, if the Son was given his power, how can we understand him to be on an equal footing with the Father? Similar supporting passages are:

> "Father, I desire that those also, whom you have given me, may be with me where I am, to see my glory, which you have given me because you loved me before the foundation of the world." [John 17:24]

> The God of Abraham, the God of Isaac, and the God of Jacob, the God of our ancestors has glorified his servant Jesus ... [Acts 3:13]

God Made Jesus Lord

There is indeed a great deal of confusion that stems from the way "Lord" is used in the New Testament. Certainly the word was used to designate God. But it was also used in a more earthly sense to represent a person of high honor or ranking (and sometimes just to mean "sir"). Thus, we will see in multiple places "God the Father and the Lord Jesus Christ." But we also see Jesus being called

"Lord" while in his public life. Surely those calling him that weren't raising him to deity!

> And there was a leper who came to him and knelt before him, saying, "Lord, if you choose you can make me clean." [Matt. 8:2]

> ... but when he was not far from the house, the centurion sent friends to say to him, "Lord, do not trouble yourself, for I am not worthy to have you come under my roof..." [Luke 7:6]

> "You call me teacher and Lord—and you are right, for that is what I am." [John 13:13]

There are numerous other such passages, all of which show a sign of great respect and perhaps awe, but not to the point of considering him God. There are also numerous other passages that highlight the more broad definition. Most of these, however, translate the Greek "*kurios*" as "master;" yet that is exactly the word used in the passage of John 13:13 just quoted that has been translated as "Lord." To cite just a couple:

> Then his lord {*kurios*} summoned him and said to him, "You wicked slave!" [Matt. 18:32]

> Peter said, "Lord {*kurioe*}, are you telling this parable for us or for everyone?" And the Lord {*kurios*} said, who then is the faithful and prudent manager whom his master {*kurios*} will put in charge of his slaves, to give them their allowance of food at the proper time?" [Luke 12:41-42]

The important point here is that calling Jesus "Lord" neither indicates nor implies that he is God. In fact, the liberal use of the term in the Gospels is much more an indication of something else. So, when Jesus is called "Lord" in the epistles, it also doesn't imply deity as so many Trinitarian apologists insist. But in Part 3 we will explore in much greater depth what it can mean.

Ultimately, as believing and dedicated Christians, we understand Jesus to be <u>our</u> Lord. We are to give him control over our lives. This is more understood in the supernatural sense. However, do we fully understand why? It's because God himself made Jesus Lord over us! For example, Peter declares at Pentecost:

> "Therefore, let the entire house of Israel know with certainty that God has made him both Lord and Messiah, this Jesus whom you crucified." [Acts 2:36]

Later, Peter and the apostles answer the high priest and the council with essentially a similar message:

> "The God of our ancestors raised up Jesus, whom you had killed by hanging on a tree. God exalted him at his right hand as Leader and Savior that he might give repentance to Israel and forgiveness of sins." [Acts 5:30-31]

God, in bringing his Son to his right hand, has also exalted him, including giving him a lordship. The full understanding of this belief is expressed by Paul in the following two passages:

> God put this power to work in Christ when he raised him from the dead and seated him at his right hand in the heavenly places, far above all rule and authority and power and dominion, and above every name that is named, not only in this age but also in the age to come. And he has put all things under his feet and has made him the head over all things for the church, which is his body, the fullness of him who fills all in all. [Eph. 1:20-23]

> Therefore God also highly exalted him and gave him the name above every other name, so that at the name of Jesus every knee should bend in heaven and on earth and under the earth, and every tongue should confess that Jesus Christ is Lord to the glory of God the Father. [Phil. 2:9-11]

God has the power, but he gives it to his Son, unselfishly making him Lord over creation and the church. But if the power originates with God the Father, then he must be greater than the Son. A claim that God has made Jesus equal in all ways to himself seems unbelievable. This both defies logic and is nowhere supported in Scripture. Furthermore, this would clearly be a case of multiple gods and a rejection of monotheism—occurring after the resurrection. Yet this claim must be true for the Trinitarian doctrine to hold!

Finally, following virtually the same vein, we hear Jesus tell us where his glory is to come from:

> Jesus answered "If I glorify myself, my glory is nothing. It is my

Father who glorifies me, he of whom you say, 'He is our God,' though you do not know him." [John 8:54-55]

"Father, the hour has come; glorify your Son so that the Son may glorify you, since you have given him authority over all people, to give eternal life to all whom you have given him. And this is eternal life, that they may know you, the only true God, and Jesus Christ whom you have sent." [John 17:1-3]

In summary, God raises Jesus from the dead, glorifies him, exalts him, seats him at his (subsidiary) right hand in heaven, and makes him Lord. None of these happened to the Son except through the power and choice of the Father. These verses clearly contradict the Church's dogma that the Father and Son are equal in power, because all power actually comes from God, the Father.

Chapter 6

Jesus' Roles Are Inconsistent with Being God

Besides the obvious separation that has been demonstrated so far, there are also various roles that Jesus takes on that either indicate a further distinction of not being God, or are inconsistent with being God.

<u>Jesus is the High Priest of God</u>

The letter to the Hebrews takes on a significantly different slant from the rest of the New Testament with regard to the study of Christ. We will come back to many more of its relevant points in Part 3, but there is one description that it gives to Jesus that strongly highlights his subordination to his Father. In Hebrews he is described as a high priest of God in chapters 5 and 6.

> Every high priest chosen from among mortals is put in charge of things pertaining to God on their behalf, to offer gifts and sacrifices for sins. He is able to deal gently with the ignorant and wayward, since he himself is subject to weakness; and because of this he must offer sacrifice for his own sins as well as for those of the people. And one does not presume to take this honor, but takes it only when called by God, just as Aaron was.
>
> So also Christ did not glorify himself in becoming a high priest, but was appointed by the one who said to him,
> "You are my Son,
> today I have begotten you";
> as he says also in another place,
> "You are a priest forever,
> according to the order of Melchizedek."
>
> In the days of his flesh, Jesus offered up prayers and supplications, with loud cries and tears, to the one who was able to save him from death, and he was heard because of his reverent submission. Although he was a Son, he learned obedience through what he suffered; and having been made perfect, he became the source of eternal salvation for all who obey him,

having been designated by God a high priest according to the order of Melchizedek. [Heb. 5:1-10]

We have this hope, a sure and steadfast anchor of the soul, a hope that enters the inner shrine behind the curtain, where Jesus, a forerunner on our behalf, has entered, having become a high priest forever according to the order of Melchizedek. [Heb. 6:19-20]

A high priest was the intermediary between God and man. Now, the author of Hebrews declares, Jesus has been designated to be the eternal high priest. But the high priest was always on the human side of that relationship; that is, he was never God reaching down but man reaching up. Certainly, if Jesus is God there is something eminently bizarre in him as a priest offering up "prayers and supplications" to himself! And Hebrews continues:

For Christ did not enter a sanctuary made by human hands, a mere copy of the true one, but he entered into heaven itself, now to appear in the presence of God on our behalf. [Heb. 9:24]

Here we see that separation between the Son and God emphatically stated, with the role of Jesus implied—as high priest.

Sacrifice and Reconciler

Coincident with being the High Priest, Jesus also offered himself as a blood offering, a perfect sacrifice to God, for the atonement of sins.

... since all have sinned and fall short of the glory of God; they are now justified by his grace as a gift, through the redemption that is in Christ Jesus, who God put forward as a sacrifice of atonement by his blood, effective through faith. [Rom. 3:23-25]

... and live in love, as Christ loved us and gave himself up for us, a fragrant offering and sacrifice to God. [Eph. 5:2]

Sacrifices always involve a second party, someone or group that receives the sacrifice, usually as a positive substitute for something else, such as a transgression or debt. But if Jesus is God, then he is making a sacrifice to himself, which makes no sense. Additionally, Jesus' sacrifice also becomes consistent with Jewish practice. In ancient Judea, only one priest each year went into Jerusalem's temple's Holy of Holies to make a sacrifice. The food that was sacrificed was then delivered to the people to be eaten. This is what Jesus does, both as high priest and sacrifice, when he, the Pascal Lamb, says of his own bodily sacrifice: "Take, eat, this is my body" [Matt. 26:26].

God enters into this action by requiring Jesus to be the sacrifice, and in a sense He helps him to carry it out. In the Old Testament Abraham, greater than his son Isaac at the time, willingly does what he can to carry out God's instruction to sacrifice Isaac. For both Abraham and Jesus, the one who sacrifices is greater than the sacrifice. That is, in the case of the human Jesus, his act of sacrificing his temporal life results in an exaltation of his divine life. But God, who ordains both sacrifices, is greater than the ones who sacrifice.

Just as Jesus' act of sacrifice is a reconciling act toward God, Jesus himself is a reconciler. With Adam's sin, mankind had been separated from God's friendship. But Jesus' sacrifice atoned for Adam's sin and brought us back to where we could have a relationship with God:

> For if while we were enemies, we were reconciled to God through the death of his Son, much more surely having been reconciled, will we be saved by his life. [Rom. 5:10]

> All this is from God, who reconciled himself through Christ, and has given us the ministry of reconciliation; that is, in Christ God was reconciling the world to himself, not counting their trespasses against them, and entrusting the message of reconciliation to us. [2 Cor. 5:18-19]

Ephesians 2:16 and Colossians 1:20-21 echo the same idea. Jesus has become not just an intermediary between God and mankind, but has taken on a larger role so as to overcome the barrier that existed prior to his incarnation. God, by an act of will, could have effected the reconciliation by fiat. But He required something else—a bridge between Himself and man: Jesus, His Son.

Messiah, Teacher, Servant and Mediator

The salvation story from Old Testament to New has as its focus a Messiah sent by God. This Messiah was to be both a king and a suffering servant, although the Jews at Jesus' time didn't understand that second role. The New Testament writers certainly recognize Jesus as that Messiah, being free in their use of the word "Christ," meaning "Messiah." For example:

> Simon Peter answered, "You are the Messiah, the Son of the living God." [Matt. 16:16; see also Mark 8:29 and Luke 9:20]

And specifically, the apostles taught that Jesus was the Messiah, not God:

> And every day in the temple and at home they [the apostles] did not cease to teach and proclaim Jesus as the Messiah. [Acts 5:42]

Of course, the New Testament is filled with attributing the title "Christ" to Jesus as in the last passage. But how is being the Messiah inconsistent with being God? The reasoning is subtle, as demonstrated through the following passage which Jesus speaks in the synagogue in Nazareth, quoting Isaiah:

> "The Spirit of the Lord is upon me,
> because he has anointed me to bring good news to the poor.
> He has sent me to proclaim release to the captives
> and recovery of sight to the blind,
> to let the oppressed go free,
> to proclaim the year of the Lord's favor." [Luke 4:18-19]

The anointed one was considered to be the Messiah, and the Spirit of the Lord rests on him. Who does the anointing but God himself? Who sends the Spirit except God himself? It is far easier to understand this Messiah as a person separate from God when the sentence structure delineates it as it does here. It also goes back to all those passages where it is clear that Jesus is sent by God, consistent with a Messiah sent by God—and separate from him. And finally, we have the strongest evidence in Peter's Pentecost speech:

> "Therefore let the entire house of Israel know with certainty that God has made him both Lord and Messiah, this Jesus whom you

crucified." [Acts 2:36]

This Messiah is also a servant, willingly doing the work of God. We see this in the fulfillment of the prophecies of Isaiah as the "Suffering Servant" (Isaiah 42:1-7; 49:1-7; 50:4-9; 52:13 – 53:12 and 61:1-3) and a message from Acts as Peter says:

> "The God of Abraham, the God of Isaac, and the God of Jacob, the God of our ancestors has glorified his servant Jesus" [Acts 3:13]

From this and many previously cited passages, it is clear that Jesus is the servant of the Father. But here is what Jesus says about servants and messengers:

> "Verily I tell you, servants are not greater than their master, nor are messengers greater than the one who sent them." [John 13:16]

Here Jesus is speaking about his apostles during the Last Supper, preparing them for their future role. But the words also apply to him, for he is both God's servant and messenger, and we will see that he amplifies this message a little later:

> "The Father is greater than I." [John 14:28]

Put in the context of Jesus' roles as servant and messenger, the superiority of the Father is vividly proclaimed! Apologists will claim that this inferiority is because of Jesus' current human state. But just as we have already seen many passages demonstrating Jesus' subordination, there are still many other passages that extend that subordination to Jesus' future heavenly state—which these apologists ignore.

One critical action that Jesus performs involves carrying out the work of salvation. First note in the following two passages how God stops his work after creation:

> And on the seventh day God finished the work that he had done, and he rested on the seventh day from all the work that he had done. [Gen. 2:2]

> For in one place it speaks about the seventh day as follows, "And God rested on the seventh day from all his works." [Heb. 4:4]

God rests after creation, so He may be sending His Son to complete the work of saving mankind from their sins. That is, Jesus is now responsible for completing any work necessary, since God is "resting." Note, however, that there is a slight conflict with these verses and John 5:17, where Jesus says that the Father is "still working."

In the same vein, Jesus' role as Messiah is a teacher, with his words originating from the Father:

> "But you are not to be called rabbi, for you have one teacher, and you are all students. ... Nor are you to be called instructors, for you have one instructor, the Messiah." [Matt. 23:8,10]
>
> "The words that I say to you I do not speak on my own; but the Father who dwells in me does his works." [John 14:10]

Jesus is also an advocate and mediator for us:

> But if anyone does sin, we have an advocate with the Father, Jesus Christ the righteous. [1 John 2:1]
>
> For there is one God; there is also one mediator between God and humankind, Jesus Christ, himself human who gave himself a ransom for all. [1 Tim. 2:5]
>
> But he [Jesus] has now obtained a more excellent ministry, and to that degree he is the mediator of a better covenant which has been enacted through better promises. [Heb. 8:6]
>
> For this reason he [Jesus] is the mediator of a new covenant ... [Heb. 9:15; also Heb. 12:24]

Another related reference can be found in Galatians 3:19-20. In a parable repeated in all three Synoptic Gospels [Matt. 21:33-45, Mark 12:1-12, Luke 20:9-19], the owner of a vineyard leases it out to tenants who won't respect their contract. After these tenants abuse the owner's servants, he sends his son, in a sense as mediator. But they kill him. Clearly the parable is about God sending his son to Israel, something that the listeners recognize.

Does it make sense that God acts as his own servant? That God acts directly as a teacher? That God acts as mediator between humanity and himself? That must be our conclusion if Jesus is God.

But instead, we see Jesus in an intermediate and intermediary role, clearly distinct from God, the Father. And the distinction is not merely because the Son, as God, became human so that he could fully understand humanity (which must be the belief of Trinitarians). No, these passages highlight a clear separation, both as persons and as roles.

Cornerstone

There are several references to Jesus being a "cornerstone." In making reference to Psalm 118:22, Jesus essentially implies he is that cornerstone:

> "The stone that the builders rejected has become the cornerstone." [Matt. 21:42; also Mark 12:10 and Luke 20:17]

This same reference is made about Jesus by Peter as he witnessed to the "rulers, elders and scribes assembled in Jerusalem." [Acts 4:5-6, 11] shortly after Pentecost. And it is repeated one more time in 1 Peter 2:6. The Letter to the Ephesians provides a very plausible definition of what "cornerstone" means:

> ... but you are citizens with the saints and also members of the household of God, built upon the foundation of the apostles and prophets, with Christ Jesus himself as the cornerstone. In him the whole structure is joined together and grows into a holy temple in the Lord; in whom you also are built together spiritually into a dwelling place for God. [Eph. 2:19-22]

Jesus Christ is the cornerstone of the Church of God—essentially God's temple—in which God will dwell. This Church is not a building, but the collection of faithful believers and followers. A clear separation between Jesus and God is manifested, with Jesus being an integral part, but still a building block, of the Church that worships God.

Holy One of God

In the act of casting out demons, Jesus has some interesting dialogue. These demons know who Jesus really is, and it comes out in what they say:

> "Let us alone! What have you to do with us, Jesus of Nazareth? Have you come to destroy us? I know who you are, the Holy One of God." But Jesus rebuked him, saying, "Be silent, and come out of him!" [Luke 4:34-35; Mark 1:24-25 is similar]]

> "What have you to do with me, Jesus, Son of the Most High God? I adjure you by God, do not torment me." [Mark 5:7]

Similar passages can be found in Matthew 8:29 and Luke 4:41 and 8:28. It is interesting that Jesus is referred to as the "Holy one of God." Note that his title really refers to Jesus as the Messiah. And along with this, the strong references as the "Son of the Most High God" by beings not of this world show a clear distinction between God and his "Holy One." This Messiah is of God, but is neither referred to, nor implied to actually be God. There is a significant negative inference that Jesus is not God when this specific language is used. So when the demons cry out naming Jesus "the Holy One of God," they are fully aware of the distinction.

<u>Word, Power and Wisdom</u>

Certainly in human terms, when one speaks there are words. These words are clearly representative of who one is, but they are not the speaker. Similarly, if one holds and wields power, the acts of that power are again representative of the holder, but they are not the person. Finally, one's thoughts are intimately related to whoever has those thoughts, but they are clearly separate as entities from the person who has those thoughts. In each case, that which issues forth from a person may distinguish who that person is, but they can in no way be concluded to be the person himself.

But in the Bible we see these same activities of God being attributed to the Son. Does that make those activities God, or does it rather point to the Son being an entire person distinct from, but truly connected to God? Here are the passages to consider:

> In the beginning was the Word, and the Word was with God, ... And the Word was made flesh and lived among us, and we have seen his glory as of a father's only son, full of grace and truth. [John 1:1,14]

> Indeed, the word of God is living and active, sharper than any two-edged sword, piercing until it divides soul from spirit, joints from marrow; it is able to judge the thoughts and intentions of the heart. And before him no creature is hidden, but all are naked and laid bare to the eyes of the one to whom we must render an account. [Heb. 4:12-13]

> But to those who are the called, both Jews and Greeks, Christ the power of God and the wisdom of God. [1 Cor. 1:24]

> He is the source of your life in Christ Jesus, who became for us wisdom from God ... [1 Cor. 1:30]

Image of God

What is an image? It is something that represents, usually visually. We think of pictures and portraits, photographs and videos. Certainly the representation can be extended to abstract things. A child will often try to draw a picture of love, or sadness, or anger. In all these representations, however, the image is distinctly different—and less than—the person or thing it represents.

But note what Paul writes:

> He [Jesus] is the image of the unseen God ... [Col. 1:15]

> In their case the god of this world has blinded the minds of the unbelievers, to keep them from seeing the light of the gospel of the glory of Christ, who is the image of God. [2 Cor. 4:4]

Note that the Greek word for "image" here, *eikōn*, is the same word used to describe Caesar's face on the coin of tribute in Matthew 22:20 (and Luke 20:24 and Mark 12:16). By stating that Jesus is the "image" of God, the language used by Paul clearly is indicative that he understands Jesus to be something less than God. There is also a very strong negative inference in this description, since Paul could have chosen entirely different language if he believed Jesus is God.

On the other hand, this metaphor also has implications of divinity, which will be explored in Part 3.

Chapter 7

Jesus' Post-Resurrection Roles

In previous chapters we have seen that the New Testament tells us that Jesus, as the Son of God, acts as mediator and sits at the right hand of God. He is also the head of the church, and the head of every person:

> But I want you to understand that Christ is the head of every man, and the husband is the head of his wife, and God is the head of Christ. [1 Cor. 11:3]

Here Paul defines a distinct hierarchy! Trinitarians will attempt to warp such a passage to allow it say that since God is part of Christ, Christ must be God. But such arguments assume that passages like this should not be read in the simple context in which they appear. There are two problems with doing this. First, it means that select passages can always be chosen by a theologian for a re-interpretation, and that means that any passage can be re-interpreted according to a predetermined paradigm. However, this nearly destroys any person's ability to read and understand the Bible, since each verse must first be interpreted by the elite. It also implies that the Bible is too complex; it wasn't written for ordinary people.

The second issue can arise whenever there is any kind of re-interpretation. What happens when the "spirit" of that interpretation is extended? For example in the present passage, if Jesus is God, and God is the head of Jesus, then it should logically follow that man is God, since God, as Christ, is the head of every man. Rather, it makes far more sense to interpret the passage in a straightforward manner, accepting the hierarchy that is stated, but which puts the Son midway.

Within Paul's writings there is a particular passage which is quite clear in its meaning, but highlights Jesus' subordination to the Father in the strongest terms possible:

> ... for as all die in Adam, so all will be made alive in Christ. But each in his own order: Christ the first fruits, then at his coming those who belong to Christ. Then comes the end when he hands over the kingdom to God the Father, after he has destroyed every ruler and every authority and power. For he must reign until he has put all his enemies under his feet. The last enemy to be destroyed is death. For "God has put all things in subjection under

his feet." But when it says, "All things are put in subjection," it is plain that this does not include the one who put all things in subjection under him. When all things are subjected to him, then the Son himself will also be subjected to the one who put all things in subjection under him, so that God may be all in all. [1 Cor. 15:22-28]

When Paul uses the expression "it is plain," he says two things. First, what follows is expected to be obvious. Secondly, his followers should <u>already</u> clearly understand that God, the Father, cannot be subject to the Son of God, Christ. He then even clarifies this further by writing that the Son himself will be subjected to God. The construction is noteworthy. It doesn't say that the Son will subject himself, as if voluntarily; instead the language indicates a hierarchy of power. God is the head of Christ, as we just saw in verse 11:3, and was earlier stated in 1 Corinthians:

... and you belong to Christ, and Christ belongs to God. [1 Cor. 3:23]

This primacy of God extends through all time, over all beings—including the Son. And this is "plain" or obvious to Paul. There is no room for re-interpretation. In fact, this is an assumption that Paul feels is so obvious that it doesn't need to be repeated in the rest of his writings! Yet those who believe in a Trinity of three equal persons seemingly ignore this passage from chapter 15.

<u>Epistle to the Hebrews</u>

There is a tremendous amount of deep theology expressed in Paul's epistle to the Hebrews (although it is commonly believed by New Testament scholars that this epistle was not written by St. Paul). In fact, much of what we should believe about the Son and his relationship with the Father, as well as his roles, is beautifully expressed in this epistle. One of the principal earthly roles was a sacrifice! Since the synthesis of all the revelation about who the Son really is requires the exploration of his divinity, most of the references to the epistle to the Hebrews will be postponed to Part 3.

However, a few post-resurrection roles should be pointed out. First, he continues to be mediator, seated at God's right hand:

> We have such a high priest, one who is seated at the right hand of the throne of the Majesty in the heavens, a minister in the sanctuary and the true tent that the Lord, and not any mortal, has set up. [Heb. 8:1-2]

Secondly, Jesus is the ultimate high priest:

> For Christ did not enter a sanctuary made by human hands, a mere copy of the true one, but entered into heaven itself, now to appear in the presence of God on our behalf. [Heb. 9:24]

And finally, the Son will act again as a savior:

> ... Christ having been offered once to bear the sins of many, will appear a second time, not to deal with sin, but to save those who are eagerly waiting for him. [Heb. 9:28]

This final act of saving will be the lifting up to heaven of the "elect," to join with God for eternity—a final victory over death.

Thus we see that even in the post-resurrection state, Jesus performs roles that are separate from, and generally subsidiary to the Father. And this extends even past the end of the world and the Final Judgment.

Chapter 8

Refuting the Apologists' Claims: Part 1

Addressing Direct "Jesus as God" Passages

Abundant evidence has now been cited that supports Jesus not being God. Yet what of the evidence that apologists use to claim that Jesus is God? What is their proof? Do they find unequivocal scriptural support to say that Jesus is God, co-equal with the Father? In this and the next chapter, the various reasons that apologists put forward for "Jesus is God" will be addressed, and reasonable explanations will be offered which significantly diminish the "obviousness" of the conclusions that Trinitarians have derived from their chosen passages. In this chapter those passages which somehow are translated to say that Jesus is called "God" will be investigated. In Chapter 9, those passages which seem to imply a Godhead (such as Jesus saying "I am" will be explored.

What, then, are some of those critical direct passages upon which apologists base so much of their Christology? Father Raymond Brown, a respected Catholic theologian, wrote a treatise supporting the Church's view entitled <u>Jesus, God and Man: Modern Biblical Reflections</u>.[1] In the first section, subtitled "Does the New Testament Call Jesus God?" Brown presents his arguments. However, while acknowledging only a handful of the Jesus-is-not-God passages, he—like most other defendants of the church's position—fails to address them! Instead, he places extreme weight on three passages he claims "clearly" call Jesus "God": John 1:1, John 20:28, and Heb. 1:8-9. Let's first look at these three.

<u>Doesn't John 1:1 Directly Claim that Jesus Is God?</u>

Apologists for the Trinitarian view put extraordinary weight on one passage: John 1:1. Most common translations read:

> In the beginning was the Word; and the Word was with God, and the Word was God. [John 1:1]

Unfortunately, this verse is almost universally mistranslated! In the Greek, the word referring to "God" at the end of the sentence is not a noun; it is considered a predicate adjective (see, for example, the chapter on the Gospel of John in The Jerome Biblical Commentary, page 422[2]). William Barclay, in his book The Gospel of John, Volume 1, has this to say about the phrase "The Word was God:"

> This is a difficult saying for us to understand, and it is difficult because Greek, in which John wrote, had a different way of saying things from the way in which English speaks. When Greek uses a noun it almost always uses the definite article with it. The Greek for God is **theos** and the definite article is **ho**. When Greek speaks about God it does not simply say **theos**; it says **ho theos**. Now when Greek does not use the definite article with a noun that noun becomes more like an adjective. John did not say that the word was **ho theos**; that would have been to say that the word was *identical* with God. He said that the word was **theos**--without the definite article--which means that the word was, we might say, of the very same character and quality and essence and being as God. When John said *the word was God* he was not saying that Jesus was identical with God; he was saying that Jesus was so perfectly the same as God in mind, in heart, in being that in him we perfectly see what God is like.[3]

In the last sentence, Barclay might be giving more of his own interpretation when he uses the phrase "so perfectly the same as." For another view, Andy Gaus, in his Unvarnished Gospels, provides a version of the Gospels in which he tries to provide a straightforward and accurate translation that is not doctrinely biased. That is, he tries to get back to the meaning of the original Greek. He translates John 1:1 as:

In the beginning was the Word, and the Word was toward God, and God was what the Word was.[4]

In this translation in the third phrase the Word shared the nature of God. John is writing that, in a sense, they are of the same "genus" or "species." Perhaps a more accurate translation for John's line should be "the word was God-like" or "the word was divine." Even the strongly pro-Trinitarian book, The Three Persons in One God, uses the latter phrase in reference to John 1:1: "He [John] speaks of a Word 'who was in the beginning with God . . . who was divine.'"[5] Although the difference may appear insignificant or subtle, it is not. John had the opportunity to use the noun form of God and deliberately chose not to do so. He did <u>not</u> say "the word was God."

It is this difference between being God and being God-like that is central to this book.

There is, perhaps, another line of reasoning, but is weaker. Recall that John was writing primarily to a Greek audience, for whom *logos*, the Greek for "word," meant something like the active, participatory mind of God. (This comes from a Greek philosophy developed hundreds of years earlier.) Thus, even though John later writes "the word became flesh," it is not necessarily definitive (although it is likely) that the pre-existent "Word" is actually Jesus. This lack of clarity also sheds some doubt on what the Evangelist was truly trying to say. In any event, we must accept that John did not say "Jesus was God," something he could have directly said.

There is one other subtle note that is evinced by Gaus' translation and is further illuminated in the Preface by George Witterschein. In the second phrase in John 1:1 this part of the verse is rendered, "the Word was toward God." By this, John is indicating a movement of the Word *toward*s God, as if in a process of becoming united.[6] Clearly this now represents a separation between God and His Word

In John 20:28 Doesn't Thomas Declare Jesus to be God?

Having missed the first of the resurrected Jesus' appearances to the apostles, Thomas is confronted a week later with Jesus' real presence. Told by Jesus to put his hands into his wounds, Thomas replies:

"My Lord and my God!" [John 20:28]

What are we to make of this declaration? The most obvious interpretation, and the one apologists claim as the only interpretation, is that Thomas actually believes Jesus to be God. But does this mean that Jesus <u>is</u> God? There are several plausible and possible ways that it would not. First, realize that Thomas at that moment is overpowered in emotion! He might not be fully realizing what he is saying.

But along those same lines, Thomas understands something extraordinary has happened. He knows Jesus is now no ordinary man, having been miraculously raised from the dead and mysteriously appearing in their midst through closed doors. But he doesn't grasp how it could happen. He has no words in his vocabulary for such a being, and so he may be addressing Jesus as "my god" (they didn't use capital letters in the original Greek so we don't know). But that doesn't necessarily mean "God," the supreme being of the universe. In a way, this may be Thomas' simple way of expressing his belief that Jesus possesses divinity in much the same way that the Gospel of John has used "*theos*" instead of "*ho theos.*" (Incidentally, *ho theos* is actually used here in most, but not all ancient manuscripts.) We will see later that there are some Church Fathers who use "god" in relation to Jesus in a similar vein—but they may lack the appropriate vocabulary.

This or a similar interpretation is supported in <u>The Jerome Biblical Commentary</u>, where the importance of emotional expression as doctrine is downplayed:

> Although the idea of truth is to be applied to the Bible primarily as a whole, it is applicable also to parts of the Bible. This does not mean however, that truth is to be found everywhere in the Bible. The Bible is the word of God in human language, and human words are not used exclusively to express truth. ... Hence, the truth quality of the Bible is not to be looked for in the places in which, for example, the Bible is exhorting or is *expressing emotion*. [emphasis mine] It is to be looked for in the places where the Bible is concerned with communicating truth.[7]

Certainly, Thomas is in a very emotional state in verse 28. Already in John's Gospel he has been shown to have had a very pessimistic view of Jesus' future by despairing on the way to Jerusalem and expecting his own death [John 11:16] and utter disbelief in Jesus' resurrection [John 20:25]. But when the proof stands directly in front of him, he is flabbergasted!

Secondly, Thomas may have meant his expression in a way akin to a prayer. That is, perhaps he means it more like "my Lord, Jesus, and my God, Yahweh." This interpretation has some merit in that the usual expression to mean only a single person would have been "my lord and God," whereas the dual use of the word "my" would include the reference to two separate persons.

Thirdly, we need to realize that this is just something one man is reported to have said. And just because an ordinary human says something doesn't mean that it has to be true. The apostles said things that weren't true.* The Jews made several such incorrect

---

* The apostles misspoke several times, in the sense that what they said either wasn't true or wouldn't come true because that apostle couldn't carry through his

statements ("Surely the Messiah does not come from Galilee, does he?" [John 7:41] "Are we not right in saying that you are a Samaritan and have a demon?" [John 8:48]). One especially important example occurs after Jesus forgives a person their sins. The witnesses state that nobody can forgive sins except God. Yet Jesus himself later confers the power to forgive sins onto his apostles [John 20:23]. The natural conclusion for those using this argument is that the apostles are God, too.

Finally, but most importantly, it is critical to look a little further in John's Gospel. Just three verses later John writes:

> But these [signs of Jesus] are written so that you may come to believe that Jesus is the Messiah, the Son of God, and that through believing you may have life in his name. [John 20:31]

So the author chooses not to expound or amplify on Thomas' statement. He is interested not in declaring Jesus God, but rather emphasizes his being both the "Christ" and the "Son of God." If Thomas' declaration is so important and definitive, why not?

In summary, what is certain is that this statement is not an unambiguous declaration that Jesus is God. If the New Testament had another twenty statements of like manner, but with a greater urgency of certainty, then we could more confidently believe this as another witness. But instead, we have only a handful of similar but usually weaker statements and over 250 statements supporting a contrary view.

Doesn't Hebrews 1:8 Refer to the Son as God?

Father Brown also cites an important passage from the epistle to the Hebrews as extremely strong evidence for declaring Jesus to be God. It states:

> But of the Son he says, "Your throne, O God, is forever and ever, And the righteous scepter is the scepter of your kingdom.

---

intent. These include Peter's declaration that he would never desert Jesus (Mark 14:29), Thomas' statement that they should all go up to Jerusalem to die with Jesus (John 11:16) and Nathanael's put down of Jesus, "Can anything good come out of Nazareth" (John 1:46). Certainly the contexts are different, so this is weak evidence against John 20:28, but it does point out that the words of the pre-Pentecost apostles weren't always reliable.

> You have loved righteousness and hated wickedness;
> therefore God, your God, has anointed you with the oil of gladness beyond your companions." [Heb. 1:8-9]

Once again, another passage is cited which has an alternative translation! For in the eighth verse, the phrase "Your throne, O God is" can be translated as "God is your throne." Also the word "your" in the eighth verse modifying the word "kingdom" is rendered "his" in several manuscripts. Thus, verse 8 could actually be rendered:

> But of the Son he says, "God is your throne, forever and ever,
> And the righteous scepter is the scepter of his kingdom.

This second translation is completely consistent with the ninth verse where God is referred to as the God of the Son, which we have seen is overwhelmingly supported in the rest of Scripture. Furthermore, how can apologists claim a co-equal status of the Son with the Father from verse 8 when verse 9 calls God the God of the Son? This is a vastly important point that is conveniently and disingenuously ignored by Brown.

Even if the first translation is correct in Brown's final "clear" passage in Hebrews, we need to dig a little deeper. The Jerome Biblical Commentary notes "The application of the name 'God' to him [Jesus] is of no great significance; the Ps had already used it of the Hebrew king to whom it was addressed." [8]

Finally, we must recognize that the author of the epistle is citing a variant of Psalm 45 when he writes "but to the Son he says '*Your throne, God, is forever and ever.*'" Here is how Psalm 45 preferentially (NRSV) reads:

> Your throne, O God, endures forever and ever. [Ps. 45:6]

However, there are two other variants that are cited:

> Your throne is God, forever and ever.

> A throne of God, it endures forever and ever.

The note from the NRSV states: "The meaning of this sentence is unclear." However, this reading is far more consistent with the second translation offered, providing greater evidence that the second is correct. So once again, there are multiple interpretations, and a strong potential for an alternative understanding of the epistle which by no means makes this passage definitive.

Other Relevant, but Disputed Passages

There exist a few other passages which are often cited as more direct references in saying Jesus is God. The epistle to the Philippians provides one such passage that has been frequently quoted. The New International Version provides a common version:

> Christ Jesus: Who, being in very nature God, did not consider equality with God something to be grasped ... [Phil. 2:5, 6]

The NRSV is marginally different:

> Christ Jesus: Who, though he was in the form of God, did not regard equality with God as something to be exploited ... [Phil. 2:5, 6]

There are two very important, but separate observations to be made about this verse. In the first part, we need to note that the original Greek is correctly translated as "being in the form of God" rather than "being in very nature God." But this isn't exactly correct either: the former is too weak and the latter too strong. Barclay points this out[9] by indicating first that the Greek word for "being" references an existence in its essence; second that Greek word for "form" used here is an essential form that never changes. Paul is saying that Jesus, before his incarnation, was God-like in his essence. This is an important distinction, for a divine Son can be in the form of God, or have the essence of God, without being God. It also points out how translations can be subtly biased to fit a theology! Furthermore, the verse needs to be parsed more thoroughly.

The Jerome Biblical Commentary translates the verse: "...Who, originally in the form of God, considered it not a thing to be clutched at to be equal with God."[10] According to Bowman and Komoszewski in their book Putting Jesus in His Place, the word in Greek that is translated as "clutched" is used nowhere else in the Bible, and is rare in extrabiblical literature.[11] Thus the meaning is not definitive. However, the NRSV contains a note indicating that the word "clutched" in the passage is more accurately translated as "seized, as in a robbery." If this more accurate translation is substituted, then the meaning of the passage is significantly altered from what we would normally surmise from popular Bibles. Paul probably means that Jesus did not deem equality with God as something to be stolen!

Indeed, these more literal translations support the statement that Jesus is divine, with the nature of God, without saying Jesus is God. The rest of the passage in the NIV version liberally implies that Jesus may have had the right to consider himself equal to God. However, it seems to be better understood that Jesus was content with his divine status, and simply did not consider it important to be equal to God—perhaps in contrast to Satan who did choose to exalt himself. Or following the appropriate analogy that God, the Father, is king, and Jesus is His son with very limited power, Jesus does not feel driven to usurp his Father's power. Remember that sons of kings are often anxious to take over power, just as David's son, Absalom, tried to dethrone David.

There exist five other passages in the gospel of John which might seem to indicate Jesus' equality with God. The first passage occurs near the end of John's prologue:

> No one has ever seen God. It is God the only Son, who is close to the Father's heart, who has made him known. [John 1:18]

There are a couple problems with this passage. First, there are several instances cited in the Old Testament where someone sees God:

> Then Moses and Aaron, Nadab and Abihu, and seventy of the elders of Israel went up, and they saw the God of Israel. [Ex. 24:9-10]

> Thus the LORD used to speak to Moses face to face, as one speaks to a friend. [Ex. 33:11]

Of course, it is pointed out in Exodus 33:20 that no one can see the face of God and live, which brings up its own contradiction with verse 11!

> At Gibeon the LORD appeared to Solomon in a dream by night ... [1 Kings 3:5]

> When Solomon had finished building the house of the LORD and

the king's house and all that Solomon desired to build, the LORD appeared to Solomon a second time, as he had appeared to him at Gibeon. [1 Kings 9:1-2]

Then Micaiah said, "Therefore hear the word of the LORD: I saw the LORD sitting on his throne, with all the host of heaven standing beside him to the right and to the left of him." [1 Kings 22:19]

In the year that King Uzziah died, I saw the Lord sitting on a throne, high and lofty; and the hem of his robe filled the temple… And I said: "Woe is me! I am lost, for I am a man of unclean lips, and I live among a people of unclean lips; yet my eyes have seen the King, the LORD {YHWH} of hosts!" [Is. 6:1, 5]

I saw the LORD {YHWH} standing beside the altar … [Amos 9:1]

Were these just vivid dreams experienced by the "witnesses," or something else? Surely they must involve something more, since the encounter with God eventually bore spiritual fruit. Isaiah's statement particularly puts him at odds with John's Gospel. Thus, the weight of these Old Testament passages indicates that we really don't know what John means when he states "No one has ever seen God." To compound the problem, if Jesus is God, then the statement must be totally false, since people saw Jesus. Perhaps it can be argued that Jesus' godhead was veiled while on earth, but if he really didn't give up that godhead (as the Council of Chalcedon claimed in declaring that Jesus is true God and true man), then John is wrong. Furthermore, would not the resurrected Jesus be considered God— especially for those who believe that the disciples worshiped him just prior to his resurrection [Matt. 28:17]? We would really need to warp our interpretation to make Jesus-is-God fit. And finally, both Catholics and Lutherans believe that Jesus is fully present (both human and divine) in the Eucharist (Holy Communion). Surely the Breaking of the Bread was celebrated prior to the writing of John's Gospel, and thus God would have been seen—if Jesus were God.

The second part of the verse is also open to multiple questions. If the NRSV translation is correct, what did John mean by "God the only Son," since this contradicts the sentence immediately preceding it? Did John merely imply a divine status when he used the word "God," and not mean the one, true God? It is possible, since John later uses the word "god" to refer to human beings—and Jesus—in quoting Jesus:

> Jesus answered: "Is it not written in your law, 'I said you are gods'? If those to whom the word of God came were called 'gods'—and scripture cannot be annulled—can you say that the one whom the Father has sanctified and sent into the world is blaspheming when I said, 'I am God's Son'?" [John 10:34-36]

The second question about this passage involves the variance amongst various manuscripts. The NRSV has chosen this translation because it is based on the oldest available manuscripts. This is, of course, a very reasonable practice since manuscripts could be changed during the process of repeatedly being copied. However, that doesn't make this method infallible. And there are other reliable manuscripts that translate the latter part of the verse either as "It is an only Son, God" or "It is the only Son." The first of these alternatives is somewhat consistent with the NRSV rendering (and its different meanings), but the second clearly is not, and essentially removes any claim of a status of godhead for the Son. Thus, we are left with contradictions, ambiguity or a reasonable alternative, all of which remove much of the power of the claim of Jesus being God for this verse.

A third perspective is given by Barclay, who translates the entire verse as: "No one has ever seen God. It is the unique one, he who is God, he who is in the bosom of the Father, who has told us all about God." But rather than interpreting this translation in a straightforward way, Barclay writes that the use of "God" in this verse is identical to that of verse 1:1, and so he quickly states "This does not mean that Jesus is identical with God; it does mean that in mind and character and being he is one with God. In this case it might be better if we thought of it as meaning that Jesus is divine. To see him is to see what God is."[12]

The second relevant passage in John occurs after Jesus had cured on the Sabbath:

> Therefore the Jews starting persecuting Jesus, because he was doing such things on the sabbath. But Jesus answered them, "My Father is still working, and I am also working." For this reason the Jews were seeking all the more to kill him, because he was not only breaking the sabbath, but was also calling God his own Father, thereby making himself equal to God. [John 5:16-18]

Is John now claiming that Jesus is making himself equal to God?

Or is he stating what the Jews *thought* Jesus was doing by calling God his Father? Here, the construction is important, since John also includes in the same sentence that Jesus "was ... breaking the sabbath." This was an important commandment, and therefore Jesus would be sinning. Thus, the most likely interpretation is that the Jews were accusing Jesus of breaking the Sabbath and making himself equal to God. But John is not making that same claim. John understands more deeply Jesus' divine relationship with God, the Father, and better understands his subordination.

As a second comment on this verse, it seems a bit strange that a Jew would claim that the son would be equal to his father. This could happen, in a sense, in a succession sort of way, such as when a son succeeds his father upon the father's death. But few persons, for example, legitimately considered David's sons (whether it be Solomon or Absalom) to be equal to their father while David was still alive. Since God won't die, it seems strange for anyone to think the Son is God's equal. On the other hand, we believe in the Son's divinity, which puts him on a level above humanity—which he shares with the Father.

Another relevant statement from John involves an argument with the Jews:

> The Jews took up stones again to stone him. Jesus replied, "I have shown you many good works from the Father. For which of these are you going to stone me?" The Jews answered, "It is not for a good work that we are going to stone you, but for blasphemy, because you, though only a human being, are making yourself God." [John 10:31-33]

Here, it is essential to note that the Jews have inferred from Jesus' previous statements that Jesus is claiming to be God. But this is <u>their</u> interpretation, and need not be taken as a fact. Actually, Jesus then refutes their assumption! More will be said about this passage in Chapter 11.

The fourth statement from John which is often used to indicate that Jesus is God occurs when Jesus declares:

> "And whoever sees me sees him who sent me." [John 12:45]

Many have interpreted this to mean that those who were seeing Jesus were actually seeing God. This is obviously too simplistic! For the verse, if literally taken, must imply that those people were actually seeing the Father; that is, the Father was "cloaked" in Jesus' body or that both the Father and the Son were the same (this latter being a Sabellian heresy). Besides the problem of a literal interpretation, this verse is being taken out of its full context, which reads:

> Then Jesus cried aloud: "Whoever believes in me believes not in me but in him who sent me. And whoever sees me sees him who sent me." [John 12:44-45]

The context now represents a contrast. Belief in Jesus' words is actually belief in the Father's words, since God is giving them to Jesus to speak. Jesus is God's representative in all things; Jesus is God's image, so the people really see the Father through Jesus, rather than simply seeing Jesus.

Two closely connected verses in the fourteenth chapter of John's Gospel have nearly the same construction as 12:45. Jesus says to the Apostles:

> "If you know me, you will know the Father also. From now on you do know him and have seen him." [John 14:7]

> "Whoever has seen me has seen the Father." [John 14:9]

Once again, the context is important. The verses that surround these statements, verses 6 through 12, follow the same pattern as in chapter 12. And the choice is still either to conclude that Jesus is the full representation of God with the Spirit of God living within him, or that he himself is the Father. Verse 10 brings out a clarification in saying that the Father is actually dwelling in Jesus:

> "... but the Father who dwells in me does his works." [John 14:10]

Literally, this makes Jesus sound like an automaton, with the Father controlling Jesus' speech and actions. But we are also aware that the context actually implies the guidance of God's Spirit directing what Jesus does. Jesus still has free will.

It is important to point out that a given translation of the Bible that you are referencing may provide a passage that looks like it supports some aspect of the Trinitarian dogma. Such verses always need to be investigated more thoroughly, since biases by the translators may have crept in. The NRSV is not immune from introducing such a bias. Besides Philippians 2:6, here is another example that could influence readers, as Jesus laments the future of Jerusalem and its inhabitants:

> "They will crush you [the city] to the ground, you and your children within you, and they will not leave within you one stone upon another; because you did not recognize the time of your visitation from God." [Luke 19:44]

But the last phrase, "from God," is not even in the Greek (a clarification that the NRSV provides in its notes). What a difference that makes! If that phrase truly were there, readers might construe this as a reference that Jesus is God, since Jesus is the one who actually appeared and is making the "visitation." But Jesus is being intentionally vague, and prefers not to be saying that the visitation is from the Son of God.

Leaving the Gospels, apologists claim several other verses in "direct" support. One verse is found in Paul's epistle to Titus:

> ... while we wait for the blessed hope and the manifestation of the glory of our great God and Savior Jesus Christ. [Titus 2:13]

Unfortunately (for the apologists), this verse is either ambiguous or extremely dependent on its construction for its interpretation. The phrase "great God and Savior Jesus Christ" can be meant as two separate persons. Alternatively, Jesus may be being referred to as "the glory of our great God." An unambiguous interpretation is not available.

In the following passage in Romans, Christ can be considered above all the patriarchs. It cannot possibly mean that Jesus is even above the Father! And the last phrase is probably just a blessing on God.

> ... to them belong the patriarchs, and from them, according to the flesh, comes the Messiah, who is over all, God blessed forever Amen. [Rom. 9:5]

Admittedly, the Greek in this passage is such that a number of different interpretations are possible. We see in the NIV, once again, a bias toward a preferred interpretation which favors the standard doctrinal view:

> Theirs are the patriarchs, and from them is traced the human

> ancestry of Christ, who is God over all, forever praised! Amen. [Rom. 9:5 (NIV)]

To their credit, the NIV provides the alternative interpretation in their notes. But the reader needs to be aware that many translations carry similar biases—without necessarily providing alternate translations. Consequently, in studying and understanding the meaning of distinct passages, it may be important to compare to other translations, and sometimes to reference the original Greek.

Finally, there are two other instances where we encounter wording that has the near-direct interpretation of calling Jesus "God." In 1 Timothy we find:

> But for that very reason I received mercy, so that in me, as the foremost, Jesus Christ might display the utmost patience, making me an example to those who would come to believe in him for eternal life. To the King of the ages, immortal, invisible, the only God, be honor and glory forever and ever. Amen. [1 Tim. 1:16-17]

And in Jude we find the verse:

> For certain intruders have stolen in among you, people who long ago were designated for this condemnation as ungodly, who pervert the grace of our God into licentiousness and deny our only Master and Lord, Jesus Christ. [Jude 4]

Both passages could lead to a possible interpretation that Jesus is God. But again, we must recognize the basic *a priori* assumption that these writers had which always put God the Father at the top—a fact that they didn't feel necessary to repeat constantly. In Timothy, verse 17 surely refers to the Father; in Jude the "only Master and Lord" would still be considered to be under the Father—who is the <u>ultimate</u> Master and Lord. (Thus again we must recall Paul's words that "it is plain" that the Father is over all.) Furthermore, an alternative translation of the phrase in question is "the only Master and our Lord Jesus Christ." So the interpretation is also ambiguous. If we foolishly accept either statement in an absolute way, then we must be denying the Father as God.

Realize, too, that there are other verse constructions which are ambiguous, and which some claim to support a Jesus-is-God theology. One such passage is:

> To those who have received a faith as precious as ours through the righteousness of our God and Savior Jesus Christ: May grace and peace be yours in abundance in the knowledge of God and of Jesus our Lord. [2 Peter 1:1-2]

In the first part of the passage "God and Savior" could be referring to Jesus, but this interpretation is based on a biased theology, since "God" could more easily be referring to the Father, in a way much more consistent with the second part of the passage. In all these latter references, if the writers wanted to indicate that Jesus is God, why did they choose to use such veiled constructions?

The Old Testament also presents some passages that are ambiguous in their interpretation. Two of the principal verses appear in Isaiah. The first, which is Isaiah 7:14 also appears in somewhat amplified form in the Gospel of Matthew:

> All this took place to fulfill what has been spoken by the Lord through the prophet: "Look, *the virgin shall conceive and bear a son and they shall name him Emmanuel,*" which means "God is with us." [Matt. 1:22-23]

To some, this is interpreted as the child being God. But the verse can also easily be interpreted to mean that God is with us *in spirit* in a special way; that indeed, the reign of God is at hand, beginning with the presence of Jesus. To a fundamentalist interpretation it should also mean that the actual name given the child was "Emmanuel" and not Jesus (whose name means "Yahweh saves"). When it comes to Old Testament prophecy, in fact, it becomes very difficult to properly and literally interpret the meaning of the passages. We are reminded that the Jews erred in their expectation of a king in regal splendor as the Messiah based on their interpretations of the Scriptures.

The second Old Testament verse of interest is complicated. Although Christians have interpreted it as part of the Messianic prophecies, the Jews did not, for they never would have considered the Messiah was God:

> For a child has been born for us, a son given to us,
> Authority rests upon his shoulders; and he is named:
> Wonderful Counselor, Mighty God, Everlasting Father, Prince of Peace. [Is. 9:6]

If this "son" is really Jesus—and the context of the verse actually points back to Isaiah's time—then he is considered to be "Mighty God." But if we cling to this designation, we also must accept the name that immediately follows in the passage as well: "Everlasting Father." (We should not have the luxury to pick and choose within a verse.) Thus Jesus would actually be the Father, too! And that is an interpretation (the Sabellian heresy) we cannot accept. We are faced with a major dilemma in this verse from Isaiah, for no interpretation seems adequate. In such cases we must try to weigh all the evidence that we have from other sources as well.

The author is unaware of any other passages in the Bible that could be somehow interpreted (unless mistranslated!) as Jesus or the Son being distinctly referred to as God. And we have seen that the primary apologists' references are at best ambiguous, and at worst mistranslations or text alterations. If the writers of the New Testament really believed that Jesus was God, why did they *never* state that clearly?

It is interesting that other authors claim extreme clarity in these passages, and state that they clearly show Jesus is called God. For example, Bowman and Komoszewski in their book Putting Jesus in His Place, cite these same passages, often admitting the existence of alternative meanings, but never agreeing with them.✦ If there wasn't the preponderance of the weight of evidence supporting that the Father is God alone, then there might be a stronger propensity toward the Trinitarian view. But these and other such authors seldom address any of the evidence that is contrary to their belief, and instead cling to the paradigm of the Trinity.

✦ since the authors[13] are attempting to prove the deity of Jesus, they will, of course, interpret all these verses to support their view. Yet when it comes to the directly contrary verses, they take some very odd views, which lack validity. For some examples, they see Ephesians 4:6 ("one God and Father of all, who is above all and through all and in all") as referring to Jesus being over all (page 256); they claim that John 17:3 ("that they may know you, the one true God") "does not deny that Jesus is also the true God" (p. 353), which ignores the use of the word "one;" they essentially ignore the distinct separation shown in 1 Timothy 2:5 ("There is one God, there is also one mediator…, Christ Jesus") (p. 166); they even insist that 1 Corinthians 8:6 (There is one God, the Father, … and one Lord, Jesus Christ) means that Jesus is God, ignoring the obvious direct separation stated in the passage (p. 272); they convolute 1 Corinthians 15:22-24 ("he [Jesus] hands over the kingdom to God the Father") by first ignoring the clear separation, pointing out that Jesus' kingdom is to last forever in other scripture (e.g. Luke 1:33, and a valid objection to the passage in general), claiming a non-existent contradiction that it implies the Son isn't currently subject to the Father, and ignoring that Jesus will finally give himself to being subject to God, who also gave the Son everything (pp. 261-263)

Another important point regarding these passages that might be calling Jesus "God" is the oddness of their construction. When these verses are interpreted to identify Jesus as God, they always omit reference to the Father. Thus, the construction actually would beg a Sabellian interpretation, where the Father is also the Son. Why would the authors leave open such a possible heretical interpretation? This is yet another problem that the apologists would have to address.

Chapter 9

Refuting the Apologists' Claims: Part 2

Addressing Indirect "Jesus is God" Passages

Apologists also claim that a number of passages indirectly indicate that Jesus is God. These may fall under the simpler arguments that Jesus performed acts that only God could do, while ignoring the fact that God could have empowered Jesus to do just about anything, as he had for many of the Old Testament figures: Moses parted the Red Sea [Exodus 14] (a feat that rivals Jesus' calming of the storm); Elijah multiplied flour and oil and cured a deathly sick boy [1 Kings 17]; Elisha caused oil and bread to be multiplied, raised a dead boy to life and cleansed a leper [2 Kings 4, 5]. Indeed, Jesus power seems to be more intrinsic, but that power can still be solely from God just as it was for Moses, Elijah and Elisha.

Other passages involve deeper implications. Various translations indicate that Jesus was worshiped, he seems to have claimed God's name when he spoke "I am," and words used to describe God were also used of Jesus. These represent many of the other articles of proof that apologists offer. And in some instances they do imply a claim of divinity for Jesus—but that does not mean Jesus is God.

<u>Was Jesus Worshiped?</u>

Many translations of the Bible have passages where Jesus is worshiped. For example, the NRSV has the story in John of Jesus curing the man born blind:

> Jesus heard that they had driven him out, and when he found him, he said, "Do you believe in the Son of Man?" He answered, "And who is he, sir? Tell me, so that I may believe in him." Jesus said to him, "You have seen him, and the one speaking with you is he." He said, "Lord, I believe." And he worshiped him. Jesus said, "I came into this world for judgment so that those who do not see may see, and those who do see may become blind." Some of the Pharisees near him heard this and said to him, "Surely we are not blind, are we?" Jesus said to them, "If you were blind, you would not have sin. But now that you say, 'We see,' your sin remains." [John 9:35-41]

After Jesus and Peter walk on water, and Jesus rescues Peter:

> When they got into the boat, the wind ceased. And those in the boat worshiped him, saying, "Truly, you are the Son of God." [Matt. 14:33]

Immediately after the Resurrection, Jesus appears to various women:

> Suddenly Jesus met them and said, "Greetings!" And they came to him, took hold of his feet, and worshiped him. [Matt. 28:9]

And at Jesus' Ascension we have passages from two different Gospels:

> Now the eleven disciples went to Galilee, to the mountain to which Jesus had directed them. When they saw him, they worshiped him; but some doubted. [Matt. 28:16-17]

> While he was blessing them, he withdrew from them and was carried up into heaven. And they worshiped him, and returned to Jerusalem with great joy; and they were continually in the temple blessing God. [Luke 24:51-53]

If Jesus is being worshiped, does that not imply that those worshiping believe he is God? Here the issue is considerably more obscure. First, the Greek word translated "to worship" is *proskuneo*, which also has the much less powerful meaning of "giving homage" or "kissing the hand."* While some Bible translations may choose to

---

* A highly regarded lexicon of New Testament Greek is the Theological Dictionary of the New Testament, edited in multiple volumes by Gerhard Kittel and Gerhard Friedrich.[1] In the fifth volume, the word προσκυνεω (*proskuneo*) is discussed (pages 758 – 766). As with the other words in the dictionary, the editor first describes the uses in the Septuagint (the Greek translation of the Hebrew Scriptures) and in the common Greek—both usages being essentially contemporary with the writing period of the New Testament. These uses range from bowing down, kissing the hand, giving homage, to worshiping. However, the editor claims that its use in the New Testament always means worship: "When the NT uses προσκυνειν, the object is always something—truly or supposedly—divine."* Yet the editor provides no explanation of why this word has suddenly taken on a much more restrictive meaning, one that would imply "worship" as the only definition. Perhaps, because the word is used only in regard to actions toward God or Jesus

use "worship," others may use the less strong language. For example, the <u>New American Bible</u> provides an alternate translation for the Luke Ascension story:

> As he blessed them he parted from them and was taken up to heaven. They did him homage and then returned to Jerusalem with great joy, and they were continually in the temple praising God. [NAB: Luke 24:51-53]

The majority of times *proskuneo* is used in the New Testament with regard to Jesus it is not translated "to worship" in the NRSV. For example, we see it used of the Magi—not worshiping, but kneeling down and giving homage as they present their gifts.

> On entering the house, they [the Magi] saw the child with Mary, his mother; and they knelt down and paid him homage. [Matt. 2:11]

We see it for people who encountered Jesus:

> ... and there was a leper who came to him and knelt before him, saying, "Lord, if you choose, you can make me clean." [Matt. 8:2]

(Note that there are several other such verses in Matthew: 9:18; 15:25; 18:26; and 20:20.) And we even see it with demons:

> When he [the Gerasene demoniac—the man possessed by a "Legion" of demons] saw Jesus from a distance, he ran and bowed down before him... [Mark 5:6]

Thus, because of this ambiguity of meaning we do not really know if the word *proskuneo* translated as "worship" is really a valid translation. If the man born blind was really worshiping Jesus, he did this act publicly in view of the Pharisees. Would it not be likely that they would have been outraged at an act of worship to a human being? Did the Apostles who witnessed Jesus walking on water really worship when they still weren't sure of Jesus' identity, which seems to be revealed two chapters later in Peter's profession of faith [Matt. 16:16]?

(with the exception of Matthew 18:26—and an attempt is made to explain it away), the editor, believing that Jesus is God and deserves worship, may be choosing this more restrictive meaning—which would be an example of letting one's belief dictate the translation.

In a similar vein, what were the women and disciples really doing after Jesus' Resurrection? Were they "paying homage?" Were they "worshiping" Jesus as God? Or could they have been doing something in between? They now knew Jesus was someone radically different than any ordinary man, but they had no words nor actions to express that extraordinariness! And they could have "worshiped" in their own way.

And what really happened after Jesus' Resurrection? There is perhaps no other set of events in the story of Jesus' life that are reported so contradictory to each other in the Gospels. A careful perusal reveals contradictions of what time the women came to the tomb, who those women were, what they saw at the tomb, who saw Jesus first, what the women told the Apostles, which Apostles went to the tomb, and where Jesus ascended from. What we can believe is that Jesus rose from the dead, he appeared to people, and he left the earth. But can we really claim any specific rendition as the absolute truth? Can we believe that Matthew's version in which people worshiped Jesus is true?

Jesus himself seems to deflect the possibility of worship when he quotes scripture to Satan during his temptation in the desert:

> Jesus answered him, "It is written, 'Worship the Lord your God, and serve only him.'" [Luke 4:8; also Matt. 4:10]

There is one place in the epistles that seems to include the strong possibility that the Son was worshiped:

> For to which of the angels did God ever say, "You are my Son; today I have begotten you"? Or again, "I will be his Father and he will be my Son"? And again, when he brings the firstborn into the world, he says, "Let all God's angels worship him." [Heb. 1:5-6]

Supposedly, the author is quoting from the Old Testament when he writes "Let all God's angels worship him." However, this reading is from Deuteronomy 32:43 in the Septuagint, the Greek version of the Old Testament. Unfortunately, the correct Hebrew versions make no reference at all to a son in these passages, and whatever worship that is referenced is intended for Yahweh. Is the author of Hebrews misquoting scripture to make a point? It is certainly not uncommon for a New Testament writer to lift an Old Testament verse out of context to apply it as a fulfillment of prophecy. But is there something illegitimate here?

And if this verse is the original writing (see Chapter 12, "Bible Inerrancy?"), what does the author mean? Does it mean that at Jesus' birth—"when He brings his firstborn into the world"—the angels paid him homage? Or is there true worship of the Son demanded by God of His angels, either at his birth or at some other time? And do these verses also then imply that there was a day when the Son was begotten, and that the Arians were right when they (are alleged to have) said "There was when he (the Son) was not?" The ambiguity of this passage really means that very little of certainty can be taken from it.

The book of Revelation raises a strong negative inference with regard to the worship of Jesus. In Revelation, clear distinctions are made between God and "the Lamb," the latter being clearly understood as Jesus, the Son of God. That is, each is named separately, particularly in the latter chapters. But then comes an admonition, which is repeated:

> Then I fell down at his feet [the angel] to worship him, but he said to me, "You must not do that! I am a fellow servant with you and your comrades who hold the testimony of Jesus. Worship God!" [Rev. 19:10]

> I, John, am the one who heard and saw these things. And when I heard and saw them, I fell down to worship at the feet of the angel who showed them to me; but he said to me, "You must not do that! I am a fellow servant with you and your comrades the prophets, and with those who keep the words of this book. Worship God!" [Rev. 22:8-9]

Certainly related to this is another reference to worshiping God:

> And I saw what appeared to be a sea of glass mixed with fire, and those who had conquered the beast and its image and the number of its name, standing beside the sea of glass with harps of God in their hands. And they sing the song of Moses, the servant of God, and the song of the Lamb:
> "Great and amazing are your deeds, Lord God the Almighty!
> Just and true are your ways, King of the nations!
> Lord who will not fear and glorify your name?
> For you alone are holy. All nations will come and worship before you,
> for your judgments have been revealed." [Rev. 15:2-4]

Worshiping "God" is used five other times in Revelation (4:10-11; 7:10-12; 11:16; 14:7; and 19:4). Thus, eight times in this book the commands are to worship "God," and not "God and the Lamb." And when the author wants to include the Lamb in other references to the almighty power, he does so, such as in Rev. 21:22, 22:1, and 22:3. It is likely that his omission of the Lamb in the command to worship is intentional. However, there is a single place where the Lamb does appear to get included in the worship activity:

> Then I heard every creature in heaven and on earth and under the earth and in the sea, and all that is in them, singing,
> > "To the one seated on the throne and to the Lamb, be blessing and honor and glory and might forever and ever!"
> And the four living creatures said, "Amen!" And the elders fell down and worshiped. [Rev. 5:14]

Because Revelation has been so careful in all the other verses that only God is receiving the worship, we need to look carefully at this passage before concluding that the Lamb is included in whom the elders are worshiping. The last sentence may seem to have the implication that the Lamb is being worshiped, but the actual construction does not explicitly say that. That is, the elders are worshiping, but they may only be worshiping God, which would be consistent with the rest of Revelation.

The honor and possible worship of Jesus brings up an important point! Does God allow us to honor, and perhaps even worship His Son? The short answer is probably yes—because that honor and worship then flows back directly to Himself. But the basis and explanation is best left for Part 3 where we explore Jesus' divinity. Thus, Jesus may indeed be worshiped, but that isn't sufficient reason to declare that he is God.

"I am" and Metaphors

There is another group of passages which apologists will claim as reference to Jesus being God. These involve the frequent uses of "I am" by Jesus in the Gospel of John. Since Yahweh used that expression to describe Himself, the claim is that Jesus' appropriation of the term to describe himself means that he is God. However, virtually all of the times that Jesus uses "I am" it is in some form of self-identification:

> "The [Samaritan] woman said to him, I know that Messiah is coming" (who is called Christ). "When he comes, he will proclaim all things to us." Jesus said to her, "I am he, the one who is speaking to you." [John 4:25-26]
>
> "I am the bread of life" [John 6:35, 48]
>
> "I am the bread that came down from heaven." [John 6:41]
>
> "I am the light of the world." [John 8:12; 9:5]
>
> "I am the gate for the sheep." [John 10:7]
>
> "I am the good shepherd." [John 10:11, 14]
>
> "I am the resurrection and the life." [John 11:25]

Weight is even put onto Jesus' declaration when in the Garden of Gethsemane the crowd says they are looking for Jesus of Nazareth and Jesus answers twice,

> "I am he." [John 18:5, 8]

But we need to especially note that the Greek words used here, *ego eimi*, are exactly the same words used by the blind-from-birth beggar cured by Jesus, when the people were trying to find the beggar. The NRSV translates his self identification as "I am the man" [John 9:9], but there is no reference to "man" in the Greek. This becomes stronger evidence that John's general use of the phrase may be his style.

Chapter 8 of John's Gospel has three instances of "I am." Two, verses 24 and 28, are oddly used, and the listening Jews do not seem to take offense. But verse 58 is different:

> Jesus said to them, "Very truly, I tell you, before Abraham was, I am." [John 8:58]

Here Jesus is expressing himself using the terminology that God used of Himself in Exodus. And the Jews are ready to stone Jesus for this apparent blasphemy. Apologists claim that the Jews were right that Jesus was claiming to be God; but in direct contrast, it is rare to hear them claim that the Jews were otherwise immediately wrong in not recognizing him as God. That is to say, that the Jews were fully right and fully wrong all in the course of two passages, so they could be trusted except when they couldn't be trusted. Were the Jews reliable when it came to understanding Jesus?

If Jesus was God, it would be totally possible that Jesus is subtly claiming to be God, for this verse definitely does have an implication of claiming divinity. But because of the subtlety, it does not have to necessarily follow that Jesus is claiming to be God. In fact, taken literally, the actual language is only consistent with Jesus claiming an eternal existence. Of course, if the premise is that someone divine must be God, then the conclusion of the Jews (and perhaps the apologists) naturally follows. Yet we have seen that this premise has scriptural problems. Because this passage is one of many that highlights Jesus' divinity, it will be further discussed in Part 3.

Finally, there are certain terms which are used both for Yahweh or the Father and for Jesus. Some simple examples are "shepherd," "light," "savior" and "the first and the last." Again apologists claim this as additional proof of the equality of the Father and Jesus. But it is important to note that a metaphor is not a declaration, and caution must be exercised in its interpretation. Since this topic, too, involves Jesus' divinity, it will be addressed with its own chapter in Part 3.

In summary, the case for the apologists is very weak and far from compelling. Of greatest importance we must note that none of their "supporting" passages comes close to establishing a co-equal status of the Son with the Father. It is true that these passages, if interpreted or translated in a particular way, would be consistent with Jesus being God. But it has been shown that the apologists' versions are not the only options for understanding these passages. In actuality they far more support only that the Son has a divine nature. Especially when faced with the large number of verses that confidently stand in opposition to the Jesus-is-God view, the traditional, Trinitarian interpretation becomes unsustainable.

Chapter 10

Negative Inferences

Abundant evidence has already been cited that supports Jesus not being God. This evidence has been directly quoted from the Bible, and although no passage explicitly says "Jesus is not God," they provide statements and descriptions that clearly point to the Son being subordinate to God, who is Father.

Now we will turn to what wasn't said, but which also strongly, if not conclusively, indicates that Jesus is not God. The first path of exploration is drawn from the writings themselves, and the second comes from an important question, which, if answered according to Trinitarian belief, contradicts what is written in the New Testament.

The New Testament Writers Never Said "Jesus is God"

Did the New Testament writers consider Jesus to be God? There is a strong negative inference indicating not! Trinitarians can cite only a handful of possibly relevant passages, but as discussed in previous chapters, each of these passages has either actually been mistranslated, there exist reasonable source manuscripts that say something different, or their interpretation is ambiguous. Otherwise, there is no such declaration. For example, as said before, John 1:1 is really better translated as "In the beginning was the Word, and the Word was with God, and the Word was divine," rather than "the Word was God" as written in most translations.

Similarly in the New Testament, God is sometimes referred to as the "Most High" or "Most High God." Yet the writers never unambiguously use either phrase to describe Jesus. These titles are even spoken by supernatural beings of God, and will be cited separately, since they represent even greater proof of the difference between God and His Son. Here are two examples which might be considered more mundane: first, that which Stephen proclaimed about God just before his stoning:

> But it was Solomon who built a house for Him. Yet the Most High does not dwell in houses made with human hands ... [Acts 7:47-48]

And second, what Jesus said in Luke's Sermon on the Plain, where he is obviously referring to his Father:

> But love your enemies. Do good, and lend, expecting nothing in return. Your reward will be great, and you will be children of the Most High; for he is kind to the ungrateful and the wicked. Be merciful, just as your Father is merciful. [Luke 6:35-36]

There are two other usages of the "Most High," Luke 1:76 and Acts 16:17, but both are ambiguous in their reference.

Was there any doubt in the minds of the apostles about whether Jesus was God? We have related in Acts, chapter 15, the First Council of Jerusalem—the first (recorded) time in which the leaders of the church assembled to discuss important matters. But they never broached the subject of whether Jesus was God, something that would be of utmost importance considering the impact that such a declaration would have on preaching the Gospel, especially to the Jews. So, we must base our knowledge on what they later wrote, and we have already seen that that writing supports only a single-person God.

For example, how does St. Paul begin his ministry? We have the answer in Acts:

> For several days he was with the disciples in Damascus, and immediately he began to proclaim Jesus in the synagogues, saying "He is the Son of God." [Acts 9:20]

Indeed, St. Paul, in all his writings had ample opportunity to make the statement that Jesus is God, and never did. Why not? Why didn't he, or any of the other writers, state something simply, such as: "Jesus is God just as the Father is God," or "the Father and the Son both are God." For most of the pantheistic gentiles, the idea of two Gods being one God wouldn't have seemed strange. So certainly if Paul, the apostles and the disciples had really believed that Jesus was God, they would have had the courage—and dedication to the truth—to proclaim such an important fact. But they did not! Were they afraid that they couldn't explain such a theology to the monotheistic Jews, and therefore just swept the entire concept under the rug? Many Trinitarians actually believe this! But based on what they did write, the logical conclusion (*modus ponens*) is that they did not believe Jesus was God. Were the bishops, then, of the Fourth Century that much more enlightened to be able to make that claim?

Similarly, nowhere is there a claim of three persons in an equal Trinity. In fact, other than at Jesus' baptism, there is only one reference citing the Father, Son and Holy Spirit within the same passage—at the end of Matthew's gospel involving Jesus' command to baptize (which, as will be discussed in Chapter 12, is likely to have been a later addition). Trinitarians claim that the benediction at the end of 2 Corinthians is also Trinitarian:

> The grace of the Lord Jesus Christ, the love of God, and the communion of the Holy Spirit be with all of you. [2 Cor. 13:13]

But note the wording carefully! God, not named as the Father, is designated <u>separately</u> along with Jesus and the Holy Spirit. That is, if the passage is properly read, God is combined into a trinity, but not with two others that are deemed God. (There is another similar but weaker passage in 1 Corinthians 12:4-7, which can be looked at in the same way. There are also other passages that Trinitarians claim as evidence, but just like the baptism passages [Matthew 3:16-17, Mark 1:9-11, and Luke 3:21-22], they involve even less personal references to the Spirit. One example is Ephesians 2:13-18.) Again, the precise wording by Paul in absolutely avoiding a designation of a Trinitarian God is further evidence that Paul didn't believe in the dogmatic Trinity. Instead, we see the New Testament authors such as John tell us specifically what we are to believe when he writes:

> Who is it that conquers the world but the one who believes that Jesus is the <u>Son</u> of God? [1 John 5:5]

This is indeed a significant negative inference that is occasionally cited by apologists, but then is ignored, as if it has no bearing on our understanding. But let us be sure to add it to the evidence so far revealed.

Finally, we can see that the consistent omission of the Holy Spirit in reference to God also bears witness. A simple example occurs at the Last Supper:

> Jesus answered him, "Those who love me will keep my word, and my Father will love them, and we will come to them and make our home with them." [John 14:23]

If the Holy Spirit were God, would he not also come to make a home in them? Could Jesus have been ignorant of this fact? Such deliberate omissions provide a strong negative inference that the Holy Spirit is also not God.

Important Testimony

We do not simply have the witness of human writers who refused to or neglected to testify that Jesus is God. We also have supernatural witnesses who testified to an identity different from God for Jesus. Since their status is closer to the divine realm than ours (they are much more familiar with God), what they say should be considered significant. At the Annunciation the angel Gabriel claims of Jesus:

> "He will be great, and will be called the Son of the Most High, and the Lord God will give him the throne of his ancestor David." [Luke 1:32]

> "The Holy Spirit will come upon you, and the power of the Most High will overshadow you; therefore the child to be born will be holy; he will be called Son of God." [Luke 1:35]

Gabriel's description hardly fits a notion that Jesus is God—which he could have done if that were indeed the case. Or at least he would have used a description that could have left open the possibility. But his clear separation between "the Lord God," "the Most High" and God's to-be-born son is definitive.

And other supernatural witnesses also neglect to identify Jesus as God. Exorcisms are frequently recorded in the Gospels, and it is interesting to listen to what the demons say. As already mentioned in Chapter 6, in the very first chapter of Mark, Jesus' true identity is given away when the exorcised demon cries out:

> "What have you to do with us, Jesus of Nazareth? Have you come to destroy us? I know who you are, the Holy One of God." [Mark 1:24; also Luke 4:34]

Similarly, another demon says:

> "What have you to do with me, Jesus Son of the Most High God?" [Mark 5:7; also Luke 8:28]

And two demons at Gadarenes (or Gerasenes) say:

> "What have you to do with us, Son of God?" [Matt. 8:29]

Ordinarily we shouldn't put too much confidence in the testimony of demons, but here their statements are totally consistent with what Gabriel has averred. And since these demons are under duress—and Jesus' power—we should at least add their witness to our evidence. Thus, even these could have identified Jesus as being God, and did not.

No Advocacy of Praying to Jesus

If Jesus were God, wouldn't the epistle writers have indicated somewhere that either their readers should pray to Jesus or that they themselves pray to Jesus? Instead, nowhere do we see any unambiguous reference. Rather, we are more likely to see something like:

> Do not worry about anything, but in everything by prayer and supplication with thanksgiving let your requests be made known to God. [Phil. 4:6]

> For this reason I bow my knees before the Father, from who every family in heaven and on earth takes its name. I pray that, according to the riches of his glory, he may grant ... to him be glory in the church and in Christ Jesus to all generations, forever and ever. Amen [Eph. 3:14-16,21]

Another ambiguous passage is Acts 1:24-25.

The best that apologists can come up with is a single reference when Stephen is being stoned:

> While they were stoning Stephen, he prayed, "Lord Jesus, receive my spirit." Then he knelt down and cried out in a loud voice, "Lord, do not hold this sin against them." When he had said this, he died. [Acts 7:59-60]

Stephen's first sentence is a prayer to Jesus. And it is appropriate since no one can come to the Father except through the Son. Therefore, Stephen is putting his spirit into the Son's care first. His second sentence is ambiguous, echoing Jesus' dying declaration to his Father on the cross. But neither are exhortations to pray to Jesus as if he were God.

So how does Jesus fit into prayer? In prayer, we see Jesus' role as intermediate and mediator, rather than the direct recipient of the prayer:

> First, I thank my God through Jesus Christ for all of you, because your faith is proclaimed throughout the world. [Rom. 1:8]

> To the church of God that is in Corinth, to those who are sanctified in Christ Jesus, called to be saints, together with all those who in every place call on the name of our Lord Jesus Christ, both their Lord and ours: [1 Cor. 1:3]

When Jesus describes to his listeners how to pray, his answer is quite clear and simple:

> "Our Father in heaven, hallowed be your name." [Matt. 6:9]

He, of course, does not include himself in that prayer. Is it because he doesn't think he should be included, or is it because he is afraid of being accused of blasphemy? In any event, we certainly don't see anywhere in the Gospels examples of praying to Jesus. But the *Our Father* does raise a distinct challenge to Trinitarians. If the Holy Spirit is God, co-equal with the Father, why would Jesus advocate a prayer only to the Father? It would be absolutely mysterious that Jesus is totally mute on an important point of theology where honor and worship should be directed if the Holy Spirit is God. Of course, the New Testament writers are also silent on this essential piece of theology. The only logical conclusion is, as with Jesus, they didn't believe that the Holy Spirit is God. The New Testament writers remain consistent with who they believe is God, and it doesn't include Jesus or the Holy Spirit.

Ecclesiastic Contradiction

Perhaps the most enduring of the Old Testament proscriptions and laws that continued into the post-Resurrection times has been the Ten Commandments. The First Commandment decrees:

> I am the LORD your God, who brought you out of the land of Egypt, out of the house of slavery; you shall have no other gods before me. You shall not make for yourself an idol, whether in the form of anything that is in heaven above, or that is on the earth beneath, or that is in the water under the earth. [Ex. 20:2-4]

Other Bible translations will render "idol" as "graven image," a man-made representation of any deity. And this included any image to represent Yahweh Himself. Deuteronomy 4:15-18 includes in the proscription any figure at all, including that of a man or woman. Yet the churches must be falling into serious error (by their own declaration that Jesus is God) because there appears to be no compunction against creating images of Jesus: crucifixes, icons, statues and paintings. In the First Commandment, God wanted to assure that no power of His would be attributed to any object, or that our concept of Him could be contained in anything finite. Why would this commandment then be superseded?

But, if Jesus is not God, then these images represent something entirely different. The crucifix becomes a symbol of God's redemptive love for us and a reminder of Jesus' faithfulness. The icons, statues and paintings become methods of story telling and honoring, just as we do for important historical figures. But they never confine God into our own image.

Can God Sin?

This sounds absurd—almost blasphemous! But this is not an irrelevant question if we want to understand if Jesus truly can be God. To look at this more closely, we must refer to the story of Jesus being tempted by Satan after fasting for 40 days in the desert (recounted in all three Synoptic Gospels). The devil tempts Jesus to 1) show his power by sating himself with bread made from stones; 2) possess all the kingdoms in the world if only he will worship Satan; 3) reveal how much God loves him by rescuing him if he jumps off the top of the Temple. Jesus appears to readily refuse and refute each of Satan's offers, but we truly cannot know just how tempting these offers were for Jesus.

Up to then, Jesus had not been known to have miraculous power. Maybe it was also a temptation to "test" that power. Being the emperor of the world certainly has its advantages, too. And perhaps the Father to that point had done little for his Son in the way of visibly showing his love. What child does not want outward expressions of love from his father? Of course, these are all conjectures, but they put significantly more power into the temptations.

But <u>could</u> Jesus have said "yes" to any of these temptations? The answer must be yes! Otherwise, these events were really not temptations at all, but just another encounter with the sinful milieu which surrounded Jesus. If Jesus can say yes to evil, then he is like us; if not, then our faith is based on emulating a being who is, indeed, not like ourselves. But in the Epistle to the Hebrews we find:

> For we do not have a high priest who is unable to sympathize with our weaknesses, but we have one who in every respect has been tested as we are, yet without sin. [Heb. 4:15]

In fact, it is so important that Jesus could say "yes" because otherwise Jesus had no free will in dying for us—that is, his sacrifice would have been totally involuntary, and his work on earth would have been nothing more than a projection, like a movie, of what the Father had scripted. But we are told that Jesus was "obedient:"

> He humbled himself and became obedient to the point of death— even death on a cross. [Phil. 2:8]

This obedience implies a free will on the part of Jesus. And this is brought out strongly in Gethsemane when Jesus says:

> "... yet not my will, but yours be done." [Luke 22:42]

If we've established that Jesus must have been able to say "yes," then we need to consider the implications if he <u>had</u> said "yes." If Jesus is God, can God go against his own will? We would be led to the conclusion that God could sin! Indeed, if Jesus had agreed to worship Satan, Jesus would be turning away from the Father and separating that unity. But God is One! He is not separable! And so we come into an incredibly important contradiction. If Jesus is God, he could not sin—even as a human being. But if he cannot sin, then he is not like us at all, and our view of him as brother utterly collapses. His sacrifice on the cross is not voluntary, and we're forced into an entirely alien theology of redemption.

Furthermore, from the story it is quite clear that Satan believes in the possibility that he can be successful. Satan, as a supernatural being and a fallen angel would certainly know Jesus' true nature, as well as the nature of God. Yet if God were truly an undivided unity of three persons, Satan would never have tried to tempt Jesus, completely knowing that he could not possibly succeed. Because Satan does try, he must know that Jesus can succumb to the temptations. And this "hope" of his is further emphasized because the devil hadn't given up, as Luke's Gospel says at the end of these temptations:

> When the devil had finished every test, he departed from him until an opportune time. [Luke 4:13]

There is a potential counter-argument that relates to the validity of the story: there were no human witnesses to these temptations. So the question naturally arises regarding its origins. It is likely that the common source of the Synoptic Gospels contained a temptation-in-the-desert reference, although it is possible that Matthew and Luke "amplified' the story by adding the nature of the temptations (Mark adds no detail). But it is unclear how the original author knew anything of the events, unless Jesus had told his disciples at some time during his ministry—or the inspiration of the Holy Spirit relayed the information. In any event, the story *could* have been fabricated. And Jesus might *not* actually have been tempted. (This then raises the legitimate question of what other stories of the Gospels are fabrications? Proceeding down that line of inquiry will eventually lead to a severe diminishing of our faith!)

Nevertheless, true or not, the spirit and intent of the story by the Gospel writers was to show that Jesus had very human qualities, and even as the Son of God he was subject to the temptations of life. And the conclusion must be the same—that Jesus could have said "yes," or else these temptations and the stories about them are meaningless.

In summary, to avoid the contradiction of saying that God can sin, we must conclude that Jesus is not God—at least in the sense of being the Supreme Being of the universe, or an equal member of a Trinity making up the Supreme Being. For God cannot sin.

Chapter 11

Jesus Himself Indicates that He Isn't God

There is one further bit of strong evidence that supports Jesus not being God, and it stems from a discussion with the Jews when they accuse him of blasphemy, as documented in the tenth chapter of John's Gospel. After Jesus states in verse 30 "The Father and I are one," some of the Jews are incensed:

> The Jews took up stones again to stone him. Jesus replied, "I have shown you many good works from the Father. For which of these are you going to stone me?" The Jews answered, "It is not for a good work that we are going to stone you, but for blasphemy, because you, though only a human being, are making yourself God." [John 10:31-33]

Apparently, the Jews have taken Jesus' previous statement quite literally! Although that interpretation could be true on the face of it, we also know that Jesus sees that his relationship with God, his Father, is one of complete unity of spirit and will.

At this point, Jesus has the opportunity to admit his godhead as part of the Trinity. But what does he do? He actually makes a plea for divinity, but worded in such a way that it is clear he isn't claiming godhead:

> Jesus answered, "Is it not written in your law, 'I said you are gods?' If those to whom the word of God came were called 'gods'—and scripture cannot be annulled—can you say that the one whom the Father has sanctified and sent into the world is blaspheming because I said "I am God's Son'?" [John 10:34-36]

To understand this more fully, we need to reference Psalm 82 which Jesus is quoting. On the surface, it appears quite peculiar. The Psalm begins:

> God has taken his place in the divine council;
> in the midst of the gods he holds judgment. [Psalm 82:1]

The Psalm states that there are others, who are called "gods!" These, apparently, are immortal beings that dwell with divinity. However, in verses 2 through 5 God takes these gods to task for not acting in love, and the Psalm finishes with:

> I say, "You are gods, children of the Most High, all of you;
> nevertheless, you shall die like mortals, and fall like any prince."
> Rise up, O God, judge the earth;
> for all the nations belong to you [Psalm 82:6-7]

These gods, "children of the Most High," are condemned to mortality. Yet Jesus, in his reply to the Jews, is putting himself in a position opposite to these disobedient gods. He, too, knows that he is a "child of the Most High" when he states that he is "God's Son" [John 10:36]. But he is different: he is truly following God's will, as shown through his works.

Ultimately, this discussion indicates that there are other levels of divinity besides simply being God. And Jesus does not claim to be God, but only that special child of God who has given his obedience to God.

John's Gospel, particularly in chapters 6 and 8, also begin to delve into Christ's divinity, without getting into any arguments of whether he is claiming to be God. However, this discussion will be left until Part 3.

There are two other passages in which Jesus indicates that he isn't God. The first is also in the Gospel of John, and it again involves a discussion with the Jews, this time after Jesus had cured a lame man on the Sabbath:

> Therefore the Jews started persecuting Jesus, because he was doing such things on the Sabbath. But Jesus answered them, "My Father is still working, and I also am working." For this reason the Jews were seeking all the more to kill him, because he was not only breaking the Sabbath, but was also calling God his own Father, thereby making himself equal to God. [John 5:16-18]

The conclusion of the Jews seems hyperbolic, since we are all sons and daughters of God. And just because the Jews are stating what they believe, that doesn't make the statement true. And indeed, Jesus answers them in a way to refute their conclusion:

> Jesus said to them, "Very truly, I tell you, the Son can do nothing on his own, but only what he sees the Father doing; for whatever the Father does, the Son does likewise." [John 5:19]

Jesus is quick to point out that his Father is greater than he is, which denies any claim of equality. Furthermore, in the verses that follow, 20 – 29, Jesus highlights roles that he has been given. And these roles are consistent with being the Messiah, someone that the Jews did not equate with God. As William Barclay notes: "But not only is this claim to be God's Messiah made in so many words; in phrase after phrase it is implicit."[1]

The other passage of note can be found in the Synoptic gospels, although the Matthew version differs slightly from that of Mark and Luke:

> As he was setting out on a journey, a man ran up and knelt before him, and asked him "Good teacher, what must I do to inherit eternal life?" Jesus said to him, "Why do you call me good? No one is good but God alone." [Mark 10:17-18]

> Then someone came up to him and said, "Teacher, what good deed must I do to have eternal life?" And he said to him, "Why do you ask me about what is good? There is only one who is good." [Matt. 19:16-17]

Is Jesus just being facetious as the apologists would have us believe? That is, is Jesus trying to coax a declaration of "Jesus is God" out of the questioner? Or should we rather take these statements at face value—that no one is "good," in its fullest sense—except God. And that Jesus is not even considering himself "good" at this stage. Based on all the evidence revealed so far, the latter explanation is more consistent, more logical, and more in keeping with the actual wording.

Chapter 12

Bible Inerrancy?

So far, nearly all the evidence presented has involved simply interpreting what has been written within the Bible, with particular emphasis on the New Testament. Thus, there has been an assumption that what is written there is without error. For most Christians the Bible is considered the inspired word of God, and there is also the belief for many of them that there can be no error in those writings. Although this may be true of most of the original writings, a problem exists with the texts that exist today precisely because they are not the original writings. Bart Ehrman, a biblical scholar provides an important insight in this regard in his book Misquoting Jesus, the Story Behind Who Changed the Bible and Why,[1] from which many of the following observations are detailed. Timothy Paul Jones in his book Misquoting Truth [2] also makes many of the same points, although he disputes Ehrman's implications regarding the relevant theology.

Although the New Testament is a collection of ancient texts, or books, the passing down of the actual words has a very muddied history. And although there are many different manuscripts of these books, if one were to count up all the discrepancies, there are more than twice as many of these than there are words in the New Testament. How could these discrepancies come about?

Originally, the author may have sent a single letter or written a single book. Upon receipt, the local presbyter may have then had copies made for distribution. Thus, in the early centuries, these books were copied over and over again—often by fairly simple people. And then copies were made of the copies. To complicate matters for the copyist, the text itself (in Greek) ran all the letters together and contained no punctuation. As a result, it was easy to miscopy the text. And once it was miscopied, this new copy could be used for future copying. And these new copies could contain further errors.

Besides the introduction of accidental changes, sometimes words or passages were changed intentionally. Perhaps this was done so that the Gospels would read more consistently with each other. There is also evidence that this could be done to support various views of how the copier viewed Jesus. Thus, the heresies of the day—or even the "orthodox" view—could be better supported if the text was altered. And, of course, biased translations into other languages could occur as well, with the translator's choice of words affecting how the Greek could be interpreted. These different texts could then be used to support various positions of doctrinal interpretation, with less-than-optimum results. The King James version was based on surviving medieval texts, which are now known to contain substantial errors.

Problems in the variance between texts of the various manuscripts were already noticed—and lamented—in the mid-Third Century. Origen writes,

> "The differences between the manuscripts have become great, either through the negligence of some copyists or through the perverse audacity of others; they either neglect to check over what they have transcribed, or, in the process of checking, they make additions or deletions as they please." [3]

By comparing manuscripts, particularly to the oldest known ones, it became obvious that sometimes whole passages, or even stories were added. These include the entire ending to Mark's Gospel [Mark 16:9–20], the story in John [John 7:53–8:11] of the woman caught in adultery, the agony of Jesus in sweating blood [Luke 22:43–44], and Jesus' saying from the cross "Father forgive them for they know not what they do" [Luke 23:34]. Although these passages do not alter our view of Jesus, they still represent changes from the original texts.

One role of biblical scholars has more recently been to determine the actual words of the original texts. They do this through a process called "textual criticism." They often base their translation on the oldest surviving manuscripts, but they also have a bias for those texts which either seem to be more unlikely (it would be odd, for example, for someone to alter the words to make Jesus look worse), or those that counter then-current heresies.

There are two major implications of these observations. The first is that earlier theology may have been influenced by the changes or additions—particularly with regard to Jesus being God. One of these has occurred in the First Epistle of John. This passage, called the Johannine Comma, reads:

> There are three that bear witness in heaven: the Father, the Word, and the Spirit, and these three are one; and there are three that bear witness on earth, the Spirit, the water, and the blood, and these three are one. [1 John 5:7-8]

Although this seems to strongly support a view of God as Trinity, the first part of the passage does not appear in the ancient manuscripts, and was certainly added later. That is, it is not something the original author wrote. Most modern, reliable translations now omit the Trinitarian reference and read something like:

> There are three that testify: the Spirit and the water and the blood, and these three agree. [1 John 5:7-8]

Another such passage is 1 Timothy 3:16, which has been interpreted similarly, for it refers to Christ as "<u>God</u> made manifest in the flesh and justified by the Spirit." Rather, it was pointed out (first by Johann Wettstein in the Eighteenth Century) that due to a simple transposition of a line segment, the passage should be read as Christ "<u>who</u> was made manifest in the flesh and justified by the Spirit." Since this change made it into several other older manuscripts, it also continued making its way into the vast majority of later manuscripts—including most of the early English translations.[4] As Ehrman writes of Wettstein's work:

> As Wettstein continued his investigations, he found other passages typically used to affirm the doctrine of the divinity of Christ that in fact represented textual problems; when these problems are resolved on text-critical grounds, in most instances references to Jesus' divinity are taken away.[5]

One other example occurs in Acts:

> Keep watch over yourselves and over all the flock of which the Holy Spirit has made you overseers, to shepherd the church of God that he obtained with the blood of his own Son. [Acts 20:28]

Wettstein was quite bothered by this verse, and published a discussion of textual problems. Ehrman continues:

> Included among the specimen passages in his discussion were some of these disputed texts that have been used by theologians to establish the biblical basis for the doctrine of the divinity of Christ. For Wettstein, these texts in fact had been altered precisely in order to incorporate that perspective; the original texts could not be used in support of it.[6]

This points out a major implication: it is dangerous for us to base our theology on single passages. The work of biblical scholars has established a great number of likely changes. But these have been based on discrepancies that already are known to exist. Furthermore, these scholars don't always agree. But there could have been changes in the earliest copies, from which all other copies came from. One writer, Randall Price, states that according to Erdman there could be as many as 400,000 variations (called "variants") in the multiple manuscripts, but also points out that most are insignificant and meaningless. He states that perhaps 1 percent may affect the translation.[7] Doing the math, that means that there can be 4000 "disagreements" about what various passages might say—a rather significant number! Furthermore, this author states that 24 percent of variants are meaningful but not viable differences, in the sense that they do not change the meaning. But one example he gives for this type of variant is the substitution of the word "Christ" for "God." This example must be considered quite important from a doctrinal standpoint and not so summarily dismissed.

In a manner similar to Price, Timothy Jones attempts to refute Ehrman, noting that nearly all of the differences are minor and of no theological consequence. He continues, "Most important, *none* of the differences affects any central element of the Christian faith." [8] Since Jones believes in the truth of the "errors," he feels confident in his assertion (note the italicized "none"), but this is engaging in circular reasoning: his belief, like Price's, is based on the theology resulting, in part, from the changes, and so the changes do not adversely affect his belief. But he is wrong here, because there are suspect passages already cited which certainly do affect the interpretation of a Trinitarian God (the Johannine Comma, 1 Tim. 3:16 and John 1:18). And there are already numerous passages indicating a single-person God. Thus, since there are extremely few passages even remotely related to the existence of God-as-Trinity, the reduction of even two or three of their number is significant. Similarly, even a few relating to Jesus' divinity should be considered significant, since very few passages outside of John's Gospel even hint at Jesus' divinity!

This doesn't mean that we now must doubt everything we see in our translation of the New Testament! But it does become more important to understand that every passage is suspect, and we need to read it in the light of other passages. We know only of the variations that have come to light. The probability that we have captured all the original writings must be very close to zero, and the probability that translators have always chosen the original text is even lower.

Perhaps the most important passage which receives incredible weight within Church doctrine is the only one that clearly references a personal Trinity—the apostolic commission which occurs just before Jesus' Ascension:

> And Jesus came and said to them, "All authority in heaven and earth has been given to me. Go therefore and make disciples of all nations, baptizing them in the name of the Father and of the Son and of the Holy Spirit." [Matt. 28:18-19]

Why might this passage be suspect? First, there is no other single-passage reference to a personal Trinity anywhere in the New Testament. (As exposed in Chapter 10, two other passages that Trinitarians misuse as evidence of a Trinity (1 Cor. 12:4-7 and 2 Cor. 13:13) don't even use the Trinitarian designation correctly.) If the New Testament writers had believed in God-as-Trinity as a major tenet of belief, they would surely have emphasized it. Instead we are usually given only infrequent and vague references, such as:

> For through him [the Son] both of us [Jews and gentiles] have access in one Spirit to the Father. [Eph. 2:18]

Second, we find no similar corroborating statement by the other Gospel writer, Luke, who twice wrote about the event of the Ascension. Surely, something as important as a major command by Jesus to his disciples would have been recorded! Third, nowhere else in the New Testament is there a reference to doing something in the "name of the Holy Spirit," although there are dozens of verses that cite doing something in the name of Jesus. Of course, this would seem a bit absurd in that the Holy Spirit hasn't ever been revealed with a name, although the colloquial use would obviously be meant, as in "under the power of the Holy Spirit." Fourth, as Father Raymond Brown points out, if Jesus had really said this, then the apostles wouldn't have had so much difficulty later on in trying to decide whether gentiles should be proselytized; the command was to go to all nations—which should include those with no Jews.[9] Fifth, this baptismal formula doesn't even appear to be used in the early church! Instead, later references to baptism declare it only in the name of the Son. Look at what happens a mere ten days after the Ascension—on the day of Pentecost. Here is what Peter says:

> "Repent and be baptized every one of you in the name of Jesus Christ so that your sins might be forgiven." [Acts 2:38]

Did Peter forget Jesus' command so soon? Did he deliberately choose to ignore it? Some time later a similar reference to baptism happens.

> Now when the apostles at Jerusalem heard that Samaria had accepted the word of God, they sent Peter and John to them. The two went down and prayed for them that they might receive the Holy Spirit (for as yet the Spirit had not come upon any of them; they had only been baptized in the name of the Lord Jesus). [Acts 8:14-16]

And what happens when Peter baptizes the very first gentiles? :

> So he ordered them to be baptized in the name of Jesus Christ. [Acts 10:48]

And this occurs after these same gentiles had received the Holy Spirit. There is a fourth, similar reference in Acts 19:5. It is also implied in Acts 22:16. Even Paul has a reference which indicates that people were baptized in the name of Jesus:

> For it has been reported to me by Chloe's people that there are quarrels among you, my brothers and sisters. What I mean is that each of you says, "I belong to Paul," or "I belong to Apollos," or "I belong to Cephas," or "I belong to Christ." Has Christ been divided? Was Paul crucified for you? Or were you baptized in the name of Paul? [1 Cor. 1:11-13]

There are also two passages where people are baptized <u>into</u> Christ: Galatians 3:27 and Romans 6:3. So even though there is reference to being baptized <u>with</u> the Holy Spirit [Acts 1:5 and 11:16] or <u>in</u> the Holy Spirit [1 Cor. 12:13], no reference outside Matthew 28:19 exists for the baptism being either in the name of the Father or the name of the Holy Spirit. This contradiction between the words of one passage of scripture and the way it was actually carried out must raise some serious doubts about the Matthew passage.

Sixth, there is something incongruent about Matthew's retelling of the Ascension. The Gospel reads:

> Now the eleven disciples went to Galilee, to the mountain to which Jesus had directed them. [Matt. 28:16]

Yet Luke relates:

> Then he [Jesus] led them out as far as Bethany, and, lifting up his hands, he blessed them. While he was blessing them, he withdrew from them and was carried up to heaven. And they worshiped him, and returned to Jerusalem with great joy. [Luke 24:50-52]

> While staying with them [just prior to his Ascension], he ordered them not to leave Jerusalem, but to wait there for the promise of the Father. [Acts 1: 4]

Note that Bethany is less than five miles from Jerusalem—unless by chance a Bethany existed in Galilee; but this location is unlikely from Luke's context. Since the Holy Spirit came (traditionally) ten days later at Pentecost in Jerusalem, it seems far more likely that Luke's setting is correct. This increases the doubt about Matthew's veracity with regard to his Ascension narrative.

Finally, we have an early Church witness whose writings indicate that verse 19 should read differently. Eusebius of Caesarea [c. CE 260-339] wrote a history of the church that covered the years up to 324. His history has provided a foundation that other church historians have consistently relied on. In Paul Maier's translation, Eusebius writes about how the apostles were "driven out of Judea by numerous deadly plots. But they traveled into every land, teaching their message in the power of Christ, who had told them, 'Go and make disciples of all nations in my name.'"[10] This construction closely follows parts of Matthew 28:19 (as opposed to that found in Luke or Acts). But Eusebius has omitted the Trinitarian formula! The most likely reason is that the version available to him at that time did not include those extra words. This likely explanation, plus the other observations provides extremely strong evidence that the Trinitarian formula did not exist in the original document. Yet how much of Trinitarian belief depends on Matthew 28:19?

As a final observation it is essential for us to understand that there was no official approved Canon of readings; there was no such thing as a "New Testament." Different leaders of the church—successors to the apostles and successors to those people—emphasized some books more than others, and gradually a list of books considered "reliable" came into being—although it still differed from the Canon we know today. Thus, each leader of the church used what was available and tried to learn from others. We can only surmise and never know how their views were colored by the culture of the day and the writings they had available.

Contradictions

Even though some Faiths believe that the Bible contains no errors, it is important to realize that there are a large number of passages which contradict each other in one way or another. Defenders of Bible inerrancy often describe this in obtuse ways, such as that one passage "amplifies" another. There is extreme danger in doing this! As an example, consider the two criminals crucified with Jesus. In Matthew we read:

> Then two bandits were crucified with him, one on his right and one on his left. Those who passed by derided him... The bandits who were crucified with him also taunted him in the same way. [Matt. 27:38, 39, 44; similar is Mark 15:27, 29, 32]

Yet in Luke 23:39-43 we hear an entirely different story, where one of the criminals is never said to deride Jesus, but requests "remember me when you come into your kingdom." An "amplification" interpretation would say that the one criminal first derided Jesus, and then changed his mind and later asked for forgiveness. What is the danger? Matthew and Mark have written something that has distinct meaning; yet that meaning becomes completely whitewashed through the amplification. How many other verses—and their meanings—don't have an "amplification" which could set an unusual passage straight? (Think of the verses in Mark (e.g. 3:5, 9:19, 9:23, and 10:14) where Jesus is downright irritable. Shouldn't those be modified since our image of Jesus is a gentle man?) If we allow these amplifications, then virtually any verse could be reinterpreted in light of it "needing" amplification, and we all fall victim to whoever is choosing to interpret the Scripture.

Consider the story of the denial of Jesus by Peter. In Matthew, Luke and John, Jesus says "before the cock crows you will deny me three times." And so it subsequently happens in those gospels. Yet in Mark (14:30), he says "before the cock crows twice you will deny me three times." And the first cock's crow occurs after Peter's first denial (14:68). Now it occurred either one way or the other, so at least one of the evangelists is wrong. Not that it matters in the telling of the story, but it does matter in terms of inerrancy.

When did Jesus come into Jerusalem and drive the money changers from it? In Matthew (21:12+), Mark (11:15+), and Luke (19:28+), this happens after Jesus' triumphant entry into Jerusalem at the end of his ministry. But in John (2:13+) it happens at the beginning of his ministry. Did it happen twice (the "amplification" explanation)? Is at least one of the evangelists wrong? Or perhaps the evangelists are changing the historical context to make a point. If we insist on inerrancy, then shouldn't we also insist on historical accuracy?

On what day was Jesus crucified? Again the Synoptic gospels agree; they say that it was on the day of Passover, after the Passover meal. John, however, says that it was on the day before Passover—prior to the Passover meal (18:28 and 19:14). Is John just using poetic license so that the sacrifice of the Lamb of God occurs at the same time that the Passover lambs are being sacrificed? Or did it really occur that way? [There is also more reason to believe John's version, since it allows the body of Jesus to lie in the tomb three full nights, consistent with the sign of Jonah. The Synoptics only allow for Friday and Saturday night.] And once again, it only matters insofar as inerrancy is important. At least one of the evangelists is wrong.

From what mountain did Jesus ascend into heaven? In the Gospel of Matthew, it occurred in Galilee [Matt. 28:16]. In Luke, Jesus leads them out "as far as Bethany," [Luke 24:50], which is in Judea. To corroborate this location, in Acts Luke says that Jesus "ordered them not to leave Jerusalem" [Acts 1:4] just before he ascends, implying that Jerusalem is where the disciples had been recently staying. One of the writers is in error.

Did Jesus always prophesy correctly? Jesus tells the story of the end of the world, and then concludes:

> "Truly I tell you, this generation will not pass away until all these things have taken place." [Matt. 24:34; also in Mark 13:30 and Luke 21:32]

Jesus makes a similar prophecy, and here the context is that it is to occur at the end of the world:

> [Jesus said] "Those who are ashamed of me in this adulterous and sinful generation, of them the Son of Man will also be ashamed when he comes in the glory of his Father with the holy angels." And he said to them, "Truly I tell you, there are some standing here who will not taste death until they see that the kingdom of God has come with power." [Mark 8:38 – 9:1]

It is clear from St. Paul's epistles that he, too, expected the end of the world to come momentarily, and exhorted his followers to act in such a manner—even discouraging marrying. Thus, the tradition of this prediction is consistent with the Gospel. Yet it did not happen. But perhaps the evangelists just recorded the words a little incorrectly, or that the first prediction really applied to the fall of Jerusalem while the second was vague in the sense that the kingdom of God may have begun with Jesus' first coming, so that the context was all wrong. In any event, some sort of error occurred.

Although there are many other inconsistencies, there is one other that is particularly relevant. In John's prologue there is a particularly interesting statement:

> No one has ever seen God. [John 1:18]

First, as discussed in Chapter 8, if Jesus is true God and true man, then the statement must be utterly false, for God cannot simply "discard" his being God. But in a broader sense the statement is false, for we have at least four records where God was seen by man. Often in the Old Testament there are references to being in God's presence, such as through angels or a burning bush. But there are several for whom God is reported to have appeared directly. These appearances were seen by Abram, Jacob, Moses (and others), Solomon, Isaiah, and Micaiah. Some of these passages have already been referenced in Chapter 8, but are repeated here:

> God appeared to Jacob again when he came from Paddan-aram, and he blessed him. [Gen. 35:9; see also Gen. 28:10-17 and 35:1]

> Then Moses and Aaron, Nadab and Abihu, and seventy of the elders of Israel went up, and they saw the God of Israel. Under his feet there was something like a pavement of sapphire stone, like the very heaven for clearness. He [God] did not lay his hand on the chief men of the people of Israel; also they beheld God and they ate and drank. [Ex. 24:9-11]

> Thus the LORD {YHWH} used to speak to Moses face to face, as one speaks to a friend. [Ex. 33:11]

> Then the LORD was angry with Solomon, because his heart had turned from the LORD the God of Israel, who had appeared to him twice. [1 Kings 11:9]

> In the year that King Uzziah died, I saw the Lord sitting on a throne, high and lofty ... And I said: "Woe is me! I am lost, for I am a man of unclean lips, and I live among a people of unclean lips; yet my eyes have seen the King, the LORD of hosts!" [Is. 6:1, 5]

> Then Micaiah said, "Therefore hear the word of the LORD: I saw the LORD sitting on his throne with all the host of heaven standing beside him to the right and to the left of him." [1 Kings 22:19]

Note especially that in the last four passages the name of God is being used. In trying to resolve the contradictions, we can play any number of "interpretation" games. These Old Testament experiences may have been visions or dreams, and no real "seeing" took place. (This seems somewhat at odds with Isaiah's experience and fear.) In Exodus 33:20, we indeed get a revision of Moses' story where God now says "you cannot see my face, for no one shall see my face and live." (Incidentally, this seems like a contradiction of verse 11.) Or maybe John is wrong—or meant, but didn't say: "no one has seen God's face."

Incidentally, it should be noted in all these "sightings" of God, that nowhere is there any indication whatsoever that the God that is being seen is anything but a single person. This is, again, additional support for God being the single person, Yahweh.

In any event, what these difficulties all point out is that we need to be careful not to tie too much of our belief to any single verse. It could be translated incorrectly, somebody's addition, or just interpreted out of context. Thus, we need to be doubly careful of the only Trinitarian passage in the entire Bible that references together the Father, Son and Holy Spirit as persons, Matthew 28:19.

Chapter 13

Summary

How much evidence is needed to be able to make a conclusion that one is confident in? The previous material has revealed that the Bible has an overabundance of evidence testifying that Jesus is not God—at least in the sense that our churches teach. Instead, God is singularly Yahweh and Father. And, except for an extremely limited set of verses, this alternative doctrine is overwhelmingly repeated throughout both the Old and the New Testaments. Furthermore, those few contrary verses can reasonably (and relatively simply) be explained in a way that do not "insist" that Jesus is God, and so they significantly lose their power in light of all the other verses.

There is also evidence that is almost so subtle that it is difficult to grasp its significance until one accepts the truth of Jesus' subordination. For example, in John's relating of the story of the Good Shepherd, Jesus says:

> "I am the good shepherd. I know my own and they know me, just as the Father knows me and I know the Father." [John 10:14-15]

If we accept that Jesus has a status that is above human beings, then we must accept that Jesus' knowledge of us most certainly surpasses our knowledge of him. But this is syllogistic of the Father's knowledge of Jesus and Jesus' knowledge of the Father. The Father, God, knows Jesus at a level that surpasses Jesus' knowledge of God. This definitely, but subtly, indicates the Son's inferiority to the Father.

Again, in summary, what we have seen from the Bible's own words is:

- Both the God of the Old Testament and of the New is depicted as a single personality, either Yahweh or the Father. Furthermore, there are several unequivocal verses which say that the Father is the God of Jesus.
- The New Testament consistently references separately the Father and the Son. In many of these verses the context virtually insists on the superiority of the Father over the Son. Jesus is <u>only</u> the son, but as such he is an heir. Rather than Jesus choosing to come to earth, he was instead <u>sent</u> by the Father. And instead of following his own will, he is <u>always</u>

obedient to the Father.
- It is equally clear that the Father holds all the power, both before and after the resurrection. And Jesus' power is derived from the Father. The Father <u>alone</u> raised Jesus from the dead; Jesus did not do it. And after Jesus' ultimate sacrifice, God—through his own choice and power—conferred on him a Lordship. The Son is exalted by God and now "sits" in heaven at the right hand of the Father—a place of inferiority to the Father.
- Jesus possesses multiple roles which are inconsistent with being God. He is, as a very special man, mediator between man and God. As such he can now act as the highest high priest of God. He is the Messiah—the holy and anointed one <u>of</u> God. He was teacher, and now acts as advocate, pleading for us at God's right hand. The Son is referenced as the wisdom, word, image, and power of God, all of which imply an issuing out from God, rather than being the integral person. Finally, he is the cornerstone of the Church of God—an essential and foundational piece of that worshiping body.
- In the end times, the Son will hand over everything he has been given and be subject to the Father.
- Jesus himself indicates that he isn't God.
- Finally, there are several negative inferences as well. If Jesus were God, certainly the New Testament authors would directly and clearly have revealed it. The truth was not something they would have veiled or hidden—unless we believe that they could have been afraid of the truth! If Jesus is like us in all ways; he must have been able to give in to Satan's temptation and sinned. But it impossible for God to sin.

As indicated before, theologians place a great deal of weight on just a handful of passages that supposedly directly reference Jesus being God. However, each of these passages has been shown to be either a mistranslation, an alternate translation, or can be interpreted in a manner—consistent with other Bible readings—that implies divinity, but not godhead. (Note: to be fair, these theologians do not solely base their doctrinal arguments on these passages. There are also several passages that indicate that Jesus has attributes of God, and he is occasionally referenced with phrases or metaphors that are used for God. Rather than insisting these mean that Jesus is God, they, instead, strongly support his divinity—something that does not have to mean he is God. Many of these references—and possible interpretations—will be discussed in Part 3.)

A study of comparative historical texts shows that it is quite hazardous to interpret any specific passage in a particular way, since we know that past errors have occurred in transcription, and that since there is evidence for passages contradicting each other, a single passage could be wrong without necessarily needing its "contradiction" to exist somewhere. Instead, firm doctrine should be based on consistent and repeated messages found in several sources. This is certainly the case with God being different, and separate from Jesus, his Son.

Yet people still hold to their old belief. The author, when bringing up this important issue, finds that those who defend the standard doctrine consistently fall back and claim those few passages that seem to support their own claim—typically rejecting any possible alternative interpretation. Furthermore, it isn't scripturally or logically possible for them to go from a claim that Jesus is God to where the Son has a co-equal status with the Father. And what is worse, they neglect to address the abundant contrary evidence. This, then, is the challenge to those who hold to the standard Trinitarian doctrine: how could Jesus have possibly been like us and been able to give in to temptation if he were God, and how are the following six passages (from multiple sources) to be interpreted if Jesus is God and equal to the Father?

> There is ... one Lord, one faith, one baptism, one God and Father of all, who is above all and through all and in all. [Eph. 4:4-6]

> [Jesus said:] "And this is eternal life: that they may know you, the only true God, and Jesus Christ whom you have sent." [John 17:3]

> Jesus said to her: "Do not hold on to me, because I have not yet ascended to the Father. But go to my brothers, and say to them: 'I am ascending to my Father and your Father, to my God and your God.'" [John 20:17]

> For there is one God; there is also one mediator between God and humankind, Christ Jesus, himself human, who gave himself a ransom for all. [1 Tim. 2:5]

> Yet for us there is one God, the Father, from whom are all things and for whom we exist, and one Lord, Jesus Christ, through whom are all things and through whom we exist. [1 Cor. 8:6]

> ... for as all die in Adam, so all will be made alive in Christ. But each in his own order: Christ the first fruits, then at his coming those who belong to Christ. Then comes the end when he hands over the kingdom to God the Father, after he has destroyed every ruler and every authority and power. For he must reign until he has put all his enemies under his feet. The last enemy to be destroyed is death. For "God has put all things in subjection under his feet." But when it says, "All things are put in subjection," it is plain that this does not include the one who put all things in subjection under him. When all things are subjected to him, then the Son himself will also be subjected to the one who put all things in subjection under him, so that God may be all in all. [1 Cor. 15:22-28]

Of course, these are but a handful of the already-cited anti-Trinitarian passages. But if a theologian can explain even those six, and the supposed ability of Jesus to sin—without reverting to intense convoluted logic (remember: the New Testament was written for normal people, not the theological elite!), then it should be easy to explain the remaining large number of anti-Trinitarian passages.

Part 3

Evidence:

Jesus is Divine

Chapter 14

Exploring Christ's Divinity

If Jesus isn't God, then who is he? Obviously, theologians cannot have been able to base their conclusion about Jesus being God solely on verses that directly say Jesus is God. Instead, they have noted a number of passages which imply that Jesus was—or is—someone greater than a normal human being, perhaps even being divine. These same theologians may have then extrapolated this to mean that Jesus must be God. But it doesn't have to be so.

In Part 3 we will explore those verses that indicate that Jesus, the Son of God, had sufficient attributes of God that we need to consider him to be divine. As we explore what the New Testament says, we will also get a better idea of what it means to be divine.

Most of the passages that we will consider can be placed into one or more of the following four categories:

1. Pre-existence. That is, that Jesus, the Son of God, existed before his conception at Nazareth and his birth in Bethlehem.
2. Divinity. In many ways, Jesus talks about, or demonstrates attributes that are appropriate only for those who live in a divine world.
3. Lordship. Jesus has been made Lord by the Father. As Lord, Jesus is also worthy of receiving extensive honor—perhaps even worship.
4. Metaphor. Many words or phrases that are used for God are also used for Jesus.

What is Divinity?

Since we are exploring the status of Jesus as being divine, it is appropriate to discuss what this means. Obviously, the topic cannot be definitive because the human mind is incapable of grasping anything but a small portion of its meaning. But we have been created in the image and likeness of God, so we also share some of God's same attributes.

First, God must exist in a supernatural "environment." Simply put, the divine environment is not bounded by three simple space dimensions and one uni-directional time dimension. Being outside these dimensions allows God to not be restricted to a specific place or time; that is, he can be everywhere in our four dimensions at once. He is omni-present.

Perhaps a person's biggest barrier in trying to "comprehend" God's attributes is his inability to understand what it means not to be bound by time! For God, time is not restrictive; he can be, and is, everywhere and every time at once. In a sense, time doesn't exist for God, except insofar as his earthly creatures must dwell in it. That is why it is appropriate for God to use the phrase "I am" to describe Himself, for all times are the present for God.

Another barrier presents itself in man's being bounded within three dimensional space. It is very difficult to imagine what life is like outside those limitations. But here, again, God provides a hint via an ability that we have that transcends those three dimensions, and represents one aspect of being "made in the image and likeness of God." We think! And where do our thoughts reside? Certainly there are neurons firing in our brains that provide a physical support for our thoughts. But are our thoughts residing somewhere as a physical entity? Or, in a sense, do they reside in another dimension? Are they part of our spiritual soul? For, indeed, most of us probably consider our true existence not in being tied to a physical body, but to "who we are," our thoughts and feelings: our soul. And God, mysteriously, can read those thoughts, penetrating even that dimension.

When a person dies and "goes to heaven," does that person then enter into a divine realm? Are there more dimensions to explore? Is the soul no longer bound by time? Of course, we cannot know, and heaven may be a place of continuous evolution as we become continually "absorbed" into God, so "that God may be all in all" [1 Cor. 15:28]. But it seems very likely that we will, indeed, enter a realm that goes beyond our simple four dimensions as we know them. We will likely become more divine! But this is conjecture, without much biblical basis, except for a few insights from St. Paul and St. John:

> And all of us, with unveiled faces, seeing the glory of the Lord as though reflected in a mirror, are being transformed into the same image from one degree of glory to another; for this comes from the Lord, the Spirit. [2 Cor. 3:18]

> What I am saying, brothers and sisters, is this: flesh and blood cannot inherit the kingdom of God, nor does the perishable inherit the imperishable. Listen, I will tell you a mystery! We will not all

> die, but we will all be changed, in a moment, in the twinkling of an eye, at the last trumpet. For the trumpet will sound, and the dead will be raised imperishable, and we will be changed. [1 Cor. 15:50-52]

> Beloved, we are God's children now; what we will be has not yet been revealed. What we do know is this: when he is revealed, we will be like him, for we will see him as he is. [1 John 3:2]

For an expanded exposition of this idea, please see the entire relevant passage from 1 Corinthians [1 Cor. 15:35-55]. Also, for those who believe that Jesus is God, John's epistle implies that we would be like God, since we would be like Jesus!

We believe angels are created beings. Yet somehow they dwell in a supernatural realm. That is, to some extent, they exist—at least partially—in a divine realm. Perhaps they exist beyond our three dimensions of space but still are restricted in uni-dimensional time. (Of course this can lead to further unanswerable questions, such as whether God can then be ministered to by angels outside of time.) The important point is that there are beings who are not God that share at least some attributes of divinity that humans presently do not have.

Another attribute of the divine God is the ability to create. The opening verses of the first chapter of Genesis describe how "the earth was a formless void" when God said, "Let there be light." We can interpret a "formless void" to mean a "nothingness." From there, God created the laws of physics, energy, matter, and then life.

So God exists outside of time and space. And there are other characteristics which we attribute to God. He is all powerful. He is all knowing. These are divine attributes which God possesses, but clearly, his angels do not. Does the Son of God also possess these attributes? To understand more about the divine nature of Jesus, we once again need to rely on God's word and investigate further. We need to see what the Bible really says about Jesus.

Chapter 15

Pre-existence

Did Jesus exist, with knowledge and activity, before he was born in Bethlehem? The evidence within the New Testament strongly suggests that this is true. In this chapter we will look at this evidence, and even address the concerns that some religions and authors have in claiming Jesus did not pre-exist his birth.

One of the richest statements which Jesus makes that supports multiple aspects of divinity occurs in his dialogue with the Jews in John's eighth chapter. Picking this discussion up at its conclusion:

> Jesus answered, "If I glorify myself, my glory is nothing. It is my Father who glorifies me, he of whom you say, 'He is our God,' though you do not know him. But I know him and I keep his word. Your ancestor Abraham rejoiced that he would see my day; he saw it as was glad." Then the Jews said to him, "You are not yet fifty years old, and have you seen Abraham?" Jesus said to them, "Very truly I tell you, before Abraham was, I am." [John 8:54-58]

There are certainly other aspects of this quote that need exploring, but we will focus on how this relates to Jesus' pre-existence. When Jesus says "I am" what can it mean? If he merely wanted to state a pre-existence, he could have said more simply "before Abraham existed, I was." His actual statement emulates God's own name: "I am who I am" {YHWH} (Ex. 3:14). What Jesus says is a very strong statement! With it, he avers not only a pre-existence, but an existence that goes beyond a simple statement of humanity. The Jews understand this to mean that he is saying that he is God, and are outraged; they pick up rocks to stone him for blasphemy. But these Jews are mistaken. Jesus claim is not one of being God, but of divine pre-existence, which the Jews do not understand. By saying "I am" Jesus is indicating that he always has existed.

We find other examples of evidence from John. The prologue declares:

> John [the Baptist] testified to him and cried out, "This was he of whom I said, 'He who comes after me ranks ahead of me because he was before me.' " [John 1:15; also John 1:30]

First, the Gospel of Luke highlights that John the Baptist was conceived before Jesus was conceived and born before Jesus was born. Yet John, who must surely recognize his cousin, declares that Jesus "was before me." And even before Jesus' baptism, the Baptist holds in awe the yet-unrecognized one for whom he is dedicating his life. Does not the following verse indicate that John recognizes Jesus' divinity?

> John answered them, "I baptize with water. Among you stands one whom you do not know, the one who is coming after me; I am not worthy to untie the thong of his sandal." [John 1:26-27]

In chapter 3, John's Gospel almost becomes explicit in indicating a pre-existence, by stating that the Son came down from heaven:

> "The one who comes from above is above all; the one who is of the earth belongs to the earth and speaks about earthly things. The one who comes from heaven is above all. He testifies to what he has seen and heard, yet no one accepts his testimony. Whoever has accepted his testimony has certified this, that God is true. He who God has sent speaks the words of God, for he gives the Spirit without measure. The Father loves the Son and has placed all things in his hands." [John 3:31-35]

In his discourse on the "bread of life" Jesus says:

> "... for I have come down from heaven, not to do my own will, but the will of him who sent me." [John 6:38]

If Jesus came down from heaven, there is a strong implication that he had existed there beforehand, conscious of his being—unless we want to believe that God pre-manufactures souls in heaven to insert into bodies before they are born. At the Last Supper Jesus speaks not only of his existence, but of his glory before the world began when he says:

> "So now, Father, glorify me in your own presence with the glory that I had in your presence before the world existed." [John 17:5]

> "Father, I desire that those also, whom you have given me, may be with me where I am, to see my glory, which you have given me because you loved me before the foundation of the world." [John 17:24]

Perhaps less direct, but still hinting at having a kingdom that exists outside of his earthly existence—which mildly implies he likely had it beforehand:

> Jesus answered, "My kingdom is not from this world. If my kingdom were from this world, my followers would be fighting to keep me from being handed over to the Jews. But as it is, my kingdom is not from here." [John 18:36]

John uses somewhat more cryptic language in his first Epistle:

> We declare to you what was from the beginning, what we have heard, what we have seen with our eyes, what we have looked at and touched with our hands, concerning the word of life—this life was revealed, and we have seen it and testify to it, and declare to you the eternal life that was with the Father and was revealed to us— [1 John 1:1-2]

Here the language implies something even stronger than pre-existence. Instead, we are told that this "word of life," which seems to be a description of Jesus, existed with "eternal life that was with the Father." We are, once again, seeing a declaration of divinity.

Some may want to cite the prologue of John's gospel to also provide support:

> In the beginning was the Word, and the Word was with God, and the Word was God. He was in the beginning with God. All things came into being through him, and without him not one thing came into being. ... And the Word became flesh and lived among us, ... [John 1:1-3,14]

Many who don't believe in Jesus' pre-existence contend that the "Word," or *logos* in Greek, meant something like the intention or active will of God. This "purpose," then, only became a living man in Jesus at his birth. Thus, by itself, this passage may not be definitive proof of Jesus' pre-existence. But in consideration of all the other statements that more strongly imply a pre-existence, we should accept that this "Word" really was the Son of God—at the beginning. And that he participated in creation. This is partially supported by the statement attributed to God "Let us make humankind in our image, according to our likeness," [Gen. 1:26], and a mildly cryptic verse in the book of Revelation that implies Jesus was present before creation:

> And to the angel of the church in Laodicea write: The words of the Amen, the faithful and true witness, the origin of God's creation. [Rev. 3:14]

The NRSV note says that this "origin" is referring to Jesus, which makes sense in the context of the other terms used in this verse.

If our evidence only comes from John, then we might be inclined toward some skepticism. However, there are descriptions by other authors which provide impetus for belief in Jesus' pre-existence. The Synoptic Gospels are quiet on this matter (except indirectly), but Luke quotes Peter in Acts:

> "But you rejected the Holy and Righteous One and asked to have a murderer given to you, and you killed the Author of life, whom God raised from the dead." [Acts 3:14-15]

When did "life" begin? Are we to take this statement metaphorically in the sense that God is initiating his kingdom with Jesus, who brings eternal life? Or does it rather mean that the Son of God participated in creation at the beginning of the world? The meaning is not definitive, but is consistent with pre-existence when seen in context with other declarations. In a stronger statement, Paul says:

> He is the image of the unseen God, the firstborn of all creation; for in him all things in heaven and on earth were created, things visible and invisible, whether thrones or dominions or rulers or powers—all things have been created through him and for him. He himself is before all things, and in him all things hold together. [Col. 1:15-17]

The language is direct: Jesus was present at creation! At the original creation, the first man, Adam, was created. St. Paul then makes a distinction between this first man as being formed from the earth, and the "second" man—or second "Adam"—Jesus, when he writes:

> The first man was from the earth, a man of dust; the second man is from heaven. As was the man of dust, so are those who are of the

> dust; and as is the man of heaven, so are those who are of heaven. Just as we have borne the image of the man of dust, we will also bear the image of the man of heaven. [1 Cor. 15:47-49]

Jesus *is* the man of heaven. And he is <u>from</u> heaven. The distinction is powerful: Adam was created as part of God's six days of Creation; Jesus was not. Or else he, too, would be a "man of dust."

There are five other relevant citations which come from epistles attributed to St. Paul, but of which most scholars agree were written by others. In Second Timothy we find:

> Do not be ashamed, then, of the testimony about our Lord or of me his prisoner, but join with me in suffering for the gospel, relying on the power of God, who saved us and called us with a holy calling, not according to our works but according to his own purpose and grace. This grace was given to us in Christ Jesus before the ages began, but it has now been revealed through the appearing of our Savior Christ Jesus. [2 Tim. 1:8-10]

Grace was given to us "in Christ Jesus before the ages began." How could this happen unless Jesus was present at that time? In Hebrews, the author writes:

> ... but we do see Jesus, who for a little while was made lower than the angels, now crowned with glory and honor because of the suffering of death, ... [Heb. 2:9]

This is a direct statement that Jesus, in heaven, was then made man. In the following, the implication is that Jesus is a builder involved in "God's house:"

> Yet Jesus is worthy of more glory than Moses, just as the builder of a house has more honor than the house itself. . . Christ, however, was faithful over God's house as a son, and we are his house if we hold firm the confidence and the pride that belong to hope. [Heb. 3:3, 6]

In involving Moses in the discussion, there is some indication that this house of God that Jesus is involved in goes beyond the simple church of the New Covenant. If Jesus had a hand in the original building of the Old Covenant, then he must have been in existence before that time. The fourth and fifth passages hints at Jesus' pre-existence:

> He [Jesus] was destined before the foundation of the world, but was revealed at the end of the ages for your sake. [1 Pet. 1:20]

> Blessed be the God and Father of our Lord Jesus Christ, who has blessed us in Christ with every spiritual blessing in the heavenly places, just as he chose us in Christ before the foundation of the world to be holy and blameless before him in love. [Eph. 1:3-4]

The Old Testament even has a relevant passage. In Micah's prediction of where the Messiah is to be born there is the explicit statement that his origin significantly predates his birth:

> But you, O Bethlehem of Ephrathah, who are one of the little clans of Judah, from you shall come forth for me one who is to rule in Israel, whose origin is from of old, from ancient days. [Mic. 5:2]

Finally, there is the implication of Jesus' pre-existence in the simple matter that the Son of God was sent to an existence on earth by the Father. How can someone or something be sent if it does not already exist? Perhaps we could be swayed by an argument that an author merely lacked adequate language to imply that Jesus, as he was conceived—and in existence for the first time—had "received a commission" for redemption. But as we have seen in Chapter 4, multiple authors use exactly the language of "sent," without modification. We would truly have to convolute our definitions to conclude anything other than that Jesus already existed before he was sent.

As indicated, there is strong evidence that Jesus pre-existed his own earthly birth. However, in most of these cited cases, there is evidence only of a pre-existence and not necessarily a divine state. And so some religions, such as Jehovah's Witnesses, believe that Jesus was created at the start of all creation. In fact, there is more evidence in the New Testament supporting that Jesus was created than there is that he is co-equal with the Father or that God is a Trinity. Here are some of those passages, some of which have already been cited to support the premise that Jesus is not God:

> He is the image of the unseen God, the firstborn of all creation. [Col. 1:15]

> For those whom he [God] foreknew he also predestined to be conformed to the image of his Son, in order that he might be the firstborn within a large family. [Rom. 8:29]

> But in fact Christ has been raised from the dead, the first fruits of those who have died. For since death came through a human being, the resurrection of the dead has also come through a human being; for as all die in Adam, so all will be made alive in Christ. But each in his own order: Christ the first fruits, then at his coming those who belong to Christ. [1 Cor. 15:20-22]

Other than Colossians 1:15, these other verses have more obvious alternate interpretations that significantly weaken their support of Jesus being created. Both the Romans and First Corinthian passages are better understood in context to mean that Jesus is the first of those who will be raised from the dead. Even the apparent directness of Colossians 1:15 can be tempered by looking more deeply into the meaning of the Greek used. Barclay writes this:

> We must be very careful to attach the right meaning to this phrase. As it stands in English it might well mean the Son was the first person to be created, but in Hebrew and Greek thought the word *firstborn (prōtotokos)* has only very indirectly a time significance. There are two things to note. *Firstborn* is very commonly a title of *honour*. Israel, for instance, as a nation is the firstborn son of God (*Exodus* 4:22). The meaning is that the nation of Israel is the most favoured child of God. Second, we must note that *firstborn* is a title of the *Messiah*. In *Psalm* 89:27, as the Jews themselves interpreted it, the promise regarding the Messiah is "I will make him my firstborn, higher than the kings of the earth." Clearly *firstborn* is not used in a time sense at all, but in the sense of special honour.[1]

There is a connection between an Old Testament passage and a New Testament verse that also implies a beginning for the Son at the beginning of creation. Proverbs 8 describes Wisdom:

> The LORD created me at the beginning of his work, the first of his acts long ago. Ages ago I was set up, at the first, before the beginning of the earth ... When he established the heavens I was there, ... then I was beside him like a master worker; and I was daily in his delight, rejoicing before him always. [Prov. 8:22-23, 27, 30]

And St. Paul writes this about Jesus:

> But we proclaim Christ crucified, a stumbling block to Jews and foolishness to Gentiles, but to those who are the called, both Jews and Greeks, Christ the power of God and the wisdom of God. [1 Cor. 1:23-24]

By implication, if the Son is the Wisdom of God as Paul proclaims, then he had a beginning at the start of creation—if we take Proverbs literally. Of course, the language of Proverbs may be figurative, since certainly God's Wisdom always existed with Him, possibly being manifested as far as humans were concerned only at creation.
Perhaps the strongest passage supporting the lack of Jesus' divinity—and by implication which would support his being created—occurs in 1 Timothy:

> ... I charge you to keep the commandment without spot or blame until the manifestation of our Lord Jesus Christ, which he will bring about at the right time—he who is the blessed and only Sovereign, the King of kings and Lord of lords. It is he alone who has immortality and dwells in unapproachable light, whom no one has ever seen or can see, to him be honor and eternal dominion. Amen. [1 Tim. 6:13-16]

The "he" in verse 14 clearly indicates God the Father. But the author claims that only this one has immortality. What does this mean if we believers are also to inherit eternal life, and hence, immortality? A reasonable argument is that God alone had no beginning, which implies that His Son did have a beginning. The earliest Arians, whose views were condemned at the Council of Nicea (and of which much more will be said) are reported to have held the belief that of the Son "there was when he was not." Yet those apologists who place so much weight on Hebrews 1:8 ("But of the Son he says, 'your throne, O God, is forever and ever' ") conveniently ignore a verse that occurs only three verses earlier:

> For to which of the angels did God ever say, "You are my Son; today I have begotten you." [Heb. 1:5]

Here the strong implication is that God can claim that there was a day when His Son was begotten. Of course, God's "day" can occur in His own divine timelessness, but we can easily see the danger of literal interpretations, especially when Old Testament Scripture is being quoted both as in verse 5 and verse 8 of Hebrews.

Over all this isn't very strong evidence of Jesus' creation, and when we look at the further evidence of Christ's divinity—to be presented in the next chapters—we must either then believe that God raised Jesus into a state of divinity after Jesus' creation—and before his conception, or that the Son of God was always divine.

Chapter 16

Divinity

To his disciples, Jesus was an enigma. A charismatic speaker, he attracted crowds to himself. Sometimes he spoke plainly, such as during the Sermon on the Mount. Other times he wrapped his message in parables so dense that his disciples couldn't understand their meaning. And he talked about the kingdom of God with authority. But in order to validate the power of these words, he also publicly performed miracles, curing the hopelessly sick, driving out demons, feeding throngs of people from meager quantities of fish and bread, and even raising the dead back to life. In private he astonished his disciples by commanding fish to be caught in waiting nets, walking on water, and calming a storm.

Despite these signs, they still needed the gift of faith before they began to understand a small bit of the truth:

> He [Jesus] said to them, "But who do you say that I am?" Simon Peter answered, "You are the Messiah, the Son of the living God." And Jesus answered him, "Blessed are you Simon son of Jonah! For flesh and blood has not revealed this to you, but my Father in heaven." [Matt. 16:15-17]

But just what did it mean to be the Son of God? Even with the gift of the Holy Spirit at Pentecost—and after—they struggled to find words to describe who Jesus was. As we saw in Part 2, they did not believe Jesus was God. Yet since Jesus possessed such attributes that only God had possessed, they struggled for ways to describe that unique individual who they had been privileged to know so well.

So as we explore what the writers of the New Testament say regarding the divine nature of Jesus, the Son of God, we frequently encounter language that is almost metaphoric. This is, perhaps, not because the disciples were uncertain of whom Jesus was, but that they had no non-God language to describe it.

Declarations of Divinity

Earlier, we had considered a number of verses which proponents of God-as-Trinity claimed proved that Jesus is God. When these verses were discussed, we learned that they did not have to be interpreted in exactly that way. Instead, many of these verses imply Jesus has the status of divinity, without being God. It's time to revisit those verses.

Of course, prominent among them is John 1:1. In that verse, we saw that the meaning of "and the Word was God" was actually a mistranslation. Instead, the modifier in front of "God" implied that the word "God" was not to be taken as a noun but an adjective. As such, a better interpretation would be "the Word was God-like" or "the Word was just like God," or "the Word was divine." To our minds, we cannot fully comprehend the difference since the divine and all it encompasses is so far beyond our understanding. But we can understand that while John is claiming that Jesus is divine, he is at the same time <u>not</u> saying that Jesus is God.

The Epistle to the Philippians makes a similar declaration:

> Christ Jesus: Who, though he was in the form of God, did not regard equality with God as something to be exploited ...
> [Phil. 2:5, 6]

Remember, again, that the word translated "exploited" actually means "seized," as in a robbery. There are two important points. First, it says that Jesus was in the "form of God." What does this mean if not that Jesus is divine? Yet, since the author could have instead written, "Jesus, being God," he must have wanted to make the distinction clear. Secondly, the divine Jesus could have wanted to exalt himself to God's level (presumably as Satan tried to do), thereby "stealing" what he did not (and could not) have—equality with God.

St. Paul is more blatant in claiming a Jesus who goes far beyond simple humanity:

> He is the image of the invisible God, the firstborn of all creation; for in him all things in heaven and on earth were created, things visible and invisible, whether thrones or dominions or rulers or powers—all things have been created through him and for him. He himself is before all things, and in him all things hold together... For in him, all the fullness of God was pleased to dwell. [Col. 1:15-17, 19]

In verse 19, what can be the meaning of the phrase "all the fullness of God?" God is divine, and so "all the fullness of God" must include divinity! Furthermore, in the other verses Paul avers that Jesus clearly participated in creation, acts which also must be totally flavored with the divine. Note, too, that this "fullness of God" was "pleased to dwell." This denotes, again, a voluntary act on God's part to dwell within Jesus; Jesus did not have it by right of his divinity.

But we also encounter something which raises the question of whether Jesus was eternally pre-existent—he is "the firstborn of all creation." Does this mean that the creation of the Son was the first act of God in the creation story? Or was something else happening besides creation? For we need to contemplate what it means for a person to be "born" from God. Here the closing of the prologue of John's gospel gives us some additional insights:

> And the Word became flesh and lived among us, and we have seen his glory, the glory as of a father's only son, full of grace and truth. [John 1:14]

Note that the words "a father's only son" can equally be translated as "the Father's only Son." Jesus is not only a son, but he is the *only* son—and sons are not created, they are "generated," as it were, "begotten." Verse 18 potentially adds corroborative meaning, although multiple translations are also possible:

> No one has ever seen God. It is God the only Son who is close to the Father's heart, who has made him known. [John 1:18]

Other alternative manuscripts read:

> No one has ever seen God. It is the son, the only begotten god, who is close to the Father's bosom, who has explained him.

If Jesus were God, then John is wrong in saying that "No one has ever seen God." Instead, we need to seek a more "diluted" interpretation if we want to avoid a contradiction. That diluted interpretation may involve a lack of vocabulary. Writers used the word *theos* to indicate both Yahweh and a pagan god. But what word could they use to indicate a divine being who dwells intimately with Yahweh? Even English, with its extensive vocabulary, has no such word. Thus, it is not unreasonable for the authors to use *theos* for that position as well. In this way, Thomas' exclamation "My lord and my God" [John 20:28] and the Epistle to Titus' "manifestation of the glory of our great God and Savior, Jesus Christ" [Titus 2:13] take on a modified interpretation that doesn't insist that Jesus is God in its fullest sense. We will also see later that the early Church Fathers occasionally used the term "God" for Jesus, but simultaneously implied his subordination.

Another more direct statement relating to Jesus' divinity is expressed again in St. Paul's epistle to the Colossians:

> For in him [Jesus], the whole fullness of deity dwells bodily. [Col. 2:9]

While this verse is sometimes claimed to show that Jesus is God, the literal meaning is different. The key modifier is "bodily." The fullness of God was present in Jesus while on earth as a man. Paul did not have to add that important word "bodily" if Jesus is God. In a sense, Jesus was totally filled with God's Holy Spirit. This certainly began with Jesus' conception, where the Holy Spirit came upon Mary and the power of the Most High overshadowed her [Luke 1:35]. But it also continued through Jesus' special union with the Father throughout his life, his obedience to the Father's will, and whatever power and grace the Father granted him. Yet there is something more, for with that union with the divine God, Jesus was able to be as close to the Father as one could be while still in human form. Jesus is the projection of the divine God unto the human universe, with the limitation of three spatial dimensions, constrained in time. It is wrong to look at that projection and claim what the real object is, just as much as it is wrong for us to see a shadow and conclude anything about the color of the object that made that shadow or to see a television image and conclude what is in the heart of the person there.

John's first epistle contains a passage that has already been cited to support Jesus' pre-existence. But we need to appreciate the importance of it as evidence of Jesus' divinity.

> We declare to you what was from the beginning, what we have heard, what we have seen with our eyes, what we have looked at and touched with our hands, concerning the word of life—this life was revealed, and we have seen it and testify to it, and declare to you the eternal life that was with the Father and was revealed to us—we declare to you what we have seen and heard so that you also may have fellowship with us; and truly our fellowship is with the Father and with his Son Jesus Christ. [1 John 1:1-3]

The use of the past tense is key, for the eternal life that was with the Father is implied to be the Son. We believers hope to gain eternal life with God, but Jesus had that eternal life before he assumed a human existence. And an initial eternal life is associated with true divinity.

There are two very subtle references to Jesus' divinity. The first occurs in the Old Testament when God asks Solomon in a dream what he wants. When Solomon asks for wisdom to rule his people, part of God's reply is:

> "I now do according to your word. Indeed I give you a wise and discerning mind; no one like you has been before you and no one like you shall arise after you." [1 Kings 3:12]

However, we know that Jesus was wiser than Solomon. Has God misspoken, or should we understand that this is only a dream and it should not be taken too literally? Or could there be more depth involved? When God says "no one *like you*," He may not just mean a person with wisdom; He may also be including ordinary human beings. This could then exclude the possibility of those outside the created realm. And Jesus, with a divine status, would certainly not be like Solomon in that regard.

The second subtle reference to Jesus' divinity occurs in Jesus' last dialogue with the Pharisees when he asked the Pharisees about the Messiah and they indicated he would be the son of David. Jesus then asks them:

> "How is it then that David by the Spirit calls him Lord, saying, 'The Lord said to my Lord, "Sit at my right hand, until I put your enemies under your feet"'? If David thus calls him Lord, how can he be his son?" [Matt. 22:43-45; also Mark 12:36-37 and Luke 20:42-44]

We know Jesus is the Messiah, and in this quote he claims to be David's lord. Since David was considered the greatest king of Israel, the implication is that Jesus' status must be even higher. And does this not also indicate a hierarchy and separation?

There is still another New Testament source that is filled with descriptions of the Son which imply his divinity. This is the epistle to the Hebrews, and the first two chapters in particular are rich in such language. However, a detailed accounting of this added proof will be postponed until Chapter 19: *Who, Then, Is Jesus?*

Divine Powers

As we have seen, Jesus possessed power to perform miracles. Similar power had been demonstrated by people of the Old Testament, such as Moses who parted the Red Sea [Ex. 14:21] and Elijah who rained down fire from heaven [1 Kings 18:36-38] and raised a dead child to life [1 Kings 17:17-23]. Yet it was always clear that Yahweh was directly working through them. With Jesus it was different, for he seemed to possess the power, as if God had given him these powers to use at his own discretion. We see this in Jesus' gratitude to the Father for all God had given him. Thus, Jesus does not fall into the same pattern as other men in this miraculous power that he possesses.

As mediator to God, a role which is present even during his earthly life, Jesus also demonstrates a power that certainly supersedes any human power. We are dependent on Jesus in order to reach the Father. In the analogy that Jesus presents of being the True Vine in John's Gospel, Jesus declares,

> "... apart from me you can do nothing." [John 15:5]

This same principle is foreshadowed in the previous chapter, when Jesus tells his apostles:

> "I am the way, the truth, and the life. No one comes to the Father except through me." [John 14:6]

Can this be anything other than a supernatural power?

There are three other powers that are important to note. First, Jesus could forgive sins. This is illustrated when Jesus cured a paralytic, but first said some startling words:

> "Take heart, son; your sins are forgiven." [Matt. 9:3]

But Jesus knowing that he was thought to have committed blasphemy continued:

> "For which is it easier to say, 'Your sins are forgiven,' or to say, 'Stand up and walk'?" [Matt. 9:5]

However, what is remarkable is the crowds' reaction:

> When the crowds saw it, they were filled with awe, and they glorified God who had given such authority to human beings. [Matt. 9:8]

(The story is also told in Mark 2:4-12 and Luke 5:18-26.) For the scribes, forgiving sins was taking upon oneself a power that only God could possess. Yet Jesus claims that very power. He doesn't specifically say that that power has been given to him; he just indicates he has the authority. However, the scribes are mistaken—at least in assuming Jesus is claiming to be God. For we know that this is a power that is transferable. After Jesus' resurrection, he grants this same power to his disciples:

> [Jesus said:] "If you forgive the sins of any, they are forgiven them; if you retain the sins of any, they are retained." [John 20:23]

If this power can be handed on, certainly God could have granted his Son that same power. This does not diminish the importance of this power; it still is a divine power. And Jesus' conferring this power on others is a defining moment in ecclesiastic history. Jesus must be special in a way that seems supernatural—divine.

Secondly, there is an interesting exchange with the Pharisees when Jesus is challenged about his disciples gathering food on the Sabbath. After providing an answer that recounts how David had done something even more drastic on the Sabbath, Jesus makes an unusual claim:

> Then he said to them, "The Son of Man is lord of the sabbath." [Luke 6:5; also Matt. 12:8]

This is truly a shocking assertion! The Sabbath was a day of rest, ordained by God in the Ten Commandments. Certainly the Pharisees in their legalism had warped the Sabbath's meaning, and Jesus was trying to straighten them out. But by declaring himself "lord of the Sabbath," he is implying power that enters into the supernatural realm. Look at the more expanded version in Mark:

> Then he said to them, "The sabbath was made for humankind, and not humankind for the sabbath; so the Son of Man is lord even of the sabbath." [Mark 2:27-28]

Mark implies that the Sabbath is man's domain, which still goes beyond the Pentateuch's strict prohibitions and restrictions—laws which God had given Moses. Of course, this becomes part of a new Covenant which Jesus brought, where the Law of Moses is being superseded by the new law of faith and love. But is Jesus just being a messenger, or does a divine status enable him to make such statements? We have been told that creation is through him and for him, with humanity being especially tied to the Son, so it is possible that the Sabbath was actually a gift by the Son to allow people to rest at least one day a week. Once again, the single incident is not definitive; but in the context of all the other evidence, it becomes highly supportive of Jesus' divine power.

The third exhibition of unique divine power comes in John's famous "bread of life" discourse. To some denominations, this text, along with Jesus' words at the Last Supper, definitively prove Jesus' real presence in the Eucharist, or Holy Communion:

> [Jesus said:] "I am the living bread that came down from heaven. Whoever eats of this bread will live forever; and the bread that I will give for the life of the world is my flesh." The Jews then disputed among themselves, saying, "How can this man give us his flesh to eat?" So Jesus said to them, "Very truly, I tell you, unless you eat the flesh of the Son of Man and drink his blood, you have no life in you. Those who eat my flesh and drink my blood have eternal life, and I will raise them up on the last day; for my flesh is true food and my blood is true drink." [John 6:51-55]

Jesus demands that we eat his flesh and drink his blood—an impossibility by any human standard, since his natural body is finite and would presumably decay. So the claim must extend beyond the natural interpretation: the body and blood possess a supernatural character that we can partake in, and this will only be possible if Jesus resides in the realm of the divine. And this divinity isn't constrained only to a post-resurrected Jesus, since the Apostles partake in the body and blood at the Last Supper while Jesus is still alive as human. Thus, Jesus cannot make this demand unless it involves Jesus' divinity.

Divine Association

The Synoptic Gospels present a story that highlights Jesus' special status. Jesus takes Peter, James and John up a mountain, where he is supernaturally transfigured [Mark 9:2-8; Matt. 17:1-7; Luke 9:28-36]. Not only is his appearance radically changed, but he converses with two major figures from Israel's past, Moses and Elijah. Jesus speaks face to face with a dead person! (Elijah was taken bodily into heaven, so we don't know his physical status.) Has it ever been recorded that either of these events had happened to another individual? No, and we need to recognize that this event is more than a simple temporary exaltation of an ordinary human being, especially when God himself calls out through the sky,

> "This is my Son, the Beloved; listen to him." [Mark 9:7]

John's Gospel is filled with statements that link Jesus to God, the Father, in ways that no present human can claim. In particular, the first, fifth, sixth and eighth chapters highlight very strong statements, most by Jesus himself, that virtually declare a pre-existent, divine relationship with God. Jesus claimed God as his father by saying he was his son, and the Jews saw in this a claim to godhead:

> For this reason the Jews were seeking all the more to kill him, because he was not only breaking the Sabbath, but was also calling God his own Father, thereby making himself equal to God. [John 5:18]

The Jews could not differentiate levels of divinity, so they saw these claims of being the Son as the same as being on the same level of God, and therefore equality. Yet so many other verses previously cited contradict this interpretation; we can conclude divinity without there having to be equality.

John emphasizes the special relationship that Jesus has with the Father and which goes far beyond any earthly bond:

> [Jesus said:] "Not that anyone has seen the Father except the one who is from God; he has seen the Father." [John 6:46]

> "If you knew me, you would know my Father also." [John 8:19]

> He said to them, "You are from below, I am from above; you are of this world, I am not of this world." [John 8:23]

> "I declare what I have seen in the Father's presence." [John 8:38]

"The Father and I are one." [John 10:30]

"And whoever sees me sees him who sent me." [John 12:45; John 14:9 is similar]

John says "No one has ever seen God" [John 1:18], yet Jesus makes that claim [John 6:46]. Is John wrong, or could Jesus be excluded in John's commentary because he really means "no ordinary human" when he says "no one?" And how can the Son be one with the divine Father unless he himself is also divine? Similarly, how can one see the Father in Jesus unless Jesus possesses the Father's attributes?

Once again, John's message is the strongest of all the New Testament writers in indicating Jesus' divinity. But we also see this idea occasionally brought out by the other authors. One less obvious group of witnesses can be found in the demons who are exorcised by Jesus. For example, one of them says:

"What have you to do with me, Jesus, Son of the Most High God? I beg you, do not torment me." [Luke 8:28]

The demon already knows Jesus' unique status as God's son, and that this son—by himself—has the power both to exorcise and torment. This power has been given by the Father, but it is a supernatural power. Luke's story continues as the formerly possessed man begs to stay with Jesus. But Jesus replies:

"Return to your home, and declare how much God has done for you." [Luke 8:39]

Of course, God is working through Jesus. So these verses aren't "proof" that Jesus, who exorcised, is God, but they do support the supernatural power and mission Jesus has.

One story, found only in Matthew's gospel, involves the issue of paying the temple tax, a tax levied on all adult Jewish males to support temple sacrifices. Jesus and Peter have this exchange:

Jesus spoke of it first, asking, "What do you think, Simon? From whom do kings of the earth take toll or tribute? From their children or from others?" When Peter said, "From others," Jesus said to him, "Then the children are free." [Matt. 17:25-26]

Here, Jesus is exempting himself from the rules that apply to ordinary Jews, because he claims he is a child of God. This thinking, by itself, was somewhat radical for an ordinary member of the "chosen people of God" to have. But Jesus already understands his mission, being the only begotten Son of God. As St. Paul says, Jesus "is the firstborn of many brothers" [Rom. 8:29]; yet this position comes first from heaven, and then is bestowed, by adoption, to others. Jesus sees his right not to be taxed because of his direct relationship with God—which is divine. For Peter, it has come already through adoption.

Chapter 17

Lordship

A constant thread that runs through the non-gospel writings of the New Testament is that Jesus is Lord. This is a fundamental tenet of the Christian faith, and is echoed in dozens of passages (many of them previously cited to show that God and Jesus are separate persons).

Yes, Jesus is Lord. But how did this happen, or was it always so? And what does it mean? We've already seen in Acts that God raised Jesus to the status of Lord. Peter says to the crowd at Pentecost:

> "Therefore let the entire house of Israel know with certainty that God made him both Lord and Messiah, this Jesus whom you crucified." [Acts 2:36]

But what does it mean for Jesus to be Lord? Previously, the status of "Lord" was held exclusively by God, the Father. Now we have a different set of relationships to deal with. God is the ultimate King, and Jesus is the Lord of humanity who serves under the king. Mankind serves the King by serving his representative. We see throughout the non-gospel books of the New Testament references to Jesus as Lord with the meaning just cited. One simple, but powerful example is written by St, Paul. And it refers to our salvation:

> If you confess with your lips that Jesus is Lord and believe in your heart that God raised him from the dead, you will be saved. [Rom. 10:9]

However, we need to realize that this status as Lord is a divine status. That is, Jesus has not merely been exalted as a human to being Lord. First, no human could transcend time and space, and we see that Jesus does exactly that. Furthermore, we are expected to act before Jesus in much the same way as we act toward God. For example, Jesus says in the Gospel of John:

> "Indeed, just as the Father raises the dead and gives them life, so also the Son gives life to whomever he wishes. The Father judges no one but has given all judgment to the Son, so that all may honor the Son just as they honor the Father. Anyone who does not

honor the Son does not honor the Father who sent him." [John 5:21-23]

Furthermore, St. Paul writes:

> Therefore God also highly exalted him and gave him the name that is above every name, so that at the name of Jesus every knee should bend in heaven and on earth and under the earth, and every tongue should confess that Jesus Christ is Lord to the glory of God the Father. [Phil. 2:9-11]

The "honoring" of the Son as we honor the Father, and the bowing of the knees—just at the <u>name</u> of Jesus—implies an honor and respect that transcends earthly power. Just as we should be honoring God and respecting His name in a sacred manner, we are expected to honor Jesus and respect Jesus' name in almost the same way.

Does this honor and respect extend to worshiping Jesus? In the passage of John, just cited, one could argue that this honoring is solely in relation to the judging activity that the Father and Son have, and does not extend to the honor—and worship—due to creation and kingship of the universe that the Father has. And as discussed in Chapter 9, the New Testament provides us with a conundrum because the Greek word used for "worship," *proskuneo*, also can be interpreted as "to pay homage," as in bowing down. Thus, within the Gospels our translation can never truly be definitive.

Yet we do see examples where whatever honoring is occurring is happening at an elevated level.

> On entering the house, they [the Magi] saw the child with Mary, his mother; and they knelt down and paid him homage. [Matt. 2:11]

> When they got into the boat, the wind ceased. And those in the boat worshiped him, saying, "Truly, you are the Son of God." [Matt. 14:33]

> Now the eleven disciples went to Galilee, to the mountain to which Jesus had directed them. When they saw him, they worshiped him; but some doubted. [Matt. 28:16-17]

> While he was blessing them, he withdrew from them and was carried up into heaven. And they worshiped him, and returned to

Jerusalem with great joy; and they were continually in the temple blessing God. [Luke 24:51-53]

Again, these verses must be interpreted with caution. Why did some apostles doubt? And what were they doubting? When they returned to Jerusalem, why weren't they blessing Jesus as well as God? Also, in the Luke version, some ancient manuscripts lack "and they worshiped him."

So we have seen that generally, the gospels do not provide anything definitive about worshiping Jesus. What do the other New Testament books say? Other than the Philippians reference, St. Paul is silent on the matter. In fact, the only possible references occur in books written late in the apostolic era: Hebrews and Revelation. In Hebrews we find:

> For to which of the angels did God ever say, "You are my Son, today I have begotten you?" Or again, "I will be his Father and he will be my Son?" And again, when he brings the firstborn into the world, he says, "Let all God's angels worship him." [Heb. 1:5-6]

Again, we have the ambiguity of the Greek providing an alternative, legitimate translation of "bowing down and honoring" the firstborn Son instead of "worshiping." The meaning cannot be definitive. But the fact that the supernatural angels are to be doing this has an implication that extends beyond what the Magi performed—once again providing evidence for Jesus' divinity.

The book of Revelation has a single passage that also hints at worship of Jesus—although we must assume that the "Lamb" is Jesus (which is sensible enough based on other texts within Revelation):

> Then I looked, and I heard the voice of many angels surrounding the throne and the living creatures and the elders; they numbered myriads of myriads and thousands of thousands, singing with full voice, "Worthy is the Lamb that was slaughtered to receive power and wealth and wisdom and might and honor and glory and blessing!" Then I heard every creature in heaven and on earth and under the earth and in the sea, and all that is in them, singing, "To the one seated on the throne and to the Lamb be blessing and honor and glory and might forever and ever! And the four living creatures said, "Amen!" And the elders fell down and worshiped. [Rev. 5:11-14]

Although as has been covered in Chapter 9, it is not clear that the Lamb is being worshiped in the last verse, it is clear that he is to receive much the same esteem as does God, the one seated on the throne.

In the book of Revelation, there are numerous references to the "one seated on the throne" and to the "Lamb." The former is clearly God, and he isn't sharing his throne! Yet, since God "highly exalted" Jesus, he has put him on a level far above everyone and everything else, so that Jesus receives something very close to what we can call worship. Nevertheless, whatever it may be still falls under—and below—the shadow of God.

It is important to note that Trinitarians have used many of these same texts to support Jesus being God. One contention is that at the time of the New Testament, the use of "Lord" for God instead of "YHWH" was the common practice. Since Jesus is also given that title, they feel that the writers are bestowing it because he is God. However, God himself gave Jesus that position and title [Acts 2:36], and thus it certainly does not have to mean that Jesus is God. Similarly, whatever honor Jesus receives—be it homage or worship—it is due Jesus because the Father commands it, and not because Jesus is God.

In summary, then, the earthly life of Jesus as recorded in the Gospels does not definitively indicate Jesus was worshiped. However, they do show he already possessed a status among his disciples that went beyond simple respect, and his claims of power foreshadowed his status as Lord. In the non-Gospel writings we see that the Son of God has been made "Lord," and this lordship extends into the eternal and divine kingdom of God. This lordship confers upon Jesus the sacred right that all others are to pay him homage—at a level that approaches, if not includes, worship. This status is indeed a divine status, and therefore requires a divine being to receive it.

Chapter 18

Metaphors and Descriptors

There remain two other aspects of Jesus which helps define his divinity. Unfortunately, there are many who claim that these aspects also "prove" that Jesus is God. These aspects in biblical writings are the metaphors and the descriptors that both God and the Son of God share. That is, there are names and phrases that are used to describe God, and which also are used to describe Jesus.

What are some of these metaphors/descriptors? Some are nouns and some represent actions. For example, in 2 Thessalonians:

> And then the lawless one will be revealed whom the Lord Jesus will destroy with the breath of his mouth, annihilating him by the manifestation of his coming. [2 Thes. 2:8]

But the breath of God was similarly powerful:

> By the breath of God they perish .... [Job 4:9]

> By the word of the Lord the heavens were made, and all their host by the breath of his mouth. [Ps. 33:6]

> ... and with the breath of his lips he shall kill the wicked. [Is. 11:4]

There are several reasons why such metaphors and descriptors are not proofs of Jesus' godship. First, most of these descriptors are applied to the risen Jesus, after the Father has elevated him to Lord. That is, the divine Jesus now sits at God's right hand and has been bestowed with many of those powers which God alone had possessed in the Old Testament. Thus, for example, God in the Old Testament is called "Lord of lords" [Ps. 136:3], and Jesus is given that appellation in Revelation 19:16. Clearly, the passage in Revelation requires a different interpretation, since it must exclude the Father because the term "Lord" is singular. The New Testament writers assume the reader understands that God Himself is at the top, as revealed in an already referenced passage from St. Paul:

> For he [God] has put all things in subjection under his [Jesus'] feet. But when it says, "All things are put in subjection," *it is plain* that this does not include the one [God] who put all things in subjection

> under him. [1 Cor. 15:27, emphasis added]

We never really see this point emphasized in the New Testament—except in this passage—because it was assumed to be obvious!

There are numerous names or phrases which are applied to both God and Jesus. To name just a few: "good shepherd" (Ezek. 34, John 10); "lord of glory" (Ps. 24:10, 1 Cor. 2:8); "light" (1 John 1:5, John 8:12); "first and last" (Is. 44:6, Rev. 1:17); "redeemer" (Is. 43:14, Titus 2:14); "hair like white wool" (Dan. 7:9, Rev. 1:14). If Jesus were God, these associations would make sense. But they also make sense if God has elevated his Son to a position of heavenly lordship and sent him on the mission of the redemption of the world. Though in the Old Testament God said "My glory I will not give to another" [Is. 48:11; also Is. 42:8], He does indeed later <u>share</u> that glory with his Son. And that glory necessarily implies a divine nature.

Thus, there is a rich body of metaphors and parallels that exegesis uncovers between the Old and New Testament. The most important one is overt: The Passover lamb is sacrificed, with its blood causing the angel of death to pass over the believers, leading to freedom from slavery and a renewed covenant with God; Jesus' blood sacrifice conquers death, allowing believers to be free and born into eternal life through a New Covenant. However, we need to be careful with the more subtle parallels, for the actions of God as demonstrated in the Old Testament are often replaced by those of Jesus in the New because God has chosen to elevate Jesus.

The second weakness in the argument is that we know that we do not have the language to express the supernatural: there are simply no words that can bridge the dimensions and timelessness of God! So the biblical writers were forced to use metaphors. If the biblical writers then wanted to talk of the supernatural Son of God, then they were forced also to use metaphors—and these, necessarily, will overlap those used for God.

A third weakness falls under the accidental use of metaphors that also describe God. That is, in searching for descriptions for Jesus, the New Testament writers may have merely chosen ones that fit, but didn't realize others had used the same metaphor to describe God.

Finally, not all metaphors necessarily have divine implications. Simon, the apostle of Jesus was called "Cephas," or "rock." Jesus is also called a "rock:"

> ... and all were baptized into Moses in the cloud and the sea, ...

and all drank the same spiritual drink. For they drank from the spiritual rock that followed them, and the rock was Christ. [1 Cor. 10:2, 4; see also Rom. 9:33]

But "rock" was a common descriptor of God in the Old Testament; we find it used in Deuteronomy 32:4; 2 Samuel 22:2, 32, and 47; and Psalms 18, 28, 31, 62, 78, 89, 92, 94, and 95. So it is somewhat presumptive to assign the use of mutual metaphors to something stronger than what they really can imply.

In summary, these metaphors and descriptors which are used both for God and Jesus provide us with a greater insight into the nature of the Son of God. For the most part, they do imply a special status for the Son that surpasses basic humanity, and supports his divinity. While many might claim that they also imply his being God, all the other evidence strongly indicates otherwise.

Chapter 19

Who, Then, Is Jesus?

There are several places within the New Testament where the divine nature of Jesus is most succinctly described. Perhaps the most straightforward of these descriptions occurs in the second chapter of St. Paul's letter to the Philippians, an epistle that most theologians and translators believe was truly authored by Paul. In verses 5 through 11, a clear elucidation is brought out: "let the same mind be in you that was in Christ Jesus ..."

"... who, though he was in the form of God, ..."
This verse attests not only to the declaration that Jesus was divine, but that he also was <u>not</u> God, since he was in the "form" of God. If St. Paul had believed the Jesus was God, there was no reason to hold back that truth, and instead use language such as "though he was God."

"... did not regard equality with God as something to be stolen [snatched, as in a robbery], ..."
Jesus was not at God's level, nor was he equal with God; therefore, he might have considered, in pride, that he might surreptitiously gain that equal status. But he did not. In contrast, perhaps this is was Satan thought!

"... but emptied himself, taking the form of a slave and being born in human likeness."
Jesus, following God's plan for man's salvation, temporarily relinquished his divine status and became man. How else can he "empty" himself unless he already was in an highly elevated state?

"And being found in human form, he humbled himself ..."
Already humbled by being a man, as a man he chose to be totally obedient to his Father and became a slave of God, embracing a human status enveloped in poverty instead of wealth.

"... and became obedient to the point of death—even death on a cross."
This obedience included a blood sacrifice which not only involved Jesus' physical death, but which entailed horrible, tortuous suffering. Thus, he willfully rejected a quiet, relatively painless death (which

most humans could possibly share). This incredible choice clearly showed the depth of Jesus' obedience to his Father.

"Therefore, God also highly exalted him ..."
Due to Jesus' act of supreme obedience just alluded to (note the "therefore"), the Father chose to elevate the status of his Son. This elevation did not simply mean his raising Jesus from the dead, but that the Father <u>highly</u> exalted him.

"... and gave him a name that is above every name, so that at the name of Jesus every knee should bend, in heaven and on earth and under the earth,   ..."
The exalting by the Father raises Jesus to a status beyond any other being—except God himself. The Father himself will enforce this rule.

"... and every tongue should confess that Jesus Christ is Lord, ..."
Just as everyone will pay supreme homage (kneeling before) to Jesus, they will recognize that God has made Jesus everyone's Lord.

"... to the glory of God the Father."
All of these actions by the Father, from the plan of salvation to the exaltation of the Son, including naming Jesus as the intermediary Lord below God but above humankind, will result in the increase of the rightful and proper glorification of the Father by mankind. The recognition by man of the role of the Son, Jesus, and his important new status, will lead humanity to a closer relationship with the Father and a greater appreciation of the love the Father has for us.

<u>The Epistle to the Hebrews</u>

A second major and succinct source of what we know about Jesus' divine status can be found in the Epistle to the Hebrews. Indeed, this letter contains some of the richest text regarding the nature of Jesus. In particular, the first two chapters provide a summary that represents what First Century (or early Second Century) Christians believed about Jesus, and these chapters are well worth reviewing. It is important to emphasize once again that these verses do not stand alone in what they state; the same message can be found sprinkled throughout the New Testament. But these verses succinctly define, in most ways, how we are to think of Jesus, the Son of God.

The opening verses read:

> Long ago God spoke to our ancestors in many and various ways by the prophets, but in these last days he has spoken to us by a Son, whom he appointed heir of all things, through whom he also created the worlds. He is the reflection of God's glory, and the exact imprint of God's very being, and he sustains all things by his powerful word. When he had made purification for sins, he sat down at the right hand of the Majesty on high, having become as much superior to angels as the name he has inherited is more excellent than theirs. [Heb. 1:1-4]

Note again, particularly, the carefully crafted distinction that the author makes between God and his Son. The Son is a "reflection" and an "exact imprint." Jesus is an "appointed heir." These are words that clearly delineate an inferiority of the Son to God, his Father, just as our own reflection or footprint is inferior to ourselves, and being an heir implies receiving something we did not have. Yet the author is quick to point out that although the Son is inferior to God, he is superior to the rest of creation. This Son, too, preceded the creation of the world, for God's creation was through the Son. To emphasize the Son's high status, the author of Hebrews goes on:

> And again, when he brings the firstborn into the world, he [God] says, "Let all God's angels worship {pay homage to?} him." [Heb. 1:6]

The reason for the Son's high status is explained later:

> ... but we do see Jesus, who for a little while was made lower than the angels, now crowned with glory and honor because of the suffering of death, so that by the grace of God he might taste death for everyone. [Heb. 2:9]

> ... let us run the race that is set before us, looking to Jesus the pioneer and perfecter of our faith, who for the sake of the joy that was set before him endured the cross, disregarding its shame, and has taken his seat at the right hand of the throne of God. [Heb. 12:1-2]

Jesus endured the cross for the joy he would *later* receive. And because of this shared experience with humanity, Jesus is now considered a brother of mankind:

> It was fitting that God, for whom and through whom all things exist, in bringing many children to glory, should make the pioneer of their salvation perfect through sufferings. For the one who sanctifies and those who are sanctified all have one Father. For this reason, Jesus is not ashamed to call them brothers and sisters ... [Heb. 2:10-11]

Jesus' sacrifice takes on even more significance than a shared humanity:

> Since, therefore, the children share flesh and blood, he himself likewise shares the same things, so that through death he might destroy the one who has the power of death, that is, the devil, and free those who all their lives were held in slavery by the fear of death. [Heb. 2:14-15]

However, this shared humanity was necessary in God's eyes for another, special reason:

> Therefore he had to become like his brothers and sisters in every respect, so that he might be a merciful and faithful high priest in the service of God, to make a sacrifice of atonement for the sins of the people. Because he himself was tested by what he suffered, he is able to help those who are being tested. [Heb. 2:17-18]

This role as the ultimate High Priest remains a theme through much of the remainder of the epistle:

> For we do not have a high priest who is unable to sympathize with our weaknesses, but we have one who in every respect has been tested as we are, yet without sin. [Heb. 4:15]

> Now the main point in what we are saying is this: we have such a high priest, one who is seated at the right hand of the throne of the Majesty, in the heavens, a minister in the sanctuary and the true tent that the Lord, and not any mortal, has set up. [Heb. 8:1-2]

> But Jesus has now obtained a more excellent ministry, and to that

> degree he is the mediator of a better covenant, ... [Heb. 8:6]

> ... but he entered into heaven itself, now to appear in the presence of God on our behalf. [Heb. 9:24]

Jesus is a divine mediator, who, by sharing humanity with us, understands man's weaknesses. He is not God, but the perfect mediator between man and God—all according to God's perfect plan. Jesus could have remained God's heavenly Son, partaking in the glow of God's glory in heaven. But instead, by obeying the Father's will, he became human, remained sinless, and became the perfect blood sacrifice. For these reasons, he was raised up to God's right hand, and has been given glory beyond what he had had previously. And he now acts as mediator and judge.

John's Gospel

To understand more about Jesus, we turn to John's gospel, which provides additional insight into Jesus' divine status and his various roles in God's plan. In his conversation with Nicodemus, he implies of himself that he came from heaven when he says:

> "No one has ascended into heaven except the one who descended from heaven, the Son of Man." [John 3:13]

But Jesus' mission and purpose is immediately revealed:

> "And just as Moses lifted up the serpent in the wilderness, so must the Son of Man be lifted up, that whoever believes in him may have eternal life. For God so loved the world that he gave his only Son, so that everyone who believes in him may not perish but may have eternal life. Indeed, God did not send the Son into the world to condemn the world, but that the world might be saved through him." [John 3:14-17]

Jesus' mission is to provide a path to eternal life, which Jesus explains at the Last Supper:

> "And this is eternal life, that they may know you, the only true God, and Jesus Christ whom you have sent." [John 17:3]

Going back to John 3, what does it mean to "believe" in the Son? Jesus came to reveal the Father that he knows, a God that differs from the Jewish conceptions of a legalistic and often vengeful force in their life. The God of Jesus doesn't demand sacrifice and rote obedience to a written law. Rather, this God commands through His Son the new law that we love one another as Jesus has loved us:

> "I give you a new commandment, that you love one another. Just as I have loved you, you should love one another." [John 13:34]

Jesus continues his testimony about God in several important sections of John's gospel, especially chapters 5, 6 and 8. First, Jesus emphasizes that he is following God's will:

> "... for I have come down from heaven, not to do my own will, but the will of him who sent me. And this is the will of him who sent me, that I should lose nothing of all that he has given me, but raise it up on the last day." [John 6:38-39]

Jesus illuminates the path to righteousness by his words and by his deeds:

> Again Jesus spoke to them, saying, "I am the light of the world. Whoever follows me will never walk in darkness but will have the light of life." [John 8:12]

Jesus is to be judge:

> "The Father judges no one, but has given all judgment to the Son." [John 5:22]

Furthermore, Jesus' role is mystically expanded, for he is to be our "bread of life" that we are to eat:

> "Very truly, I tell you, unless you eat the flesh of the Son of Man and drink his blood, you have no life in you. Those who eat my flesh and drink my blood have eternal life, and I will raise them up on the last day;" [John 6:53-54]

This last role is truly remarkable, as it connects today's believers to Jesus in an intimate, and continuing way. Jesus is the dynamic sign of the new covenant as we celebrate this mystery and do it "in memory" of him [Luke 22:19 and 1 Cor. 11:24].

Ultimately, with these passages from three disparate books of the New Testament, as well as other testimonies of similar witnesses, the evidence is convincing: Jesus is divine. His original divinity does not seem to be conferred on him (in the same sense as all of us will have a form of divinity conferred on us when time ends and we enter heaven). Instead it existed before time—at the beginning [John 1:1]. However, his divine status has been elevated as a result of his obedience in becoming human and dying on the cross.

How can Jesus be divine if he isn't God? Ultimately, this is a mystery that isn't explained in the Bible. We know that Jesus is the only begotten Son of God, but we cannot possibly grasp what this means, since it extends so powerfully beyond our four dimensional experience. Perhaps, in some way in the other dimensions God can "beget" a Son outside our perception—outside of our time—but not God's. This possible approach to the mystery of God's "begotten" Son is no more incomprehensible or incredible than the mystery of God's own eternal existence. And it is far more plausible (and consistent with the Bible) than one God existing as three equal, divine persons.

Analogies about God are always incredibly inadequate. But perhaps the following model might serve to provide a shadow of some insight into the nature of the Son of God relative to his Father. God is like a large river which has no beginning and no end. In the course of eternity, a small creek was intentionally separated from that river. This creek was an entity separate from the river, yet obtained all its water from the river. Thus, this creek, too, had its origins in eternity. The creek, in obedience to the will of the river, entered a strange land, with the knowledge that it had to fall over a tall cliff. The creek could have chosen to totally separate itself from the river, but did not, and willingly cascaded over the cliff. Later, the creek rejoined the river in a special way, still separate, but now running parallel to it, even touching it, and being supplied by the river with more water than ever before. From a distance, the creek and river look to be one. Jesus, as part of the original God (begotten), could have separated himself from God through giving in to the temptation of the devil. But he did not. And now he has rejoined his source, his Father, and his God.

Two Gods?

In the earliest Christian years, serious debate resulted from the attempt to understand Jesus' nature. If Jesus is divine, doesn't that mean that there are two gods instead of one? And how can that possibly be consistent with Israel's centuries of monotheistic belief? As a result, some factions postulated that the Son was actually God, the Father, in human flesh. Others claimed that he was just a man who, by his holy nature, was infused with the Holy Spirit at his baptism. Multiple alternative theories arose, and extensive arguments against them were written down and preached by those who are commonly called the "Church Fathers," the Second and Third Century theologians who won the ecclesiastic battles and destroyed the evidence of their opponents' arguments, other than what they themselves had written about them.

But virtually nowhere is there evidence that they ever considered that there might be different levels of divinity. The supernatural realm appears to them to be in one homogeneous realm, just as the natural world is. Yet, even using the example of the natural world we see that there are different levels of animal life. Why, then, can it not be so that there are different levels of divine life? And why is man so knowledgeable (or so full of pride) that he can describe completely the supernatural world and what constraints that world must exist with? We can no better describe God than a flea can describe a human!

Should we then consider Jesus a second god, a kind of demigod? In simple terms, no. The Son of God is so united with the Father, that there is no separation of will or action. God's will is his Son's will. That is why Jesus can say that we see the Father when we see him [John 12:45, 14:9]. There is no God beside Yahweh, and his Son continues to serve him.

God, the Father, is the creator of the universe and the willful begetter of His Son. All things and beings have their origin in the Father, and He wants all things and beings to be returned to Him. In a real sense, everything is divine because of this. (The condemned to hell will be the exception.) But there is a hierarchy, with the Son and Spirit below the Father, and angels and humans below them. Yet all answer to the one, true God.

As we have seen, the biblical evidence is overwhelming that there is one God, who is Father. The biblical evidence is also overwhelming that Jesus is a god-like being, whose nature is best described as being divine. That does not mean he is God. Instead, he obtains his divinity from God and through God. His god is <u>the</u> God—the "only true God"—the supreme being of the universe. If we confuse Jesus' divinity with implying polytheism, then we truly are unable to appreciate the real power of God and the realm of the supernatural, both of which surpass any possibility of human understanding.

Part 4

The History of the Dogma

Chapter 20

The Historical Perspective

If the Bible seems to clearly say that there is one God, who is Yahweh, and one Lord, Jesus Christ, who is God's Son, then the question naturally arises as to how the doctrine of the Trinity ever became the Church's position. Was this the traditional teaching of the Apostles which only was handed on verbally, later to be written down by future generations? Was it the belief of the earliest theologians who followed in the Second and Third Centuries, thus establishing a Tradition that could be referenced by the bishops who later ratified the Nicene documents? Or was there a new revelation that occurred in the Fourth Century that brightly illuminated the nature of God for all to see? Unfortunately for the Church's credibility, the answer to all of the above questions is in the negative.

But to truly understand the answer to these questions, one has to go beyond what the Bible says and look at the earliest non-scriptural writings of the Church. These include those credited to the generations immediately following the Apostles, who were called the Church Fathers, and Third Century theologians such as Origen. They also include writings which were opposed as heresies, but which had a profound impact on the way the Church developed its own theology.

Even more importantly, one needs to look at how the foundation of the doctrine of Jesus-is-God, co-eternal and co-equal to the Father, began to be established during the Fourth Century. For this did not occur simply through a convocation of representative bishops who saw the truth and amiably agreed. Instead, the establishment of the doctrine was totally enmeshed in a web of politics, power and wealth. If we fully understand the historical perspective, then we can better comprehend and judge the validity of the Nicene and Constantinople Councils' doctrines, particularly expressed through their creeds.

Chapter 21

Early Church History

The Roman Catholic Church puts a great deal of emphasis on what it calls "Tradition." This Tradition involves a whole host of stories and beliefs that occurred in its early history, including writings that were not included in the New Testament Canon. Many of these early writings come from the first two and a half centuries after Jesus' resurrection, and it was often a matter of controversy about which of these to believe.

During this same time a number of prominent men involved in the Church—usually bishops—wrote somewhat extensively about this new Christian faith. For as the Church grew and spread, multiple questions came up regarding everything from Christianity's relationship to Judaism (i.e. what of the "old" scriptures should be believed or revered) to liturgical issues (i.e. how and when to baptize or how to celebrate the Lord's Supper) to cultural issues (i.e. incorporating Greek logical thought versus either Jewish tradition or Roman imperial confidence) to theological issues. Amongst the most difficult of those theological issues was the mystery of the nature of Jesus.

Although it would be convenient for the Church to be able to cite those ancient theologians to support the belief that Jesus is God and co-equal to the Father, the evidence is extremely mixed. In fact, rarely did anyone conjecture that Jesus was the Supreme Being of the Universe, much less that God was a trinity which included the Holy Spirit. In fact, the first record we have of someone mentioning a "Triad" was Theophilus of Antioch in about the year 180[1]. Thus, for the most part, this belief is not based in the Tradition of the first three centuries of Christianity, but rather in the proposed theology of the Fourth Century, where a bitter controversy arose, and was resolved only after many years of Church councils, politics and violence. This Nicaean controversy will be discussed in detail in the next chapter. As Brox states it in <u>A Concise History of the Early Church</u>:

> In brief, hitherto this relationship [between the Father and the Son] had been seen as one between a Son who was also 'God' (or divine) and a Father to whom he was subordinate. This relationship of subordination was expressed in different ways, but the question had not been clarified in principle: there was

evidently no need for this. The subordinationist view was first of all the whole church's way of believing in the Father and the Son (as yet no similar statements were made about the Spirit). It arose consistently out of the biblical-Jewish monotheism of Christians. Faith in the one God was taken for granted. Talk of the divine Logos and Spirit were compatible with monotheism in the model of subordination to the one God.[2]

We even see in the Apostles Creed no evidence of a triune God, nor even the divinity of the Son. This statement of faith, believed to have its roots in the earliest church (potentially by the year 110), states clearly "I believe in God, the Father Almighty." The Father alone is considered God in this statement. When it mentions Jesus, it is another belief "in Jesus Christ, His only Son, our Lord." The Creed proceeds with Jesus' history, and how he sits at the right hand of "God the Father Almighty," but nowhere does it imply a divine status for him. And the belief in the Holy Spirit doesn't even indicate that that is a person. Perhaps this Creed represents the essential basis of belief from which Church Fathers would refine their theology.

For this chapter, it is important to highlight who were the great post-apostolic leaders of the Church during those two centuries and what they are attributed to having believed. Of course, since only a limited selection of actual writings survived the ravages of time, we are forced to use those works and references which have survived, a fact that always puts us at risk of missing something important or can result in misinterpreting what was written. For this review, it is likely to be useful to know when these Church "Fathers" lived, for then the history and development of the theology can make more sense. Here is a list (in many cases the birth date is unknown or estimated):

Clement [? – 100]
Ignatius of Antioch [50? – 107]
Polycarp [69 – 155]
Justin Martyr [100 – 165]
Irenaeus [130 - 202]
Tertullian [160 – 225]
Hippolytus [? – 236]
Origen [185 – 254]

What is recorded from these individuals about the nature of Jesus?

Clement, the third bishop of Rome wrote little which survives.

But in his first epistle to the Corinthians he seems to follow St. Paul's delineation of the Father being God alone when he references the three persons:

> Have we not one God, and one Christ, and one Spirit of Grace poured upon us? [1 Clement, 46][3]

Other passages that reveal Clement's Christological thought are[4]:

> Through him [Jesus] the Master willed that we should taste of the immortal knowledge; Who being the brightest of His majesty is so much greater than the angels, as he hath inherited a more excellent name. [1 Clement 36]

> The Apostles received the Gospel for us from the Lord Jesus Christ; Jesus Christ was sent forth from God. So then Christ is from God, and the Apostles are from Christ. Both therefore came of the will of God in the appointed order. [1 Clement 42]

> ... that we may know thee [God], who alone abidest Highest in the lofty, Holy in the holy; ... who alone art the Benefactor of spirits and the God of all flesh; ... who multipliest the nations upon earth, and hast chosen out from all men those that love Thee through Jesus Christ, Thy beloved Son, through whom Thou didst instruct us, didst sanctify us, didst honor us. ... Let all the Gentiles know that Thou art God alone, and Jesus Christ is Thy Son, and we are Thy people and the sheep of Thy pasture. [1 Clement 59]

One pro-Trinitarian author writes "But of the problem of the relation of the Three to each other he seems to have been oblivious."[5] But it is clear from these four passages that the author considered God to be a totally separate person and entity from Jesus. In 2 Clement, which may not even have been written by Clement, the opening deems Christ to have a divine status when it advises readers to "think of Christ as of God, as of the judge of the living and the dead,"[6] but this, too, avoids making a judgment regarding either equality or a trinity.

Ignatius of Antioch much more echoes the gospel of John in his writings, saying, for example "There is one God, Who has revealed Himself through His Son Jesus Christ, Who is His Word emerging from silence."[7] For Ignatius, the Son is both an emanation of God and a separate person, and he even can describe the Son as "God

Incarnate" and worthy of our prayers.[8] Another of his writings include, "there is one physician, of flesh and spirit, generate and ingenerate, God in man, true life in death, son of Mary and son of God."[9] In fact, extant translations of his epistles occasionally reference Jesus, the Son, as God, as in the following:[10]

> ... united and elect in a true passion, by the will of the Father and of Jesus Christ our God; [To the Ephesians, intro]

> Ignatius, who is also Theophorus, unto her that hath found mercy in the bountifulness of the Father Most High and of Jesus Christ His only Son; to the church that is beloved and enlightened through the will of Him who willed all things that are, by faith and love towards Jesus Christ our God; ... abundant greeting in Jesus Christ our God. [To the Romans, intro]

> I give glory to Jesus Christ the God who bestowed such wisdom upon you; for I have perceived that ye are established in faith immovable, being as it were nailed on the cross of the Lord Jesus Christ, in flesh and in spirit, and firmly grounded in love in the blood of Christ, fully persuaded as touching our Lord that He is truly of the race of David according to the flesh, but Son of God by the Divine will and power, ... [To the Smyrnaeans, 1]

Note the questionable (and probably blasphemous) use of calling "Jesus our God" without equally referencing the Father, unless either Ignatius means something quite different—such as a form of divinity for the Son—or that the translations that exist, most of which are from the Middle Ages or later, have been altered to render a more Nicene view. There is also a significant problem if one tries to interpret the language to mean "Jesus is the Supreme Being God" or "Jesus is equal to the Father" when, as in the Romans letter, he references the Father as "Most High" or in the Smyrnaean letter that Jesus is the "Son of God by the Divine will and power." Also with a Jesus-is-God interpretation, how can he write the following?

> Ignatius, who is also Theophorus, unto her that is beloved by God the Father of Jesus Christ [To the Trallians, intro]

Ignatius falls far short of declaring an equality of the Son with the Father, and it doesn't seem possible to determine exactly what Ignatius' views are, since his writings appear too often contradictory.

Polycarp left little record of his view of Jesus' relationship with God. One thing that survives is that he is reported to have used a Trinitarian formula when praying just before his martyrdom: "I glorify thee through the everlasting and heavenly high-priest Jesus Christ, Thy beloved Son, through Whom be glory to Thee together with Him and the Holy Spirit."[11] But this does not indicate a belief either in an equality between the persons of Jesus and the Father or a belief in a God as Trinity.

In an Epistle to the Philippians which is attributed to Polycarp, the author refers to Jesus as "God," but the context obviously implies a different definition than the Supreme Being of the Universe:

> Now may the God and Father of our Lord Jesus Christ, and the eternal High-priest Himself, the [Son of] God Jesus Christ, build you up in faith and truth, and in all suffering and in patient endurance and in purity; and may He grant unto you a lot and portion among His saints, and to us with you, and to all that are under heaven, who shall believe on our Lord and God Jesus Christ and on His Father that raised Him from the dead. [Polycarp's Epistle to the Philippians, 12][12]

Polycarp's dual use of the word "God" may be best attributed to the lack of a word to express Jesus' unique divine status, since the Father is declared the "God... of our Lord Jesus Christ."

Related to the earliest writings was Hermas' *Shepherd*, which was almost included in the Church Canon, but was probably rejected because it couldn't be traced back to an apostolic origin. In it, God is clearly Father. The pre-existent Son is associated only with the Holy Spirit until the actual incarnation. And then the Son is elevated to be the companion of the Father and the Spirit only after his obedient works of salvation.[13]

Thus, in the earliest writings of the Church Fathers, Christ was still very much a mystery, and there was essentially no sign of a doctrine of the Trinity.[14] These early men were still struggling with the philosophical term "Logos," which appeared in the prologue of John's Gospel, and had its roots in the meaning either of "God's Word" or "God's Reason."

The next churchman of importance was Justin Martyr, who left somewhat contradictory statements regarding the Son. For Justin, the Son is God's Reason (another definition of *logos*), and therefore sees the Son as pre-existent, evidenced in many Old Testament's references to Wisdom. This Son is indeed separate, and took on a special role to be the visible "God" in his appearances, such as to Abraham [Genesis 18]. Thus, he could write describing the Son: "below the Creator of all things, there is Another Who is, and is called, God and Lord;" but despite this appellation, this Son is subordinate, for Justin could not believe that "the Master and Father of all things should have abandoned all supercelestial affairs and made Himself visible in a minute corner of the world"[15]. Rather, God was completely above the world, timeless and unknowable, so that any revelation about himself, including creation, required an agent, the *logos* who became Jesus.[16]

At this point, the Christology was becoming more complicated and more detailed, yet wholly consistent with the writings that were considered valid and with monotheism in its strict sense. Justin and his contemporaries viewed the Son as the original "Logos" of the Father before there was a generation or begetting of the Son. For example, Tatian, Justin's disciple proposed that this Logos ever-present within the Father leaped from Him prior to creation as his "primordial work."[17] Thus, they thought of the Father as the one God responsible for creation, and they didn't recognize the Son as Son until his issuing forth from the Father for the works he is scripturally assigned: assisting creation, revelation of his Father and redemption. For Justin, veneration of the Son and Spirit were secondary to the Father.

With Irenaeus we see only a little change in theology from his predecessors. There seems to be a little more emphasis on the Word being intimately entwined with the Father before creation, as if there is no distinction. Kelly states of Irenaeus' view of the Father: "His thinking is his Word, and His Word is His intelligence, and the Father is that intelligence comprising all things."[18] Similar to his antecedents, Irenaeus states "What is invisible in the Son is the Father, and what is visible in the Father is the Son."[19] But he goes a little further toward the Nicene view when he claims divinity for the Son, since he believes that "whatever is begotten of God is God."[20] Yet this must be interpreted in light of his apparent belief that both Son and Spirit are extensions of the Father's reason, wisdom and spirit.

Eusebius of Caesarea cites an unknown source from near the end of the Second Century that provides insight into at least one churchman's belief in defense of a heresy going on at that time—that Jesus was only human. What is relevant to the present discussion is this excerpt:

And Christian writers before Victor also defended the truth against both the pagans and the heretics of their own day—I mean the works of Justin, Miltiades, Tatian, Clement, and many more, in all of which Christ is treated as God. For who does not know the books of Irenaeus, Melito, and the others who proclaim Christ as God and man or all the earliest psalms and hymns that sing of Christ as the Word of God and regard him as God? When the church's understanding has been proclaimed for so many years, how then is it possible that Victor's predecessors can have preached as the people claim? Are they not ashamed of slandering Victor in this way when they know well enough that he excommunicated Theodotus the shoemaker, the father of this God-denying apostasy, when he first said that Christ was merely human?[21]

There are a couple objections to taking this passage literally—that is, that Jesus is God, in the sense of being the supreme God of the universe. First and most importantly, the defense is against the claim that Jesus is only human. The author is certainly claiming that Jesus is greater than that, and his words of treating Jesus as God may represent the available language he has of stating Jesus' divinity. Second, we do not have extant any unequivocal claims by the author's cited referenced Church fathers that they considered Jesus being supreme God. This author may be saying "Jesus is God" in order to treat him as a divine being with divine perquisites, which most closely represents anything (including the New Testament) that was written in those first two centuries. Finally, this is only one man's writings that Eusebius chose to quote, which echoed somewhat the doctrinal arguments Eusebius favored when "the History" was written about 324.

Hippolytus is perhaps more insistent on a type of unity within the Godhead. He, too, agrees with some of his predecessors that the Son and the Spirit were essentially indwelling within the Father as God's Reason and Wisdom, and then became manifest for creation and redemption through an act of will. He recognizes the begotten Son, then, as "another," but completely in unity with the Father: "when I speak of 'another,' I do not mean two Gods, but as it were light from light, water from its source, a ray from the sun. For there is only one Power, that which issues from the All. The All is the Father, and the Power issuing from the All is the Word. He is the Father's mind."[22]

Tertullian is essentially in agreement with Hippolytus, using similar language of the Son such as "water from its source" and "light from the sun." He, too, claims the essential unity of Father and Son, and refines his thought in claiming that though they are distinct as persons, they are of the same substance, with the Son being an extension of the Father rather than a division from the Father.[23] Some interpreters would conjecture that since Tertullian considered God as one, Tertullian would then say that the Father, Son and Spirit are one identical being[24], and yet in his arguments against Monarchism he seems to dispute nearly that exact same language.

It is extremely important to realize that these second- and third-century churchmen just cited did not possess a monopoly on theological thought. In fact, their primary recognition occurs because their particular line of thinking would eventually be used to point to the doctrine of the Trinity of three equal persons. Numerous other veins of interpretation of the Triad (Father, Son and Spirit considered in a more separate context) were also often popular, and frequently it was in opposition to these trains of thought that these churchmen applied their thought and came up with their theological view. Amongst these views were (in very simplified form):

- Docetism: Jesus did not have a physical body, and only seemed to die on the cross.
- Marcionism: there were two Gods, one evil one of the Old Testament and a good one who finally took over at the time of Jesus.
- Sabellianism: the belief that the Son and Father were the same, and so the Father actually came to earth for the act of redemption (although he didn't actually suffer).
- Gnosticism: special knowledge about God could be known to an "elite" group; there are two separate realms, one totally material and dark in which man dwells, and the other of spiritual light ruled by God.[25] There are some who have a spiritual nature, and only these, through knowledge (*gnosis*) can come to a redemptive state and return to the "light."
- Adoptionism: Jesus was a mere man upon whom God's spirit descended. Some Adoptionist then believed that God deified the Son upon completion of his redemptive work.
- Monarchianism: Christ is divine, but only insofar as the Triad is three manifestations of a single divine being, rather than distinct persons.[26]

- Montanism: a belief springing up around the year 200 that the world's end was imminent, and that an ascetic life was called for to achieve salvation.

Of course, none of these theological strains won the historical battle, and so became relegated to the status of "heresy." (Also, unfortunately, most of what we know of these strains is from writings by the victors, who may not have felt it necessary to represent their opponents' arguments validly. Still, there is some evidence that they were honest.) Yet each has its own set of scriptural support, and answered, to various degrees, some of the pressing questions—not the least of which was attempting to be consistent with monotheism in the face of a second "God" if Jesus is divine. Even Tertullian was converted over to Montanism. Of these strains of thought, perhaps Gnosticism is most connected with the mysteriousness of God and the special "knowledge" needed as shown in scripture, such as when Jesus says at the Last Supper, "no one comes to the Father except through me. If you know me, then you will know my Father also." [John 14:6-7]

To complicate matters, it was still uncertain as to how much theological authority one could place on the accepted writings. Tertullian had argued that scripture could not be the sole source of authority. On the other hand it was argued that even the bishops must remain faithful to the scriptures in their interpretations.[27] And even then, how was that scripture to be interpreted? Just as now, cultural influence usually colored people's thinking.

Origen provides a significant departure from his immediate predecessors, both in postulating more about the relationship within the Triad, but also declaring a subordination of the Son to the Father. He declares that the Father alone is God in the strict sense. Outside of time, the Father begets the Son by an eternal act, so that in a sense the Son is also God, but his deity solely derives from the Father. Along with the Spirit, these are three distinct persons from all eternity, but united "in unanimity, harmony, and identity of will."[28] Origen expresses "we are not afraid to speak in one sense of two Gods, in another sense of one God."[29] Origen echoes his predecessors in making an analogy that the Son is like an act of will issuing from the Father, but he maintains both a separateness and subordination.

Around the year 250, Novatian wrote the treatise *On the Trinity*, but rather than define that entity more directly, concentrated on the Father and the Son. According to Sloyan[30], Novatian taught that the

Father generated the Son, His Word, through an act of will, before time and apart from it. He continues:

> This Word has his own subsistence (*substantia*), being a second person. This is the first time that the pre-temporal Sonship of the Word is set free from the idea of creation. The Son receives his being from the Father in a "community of substance." As a "second person after the Father," he forever harks back to the Father. He is saved from being a second divine principle by being other than the Father only as a Son. The *monarchia* is preserved, and in God there are Two. ... Even though the closest he came to the idea of eternal generation was to say that the Father always had his Son, and though he tended to subordination of the Son in his phrasing, he nonetheless set the inner life of God free from any consideration of time.

The view of the Son's subordination continued. Of course, there were other developments after Origen and Novatian as different factions argued their cases to bishops of different regions. Bishop Dionysius of Alexandria found both common ground and differences with Bishop Dionysius of Rome around 260. In Antioch, Bishop Paul of Samosata argued with Lucian about subordinationism. Paul had supported the Greek term *homoousios* to describe the oneness of substance of the Father and Son (and which term was at the center of the Nicaean belief later ratified at that council in 325). But Paul was condemned by the church at Antioch in 268 for his beliefs, indicating that at that time, the larger (local) church didn't subscribe to what would become the Nicene view.

It is interesting that Eusebius in his "History of the Church" never discusses the nature of Jesus, other than in the brief expositions of churchmen dealing with the heresies already highlighted. Considering that he finished his History very close to the year 324, apparently he did not deem the Arian controversy worthy of mention. We can get some idea of at least Eusebius' thoughts with regard to God and Jesus in the lengthy panegyric he included with his History. In it he avers:

> But they [the new Christian emperors] acknowledge as the one and only God, the Benefactor of all and Christ as Son of God and sovereign King of the universe, naming him "Savior" on monuments and inscribing in imperial characters in the center

of the city that is empress among the world's cities an indelible record of his victories over the wicked. The Jesus Christ our Savior is the only person in history to be acknowledged—even by earth's most exalted—not as an ordinary human king but worshiped as the true Son of the God of the universe and as himself God.[31]

The whole temple he [Constantine] adorns with one mighty gateway: the praise of our one and only God and King, flanking the Father's supreme power with the secondary beams of the light of Christ and the Holy Spirit.[32]

As to the great and unique altar, what might it be but the spotless Holy of Holies of [Christ], the common priest of all? Standing beside it on the right side, the great High Priest of the universe, Jesus, the only begotten of God, joyfully receives the sweet-smelling incense and prayers of all and forwards them to the heavenly Father and God of the universe. Adoring the Father, he alone renders him the honors due and implores him to continue favorable toward us forever.[33]

    The interpretation of these three passages, written just prior to the Nicene Council, should be clear. Eusebius, a notable bishop of his time, believed in the subordination of the divine ("*as* God") son to the "one and only God." Also, we must be careful with the interpretation of the word "worshiped" in the first quote, since this was originally written in Greek, with its spectrum of meanings for that word. We occasionally see references to Jesus as "God," but we must also recognize that the contexts will often call the Father "God of the Son" or "Almighty God," terminology which emphasizes the Father's dominion over His Son. Caution must always be taken when apologists quote a reference to Jesus as God and neglect the more important subordination language.

    There is, of course, one other important consideration. Typically, what has survived to this day was either hidden (such as the Gnostic writings only recently found in desert caves), or what was allowed to survive through all the censorship that the Church would later apply to writings that it didn't agree with. Other than the contents of recently unearthed documents, most of what we know about the different heresies of the time involve the refutations by the churchmen who wrote against them, and who thus had to describe them—admittedly a very biased way to pass on information. For example, we will see in the next chapter that much of what we know about the Arian belief comes to us through the writings of Athanasius, the arch-enemy of Arian thought. Thus, it would be extremely likely that writings of key churchmen that expressed beliefs that did not conform to Trinitarian dogma would have been destroyed when discovered. Censorship has a way of clouding the truth.

These were the churchmen who had the greatest influence on the Church in its first 270 years of existence, well after the apostles and immediate disciples had passed on. This also represents at least one view of the Tradition of the Church and shows both that there was no unanimity of thought about the relationship of the Son to the Father, but also that there tended to be the belief in the Son's subordination to or emanation from God, the Father, rather than any Trinitarian belief of co-eternal and co-equal persons comprising one God. The important point is this: the Tradition of the early Church cannot be claimed to be the basis for what would eventually become doctrine. Thus, the doctrine which eventually would emerge was an extrapolation, and even contradiction, of what these men believed.

Chapter 22

The Politics of the Establishment of the Trinity

How did the Church declare "Jesus is God," and how did this belief become doctrine? Furthermore, how did the Church declare "Jesus and the Father are equal in all things?" The answer is far less theological than one might think. In fact, the development of that doctrine was deeply influenced by the politics of a tumultuous time in the Roman Empire.

In the first three centuries of its existence, prior to the time of Emperor Constantine, the new Christian sect had experienced persecution. At some times, this extended to outright attempts at extermination, but usually it followed a pattern of discrimination. Thus, the Church was able to grow, establish bishoprics, and even create vibrant regions of converts against the pagan background of the time. As the number of converts grew, the power of the bishops also grew. Yet their power was primarily ecclesiastical.

The global role of the Church all began to change in October 312 when Constantine achieved a major victory over his rival at Rome, Maxentius, and essentially became Emperor of the western Roman Empire. His power was consolidated in 324, when a victory over Licinius in the East confirmed Constantine as Emperor of the entire Roman Empire. With regard to religious matters the "cult" of acceptable religious practices had usually been dictated by the emperor. Constantine remained consistent with his predecessors. He, too, intended to maintain a strong hand in the control of the religious beliefs of his empire. However, Constantine was also strongly influenced by his perception that Christianity had brought him to power. And so the emperor threw his support behind this rising religion. The result would bring an enormous change to the Roman empire, for Constantine was not only the first Christian emperor, but he also elevated the Christian religion to that of the preferred religion.

Constantine's support had supreme significance for the Church. As a vigorous Church supporter, Constantine not only provided magnanimous public funding for the Church, he also granted a great deal of political power to the Church leaders. Yet being the emperor, he believed that he personally should define the relationship between Christians and himself—not the Church.[1] Since Constantine understood his role as unifier of the empire, he was sensitive to anything—whether civil, secular or religious—which threatened that unity. So when he became aware of religious disputes that seemed to be tearing at the fabric of Christian unity, he decided to intervene. The first intervention occurred around the year 311 when he worked to resolve the Donatist controversy (which involved whether the sacraments ministered by a sinful bishop were still valid).[2] But another more significant disagreement was brewing between the Church leaders. Consistent with the imperial policy of being in control over religious matters, Constantine felt his involvement in this Church dispute was essential.

Prior to and during Constantine's rise to power, a number of theological ideas had been generated about the nature of Jesus. For example, Sabellianism asserted that the Father and Jesus were simply personalities of the same undivided reality; therefore the Son was not really human, or perhaps only his body was human while his mind was divine. Other theological ideas, already highlighted in the previous chapter, ran the gamut from Jesus being just a man to Jesus being the one and only God. Although bishops and local councils frequently addressed these issues as challenges to what they felt should be believed, at that time there had been no formal procedure for the Church as a whole to rule on orthodoxy.

One proponent of what became a very popular conception of Jesus was a priest (presbyter) named Arius. Since his ideas seem to have developed over time, it is difficult to be specific about what the Arians, the followers of Arius' ideas, truly believed when Constantine took power, but at one point Arius wrote *The Banquet* in which he wrote:

> The Unbegun made the Son a beginning of things made and advanced him as His Son by adoption.
>
> Understand that the Monad was, but the Dyad was not, before it came to exist.
>
> Thus there is the Triad, but not in equal glories. Not intermingling with each other are their substances.
>
> One equal to the Son, the Superior is able to beget, but one more excellent or superior or greater, He is not able.
>
> At God's will the Son is what and whatsoever he is.
>
> God is incomprehensible to His Son. He is what He is to

Himself: Unspeakable.

The Father knows the Son, but the Son does not know himself.

(Note that this poetry was taken from the work of Arius' arch-enemy, Athanasius, in his *Oration Against the Arians*[3], and has the possibility that it contains biases.) *The Banquet* seems to be an earlier treatment by Arius regarding his views of Jesus, and he puts more emphasis on the human aspect of Jesus, while distinctly reflecting a subordination of Jesus' power to the Father. Eusebius of Nicomedia, a bishop, supported Arius while toning down some of the more extreme views of Arius.

The initial views of Arius involved two major points. First, that there was a time when the Son didn't exist, coming into being begotten by the Father. Second, that the Son was promoted to a divine status through moral growth and obedience to God. Arius' first point had sufficient evidence both in scripture and in Greek philosophy. As elaborated in Chapter 15, scripture has several supportive references. Similarly, the Greeks' interpretation of *logos* was that is was the mind and reason of God, and since Jesus was God's *logos*, he was also the physical/spiritual manifestation of his Wisdom; and therefore scripture, such as Proverbs 8:22, would support the Son having a beginning:

> The LORD created me [Wisdom] at the beginning of his work, the first of his acts long ago. [Prov. 8:22]

Furthermore, they believed that God himself could not suffer, and so a subordinate being, his Son, would need to perform the work of redemption. For humans, the advantage of such thoughts was that they, too, could attain a divine status.

These views—and thus, the views attributed to Arians—evolved over time, and so it is difficult to define a specific "Arian" belief. However, what is believed to be the essence of their belief can be briefly summarized in three points:

1) With the Christian symbolism of Father and Son adapted from human procreation, the implication is that the Father preceded the Son. Thus, since the Son was the only-begotten offspring of the Father, the Son could not be equal in eternity with the supreme God;
2) God, the Father, was so far beyond the world that He could

not be known by human beings. The Son, as mediator between God and man, must be different, entering into communication and interchanges with the world;

3) The Father could not change, and was therefore incapable of suffering; therefore God is insulted by those who insist that the supreme deity could be born, suffer and die. Since the Son had suffered, he must be different.

The Arians believed in an essential difference—indeed a subordination—but most still understood the Son as being fully and completely divine. These Arian views were essentially consistent with Origen's theses in the Third Century.

In opposition to the Arian view was a faction represented by the bishop Alexander of Alexandria (Egypt) who believed that Jesus was really God—that since the Father and Son were of the very same essence, they could not be different in power. He convened a council of Egyptian bishops which declared that the Son was both co-eternal and co-equal to the Father.[4] Alexander's protégé, Athanasius (a much younger man at the time) would become a key figure in the struggle between the beliefs of Alexander and the Arians. Athanasius was a supreme politician with excellent oratorical and writing skills. As shall be indicated later, Athanasius apparently also had a very violent side.

To some extent, the beliefs reflected the culture, for the supporters of Arius generally followed the more Aristotelian approach, trying to put logic first. Furthermore, a clear ordering of power, with Father first, then Son, and then Spirit also appealed to the rank-minded people of the East. Finally, the Arians were attempting to make sense of Jesus being "begotten" of the Father. If there was any literalism to that term, then the Father had to precede the Son—whether inside time or outside time.

The Alexander/Athanasius view rebelled against the possibility of there being someone (Jesus) between God and man, since this seemed too much like the paganism of the day, where demigods were formed when the gods impregnated mortals. Nor could they see Jesus as a second God, since that violated monotheism. However, a decisive paradigm in their theological interpretation involved the belief that only God himself could redeem mankind.

What ensued was violence. The people of the day often resorted to force to defend their beliefs, and many riots broke out because of the differences. Leaders of the two groups do not appear to have acted "Christian" when it came to supporting this violence. So these differences began to tear at the unity of the Church.

To this end, councils were called. In one that took place in Alexandria (where the bishop Alexander had substantial power) in 318, Alexander asserted that Jesus was no less than God on earth, the Creator becoming human to redeem our sins (this view of God being simultaneously both Father and Son is considered to be the Sabellian heresy, and was later condemned by the Church!). Arius maintained that Jesus was divine (whether by will or adoption), but subordinate. Arius' views were in the minority, and so Arius was excommunicated. A brief while later in a less hostile setting, another council was called at Nicomedia in 319 or 320, in which Arius' views (after some toning down) were declared "orthodox" (within the range of ideas that a Christian could hold), and therefore that he should be reinstated.

Eventually, in the hope of bringing greater unity to his empire by establishing greater unity in the Church, Constantine called a "great" council at Nicaea in 325, just one year after consolidating his eastern power. Under the prior influence of Eusebius of Caesarea, the Emperor felt particularly divinely gifted. Specifically, he thought of himself as the friend of God, "the interpreter of the Word of God," and even a mediator between God and man—an attitude still consistent with those pagan emperors who had preceded him. The Emperor assumed the special privilege of calling councils <u>and</u> directing them. By calling this particular council, he hoped, for the first time, to bring agreement within the entire Church on a matter of orthodoxy.

The council was attended by about 250 bishops (mostly all from the East). Prior to the Nicene Council, Constantine's chief religious advisor had been Hosius of Cordova, a strong anti-Arian. And he made sure that Constantine's own beliefs were sufficiently biased against the Arians. Since the Emperor was in attendance at the council, Constantine's politically "theological" influence was substantial, and his "demand" for unity was paramount. The evidence of this came when the pro-Arian Eusebius of Caesarea recited a creed that he was using locally. David L. Dungan writes of a critical scene:

> Constantine immediately indicated his approval, and went on to ask Eusebius point blank whether he could accept the term *homoousios*, "of one substance," to explain the relationship between the Son and the Father within the divine Trinity. Thus put on the spot, Eusebius reluctantly agreed. With his acquiescence, the position of the Arian party, which had been

holding out for some sort of subordinate position for the Son, collapsed.[5]

Constantine immediately agreed to accept the creed, provided that that special term be used. Thus, the phrase that resulted was that "the Son was of identical essence (*homoousios*) with the Father."[6] So in the context of Constantine's current beliefs, it turned out to essentially be "agree against the Arians . . . or else!"

The anti-Arians had interpreted this unscriptural Greek word to mean that the single essence of God was composed of the two persons, Father and Son. This phrasing was in opposition to a proposed alternative word, *homoiousios*, which means "of like substance," which carried the potential meaning of two totally different persons.[7] For some, this violated the tenet of monotheism, which was totally unacceptable.

But what does the "essence" of God really mean? After all, it could just mean divinity, which most Arian supporters already believed applied to the Son. And the "*ousios*" word could also simply mean substance, reality, being or type. Thus, most of the pro-Arian believers (in their own minds) provided their own "acceptable" interpretations! Along these lines, many of the bishops may have been following Paul of Samosata's theology who also claimed a *homoousia* between the Father and the Son, yet who conjectured that the Son's essence was infused by the divine wisdom of the Word of God.[8] With other modifications, the creed was ratified by all bishops but two. To show the danger of disagreeing with the emperor, the dissenters, including Arius, were exiled. How many bishops would be willing to give up their lofty status over the Greek letter *iota*, especially when they might be able to justify some kind of acceptance in their own mind? But rather than establish the unity that Constantine had intended, the arguments continued for decades.

The exact wording of this Nicene Creed was:

> We believe in one God, the Father, almighty, maker of all things visible and invisible;

> And in one Lord Jesus Christ, the Son of God, only-begotten from the Father, that is from the substance of the Father, God from God, light from light, true God from true God, begotten not made, of one substance [*homoousios*] with the Father, through whom all things came into being, things in heaven and things on earth, who for us men and for our salvation came

down and became flesh, becoming man, suffered and rose again on the third day, ascended into heaven, and will judge the living and the dead;

And in the Holy Spirit. But as for those who say, "There was when he was not," and "Before being born he was not," and that he came into existence out of nothing, or who assert that the Son of God is of a different reality or substance, or is subject to alteration or change—these the catholic and apostolic church anathematizes.

Obviously, this creed skirts any attempt to define what "begotten" means, but the intent of later interpretation was essentially to ignore, and essentially deny, what it could mean in terms of an actual generation of the Son.

With the imperial power strongly backing this new creed, it was difficult for the bishops to oppose it. Make no mistake; Constantine was a powerful Roman Emperor, who acted decisively in destroying his enemies and subjugating his opponents. The year after the Council, he even ordered the execution of his first son, Crispus, and his own wife Fausta (the reasons have been erased from the historical record). Constantine chose to avoid baptism until he was on his death bed because he wouldn't be able to act as politically ruthlessly as he felt he would need to if he was a "true" Christian. Delaying baptism, which would absolve all one's sins, would get Constantine a sure entry to heaven if he could time it right. (Still, even though he was considered Christian, he didn't completely reject pagan symbolism.) He was an Emperor who got what he wanted and the bishops were right to fear him!

Daniel L. Dungan writes of Constantine's influence:

The Church had long been fiercely loyal to its traditions. After the Edict of Milan in 313, and as a result of Constantine's bountiful gifts and numerous direct interventions and the eager cooperation of the Catholic bishops, virtually all of Catholic Christianity's most important elements—traditions, staff, institutions, regulations, customs, rituals, calendar, places of worship—were replaced by the elaborate customs, values, prerogatives, rituals, calendar, places of worship and governmental machinery of imperial Rome. The most important change, of course, was the acceptance of the Christian emperor's aspiring to act as master and director of the church of Jesus Christ and the apostles, with all the changes in value, outlook, and theology that that entailed.⁹

Furthermore, after being in the shadows of society for so long, Christians, and especially the elite clergy, were beginning to experience the benefits of imperial solicitude. For many, following the emperor had significant advantages. This would later manifest itself in outright ostentatiousness by many. Ambrose of Milan would ring his city with Basilicas; Roman bishops were reported to "dress splendidly and outdo kings in the lavishness of their tables." Vying for open sees could become violent.¹⁰

Another act of Constantine that had a profound impact was his commissioning of Eusebius of Caesarea to make 50 copies of the Holy Scriptures, ostensibly for use by the churches in the empirical capitol Constantinople. These were to include appropriate writings of the Apostles. Although there is no indication that Constantine himself decided which books should be included, with the publishing of the Bibles the (unofficial) Canon of the New Testament became most firmly settled, for who would oppose the emperor's own Bible? Afterwards, there was little opposition discussion regarding what should be the official Canon. Furthermore, with imperial edicts that proscribed "heretical" writings, opposition thought lost much of its force.¹¹

However, with regard to the Arian controversy nothing was really settled because of the Nicene Council. More variations would soon occur. In 328, another council of bishops in Nicomedia reviewed a creed prepared by Arius and pronounced it "orthodox," and reinstated Arius. Most churchmen did not want to get too detailed in defining the relationship of Jesus to his Father or in the definitions of Jesus' divinity and humanity. Interestingly, this time Constantine sided with their decision. And so the anti-Arians fell into disfavor only a couple years after the Great Council for unification.

Athanasius, now a supreme politician, maneuvered to place himself as the next bishop of Alexandria. In what appears to be a devious move, he persuaded a small group of bishops to name him to the Alexandrian See, while evading a different discussion being held by 50 other bishops about a future Alexandrian bishop. However, Constantine, still in control, approved of the appointment—although his decision was not fully informed. What ensued was a rebellion of some bishops, and Athanasius responded with violence. Constantine insisted that Athanasius accept back Arius, and Athanasius refused.

By this time the two sides had drawn battle lines. Of the two theological positions, the Arian view was far more benign. They maintained that there wasn't enough evidence to declare the true nature of God and Jesus, but that we can only surmise from the scriptures what these might be. This was reflected in the multiple statements of belief that represented a wide spectrum of speculation. On the other side, Athanasius was extreme, holding that if you didn't believe Jesus was fully God, then you were a heretic, and so divisive to the Church that you should be thrown out. His language was frequently inflammatory. (See the next chapter for examples of his rhetoric.) In one letter he likened Arians to the crucifiers of Christ. If force was needed, he could support it.

One historian characterizes Athanasius thusly:

> But in his writings, Athanasius ... systematically distorted and misrepresented both the arguments and characters of his opponents, selected his evidence in a one-sided way, could be evasive and incomplete in his descriptions of events, suppressed vital pieces of evidence inconvenient to his position, painted himself as unjustly persecuted, and portrayed attacks on himself as attacks on the whole Catholic Church. Unrelenting in his defence of what he conceived to be Christian orthodoxy, he was frequently lacking in many of the virtues extolled by his faith such as humility and patience. In his own town of Alexandria he was also quite prepared to employ intimidation and physical violence, unleashing organized gangs of thugs onto his local opponents.[12]

Charges of sexual misdeeds, violence and malfeasance were thrown back and forth. Establishing the truth was nearly impossible, as each group provided their own supporters and witnesses. Torture, whether to get information or to prevent getting information, was not uncommon. In one classic example, Athanasius was accused of ordering an Egyptian priest, Ischyras, beat up—a charge that he apparently did not deny, but defended on the grounds that the priest hadn't been ordained to his own specifications.

The power of the emperor was still supreme—even in the Church. But Constantine's vacillation between the two factions, often based on trying to achieve peace and harmony, further complicated the matter. After Arius had been officially cleared of heresy by the emperor and had orders to be re-accepted into Alexandria, nothing still had happened after four years. When Arius wrote an angry letter to Constantine in 333, the emperor, in one of his frequent fits of rage, re-branded Arius as a heretic and ordered all of his writings burned everywhere! However, after meeting with Arius and becoming convinced of his sincerity, the fickle emperor forgave him. Athanasius also fell in and out of favor with the emperor. So it happened that at different times, both Athanasius and Arius were exiled—Athanasius five times.

By the year 336, Arius was to receive (again) full reinstatement into the Church. But in a bizarre turn of events, Arius (over the age of 70) was stricken with bowel problems and died on the toilet the day before his official reinstatement. To the superstitious (and there were many), this was a sign of the disapproval by God of Arius. On the other hand, given the enmity and violence surrounding the controversy, it could have also been the work of poison—the murder weapon of choice in those days.

Further chaos was to occur. In 337, Constantine grew sick, and finally agreed to be baptized. He died shortly thereafter, and the Empire was divided between his three sons. They, too, would become drawn into the theological controversy.

Council and counter-council continued. Around 337 in Antioch, bishops found Athanasius guilty of new atrocities and ordered him deposed. Athanasius called his own council of 80 Egyptian bishops in 338 (and Athanasius had huge support in Egypt), which cleared him of all charges. This was countermanded in 339 by another council in Antioch, which assigned military force to depose Athanasius in Alexandria. While Athanasius fled, riots broke out.

Each group attempted to get the political backing of the three sons. Constantine's eldest son died early enough to not get too involved. In the Eastern empire, Constantius supported the Arians. He had allied with Eusebius of Nicomedia—then bishop of Constantinople. When Eusebius died in 342, and Constantius had become embroiled in foreign enemy problems, his ability to support the Arian cause diminished. Meanwhile, Athanasius courted Constans, the Western Emperor (while in exile), and played the politician by equating Constantius as a Pilate, a Judas Iscariot, or a Nero. Although the theology was of far less interest in the West, the political opportunities for pressure were appealing to Constans. At this time, Julius, the bishop of Rome became involved. (During the early years of the Church, no one was considered the solitary head of the Church. In the mid-Fourth Century, there were between three and five chief bishops, three of the most important being located at Rome, Alexandria and Antioch, who were essentially considered equals. However, the machinations surrounding the resolution of the Arian controversy would eventually provide the bishop of Rome with an excuse to claim supreme authority over the Church.)

Of course, there were other reasons for Constantius' support of the Arian cause besides the political. There was a rationalistic approach to the Arian philosophy, and it seemed reasonable to have an optimistic view of people's ability to make moral progress and have a hand in their own salvation. The Arians were now moving toward the middle—no longer insisting that the Son was created from nothing and agreeing that he was fully divine. On the other hand, the pro-Nicene supporters were radical in their insistence (presumptuousness?) and confidence in the "truth" that Jesus is God, yet content with the paradoxes that their beliefs created.

In an attempt to end the disunity, the more powerful Constantius convened at least 9 councils in the years 351 to 360. Creeds were also developed, with the Arian (but not radical Arian) views incorporated. Both Eastern and Western bishops agreed, but again it was under political pressure—although not as strong as under Constantine. One such Creed was developed in the council of Sirmium in 357, with the essential difference being that the insistence of the Father and Son being of the identical essence (the Greek word, *homoousion*) was omitted, as had been present in the Nicene Creed, Athanasius was also condemned. The creed began by professing the belief in:

> One almighty God and Father ... and his only Son Jesus Christ the Lord, our Saviour; but there cannot be two gods nor should that be preached ... Therefore there is one God of all.

It continued:

> There is no uncertainty about the Father being greater; it cannot be doubted by anyone that the Father is greater in honor, in dignity, in glory, in majesty, in the very name of "Father," for he himself witnesses ... [that He who sent me is greater than I] [13]

Also significant in this Creed is the insistence that no one can know about the "substance" of the Son, nor how the Son was begotten, since scripture says nothing about it! This directly condemned the Nicene declaration as fabricated theology. The Creed also stated that the Holy Spirit "is through the Son" rather than being co-equal with the Father

Imperial power was once again in evidence in 359, when Constantius essentially persuaded or coerced agreement by all sides favoring a pro-Arian interpretation at separate councils at Seleucia (Asia Minor) and Rimini (Italy). For once, however, bishops from both the East and West had participated in large numbers, bringing—at least as far as Constantius was concerned—a unification of the entire Church.

Not to be suppressed, Athanasius also called a council in his friendly, native territory, Alexandria, in 362, which declared "The Trinity of one essence (*homoousios*) true God who became man of Mary. Let all who disagree be anathema." Still, the council attempted to placate some of the Arian thought by admitting that even though the Trinity was of one essence, they were still separable, and as such, Jesus could maintain the humanness of his character.

Once again, the turning of tides in the Imperial realm markedly changed the flavor of the debate. Julian, Constantius's nephew assumed power in 360. Julian favored paganism! To weaken the Church as a whole, he did what he could to incite the factions into greater disagreement, hoping that the Church might collapse from within. To increase the tension, he even reinstated Athanasius as bishop of Alexandria.

When things didn't go quite as planned, Julian deposed Athanasius in 362, but the reversal was temporary with Julian's death in 363. Jovian, a pro-Christian, succeeded Julian. But dying accidentally only months later, he was succeeded by Valens. Valens was staunchly pro-Arian! However, the new Eastern Emperor was considerably more conciliatory, somewhat avoiding the theological squabbles that preceded him.

Added to all this controversy and confusion was the fact that the Church had never agreed on a common Canon—the "acceptable" books of both the Old and New Testaments. Certainly, a majority of New Testament writings was commonly accepted, but many—including the books of *Revelation, 2 Peter* and *Hebrews*—were not. And some wanted other writings, such as the *Shepherd of Hermas*. Thus, supporting scripture could be found for either side from the extant writings—although the Arian side could claim far more scriptural support for their assertions. Athanasius, in his inimitable authoritative style, insisted on what is now the present Canon in a letter to the churches of Egypt in 367 writing "in these alone the teaching of godliness is proclaimed. Let no one add to these; let nothing be taken away from them." Disputes continued about this

Canon throughout Christian communities, although there tended to be general agreement by the end of the Fourth Century. But not until the Council of Florence did the Church issue a definitive list of the 27 books of the New Testament, and not until the Council of Trent in the mid-Sixteenth Century was there a binding (to Roman Catholics) pronouncement on the Canon.

But realize that the creation of the Canon itself over those three and a half centuries significantly influenced what would eventually become creed. As Bart Ehrman writes:

> We can probably say with some certainty that if the other side had won—Marcionite, Ebionite, some form of Gnostic—there would have been no doctrine of Christ as both fully divine and human. As a consequence, there would have been no doctrine of the Trinity.[14]

During this time, Arian views also became divided into factions. One faction held that the Son was "unlike" (*anomoios*) the Father, was fallible, and might sin. A second held the view that the Son was "like" (*homoios*) the Father. A third, termed the "semi-Arians," went along with the Son being "of similar substance" (*homoiousios*) as the Father, but wouldn't go as far as "identical substance."[15] This divisiveness would later hinder the Arian cause.

The flavor of the argument changed under the influence of three "new" individuals on the scene, known as the Cappadocians: Basil of Caesarea, Gregory of Nyssa (his brother), and Gregory of Nazianzus. The third of these three provided five "orations" in 380, which attempted to support the Nicene view and oppose the beliefs of subordinationists and others. Although these arguments were full of depth, one modern author writes: "the proposed solutions are often incomplete or fail to convince."[16] Being less belligerent than Athanasius, the Cappadocians tried to refine the Nicene view to be more acceptable to the Arians. Their success was due, in part, to its resolution of an additional theological controversy that had arisen: the question of what or who the Holy Spirit was. But ultimately, by claiming three equal persons in one God, they still relied on an unexplainable paradox. This was still upsetting to the Arians, as they were predisposed to follow the Greek way, seeking understanding in a logical way. On the other hand, this did somewhat placate moderate Arians who feared the Sabellian tones that often resonated from the Nicene supporters: belief that the single person God became Jesus on earth.

Understand too, that the arguments had been based on separate denotations of the persons. This new Trinitarian paradox superseded the separateness in a novel way, one that could act as a compromise for many. But there was sufficient vagueness in this mystery that allowed many conservative Arians to at least not oppose it, if not embrace it.

In 373, Valens became more interventionist, attempting to instate pro-Arian bishops into sees held by the pro-Nicene supporters. But again, enemies from outside turned the attention and power of the Emperor away from the theological debate. And in 378, the Visigoths defeated the Romans, killing Valens.

This radical new weakness in the Roman Empire caused a crisis of conscience for the Arians. Since Jesus the divine person became human, the City of God on earth seemed a possibility. But with the pro-Arian Emperor defeated, and things looking substantially more bleak, the Kingdom of God on earth became more doubtful. Concern for the salvation of the immortal soul increased, and this seemed to be better embodied in the more divine focus of the pro-Nicenes.

The largest impetus for a change back to the Nicene view began in 379, when a general named Theodosius became the new Eastern Emperor. He was staunchly pro-Nicene and considered his rise to imperial power due, in part, to his beliefs. A violent man, he outlawed Arianism and ordered that all subjects must believe in "the deity of the Father and the Son and the Holy Spirit of equal majesty in a Holy Trinity." Unlike the emperors before him, his religious stand would become the law of the land by both commercial and violent force. Tax exemption for churches was granted only for those following the Nicene formula. Those who opposed the Nicene view were forbidden from attending church or being bishops. This persecution, along with the newer version of Nicene understanding, significantly diminished the Arian fervor.

To consolidate his religious views he called a council in Constantinople in 381. It did not have a good representation of the various bishops at the time (especially those from the West and those who might favor a subordinationist view). Furthermore, it was wracked by bitter disputes. The original presider of the council, Meletius of Antioch died, and the new presider, Gregory of Nazianzus, obstinately argued for inclusion of the Holy Spirit into the Godhead, a view that was unpopular and refused by council members. Eventually, a modification of the Nicene Creed was adopted—the one principally used today. Interestingly, even though the Cappadocians had been garnering support from Arians by advocating a different description of Jesus by using the word *homoiousios* (note the added "i," that is, "of like substance"), this wording never made it into the Creed—although there was general agreement that "of like substance" was the same as "of identical substance!" This tacit agreement was enough for the Eastern bishops, for it acknowledged the separateness of the Father and the Son.

One further significant distinction arose from the final creed, and that was the line that read: "And we believe in one holy catholic and apostolic Church." The authority of the Church had now become an article of faith. Although this idea had been articulated as early as 246 by Cyprian, bishop of Carthage, when he wrote, "He cannot have God for his Father who has not the Church for his Mother,"[17] this creed now ensured that the Church had the right to exercise power over the people in spiritual matters just as the emperor had done in worldly matters. Thus, instead of spirituality existing in Church members, true holiness resided in the Church. And since apostolic succession was assumed to be essential to the Church power, the bishops were able to claim increased power over the Church. This power would manifest itself in a clear separation in function between clergy (only they could address the congregation) and laity (the people couldn't speak as the Spirit moved them).[18]

During this time, the full force of politics seems to have overshadowed the power of the Church. Previous to Theodosius, the emperors had directed the theology but had typically not enforced it. Theodosius did both. And for this new emperor it would be more popular and expedient to consider Jesus to be God, rather than a Jewish insurgent fighting Rome. Beside, just as Constantine had seen his new role as mediator between God and man—since Jesus was now "God," subsequent emperors could also claim that powerful, theological position as mediator.

One example of this political influence occurred at Constantinople itself. Gregory was essentially ousted from the position of bishop of Constantinople, and the politically expedient candidate Nectarius was named. Interestingly, this popular statesman knew little of theology and hadn't even been baptized! (Ambrose was another who was nominated as bishop, in Milan, who hadn't been baptized at the time; he would become an enthusiastic supporter of Nicene theology.)

A second example of the politicization of the Church that occurred involved rules passed at the council that were established to prevent bishops from interfering in jurisdictions outside their own sees. The see of Constantinople was elevated in power behind Rome, essentially snubbing Alexandria. As one modern historian writes: "the council had been used to mount a coup that had reinforced the emperor's role as head of a politicised Church and arbiter of religious affairs in general."[19]

Persecution of Arians increased, with Arian bishops summarily excommunicated wherever they did not have significant popular support. Possession of Arian writings became a crime punishable by death. Now that the traditional monotheism was broken (that is, one God as one person), Christianity saw a clean break with Judaism: the Jews didn't believe in the same God! Thus, shortly after this total "conversion" of the Roman Empire to the pro-Nicene formula, persecution of Jews and pagans broke out. By deemphasizing the human element of Jesus, the former ties with the more earthly elements were broken, and a greater intolerance ensued. Even Augustine in 412 would condone punishment against opponents: "certain wars that must be waged against the violence of those resisting are commanded by God or by a legitimate ruler and are undertaken by the good."[20]

Sadly, with a "defined" theology, adherence to orthodoxy generated even more friction, even among the Nicene believers. A definition of heresy was provided by a new emperor in 395 as being to "deviate even in a minor point of doctrine, from the tenets and path of the Catholic religion," and heretics would be subject to the sanctions against them.[21] In 409 a law requiring that heretical books be burned was enacted; those who intentionally hid such books had committed a capital offense. But what was heresy, and how much heretical content made a book heretical?

Controversies were to continue, however, as the nuances of language haunted the theological positions. In the early Fifth Century, arguments arose over whether Mary was a "God-bearer" or a "Christ-bearer." Cyril, the chief supporter for the former view lashed out against Nestorius, the chief supporter for the latter language. Part of the impetus for increasing Mary's status involved the need for more mediators between God and man—since Jesus was now considered God. Again, councils met and remet, vacillating in support of the two views. Again, the politically stronger won, and Nestorius was sent into exile.

Eventually, in 451 at the Council of Chalcedon (convoked by another Roman Emperor) Jesus was declared true God and true man, with the full implication that he was equal to the Father.

As a postscript, though by imperial decree the role of Jesus had been clarified—admittedly in a far more obscure way—the full role of the Holy Spirit was still in dispute. And the disagreement there between East and West would someday provide the basis for a permanent schism between the two areas.

Chapter 23

Athanasius' Discourses Against the Arians

Note: The following observations are mostly based on the writings of Athanasius as printed in the book, <u>Nicene and Post Nicene Fathers of the Christian Church, Volume IV, St. Athanasius Select Works and Letters</u> by Philip Schaff & Henry Dace.[1]

One of the most famous surviving documents regarding the Arian controversy was a treatise that Athanasius wrote: "Against the Arians." The purpose of this set of four chapters called "discourses" was to point out the errors of the Arian position, while defending the Nicene theology. These discourses are noteworthy in many respects. First, we can surmise what Athanasius thought the Arians believed, although great caution is required since the author is biased to the extreme. We are also exposed to Athanasius' rhetoric. But what is most interesting is how Athanasius argues and the substance of his evidence. Gerard Sloyan, in his extremely doctrine-supporting <u>The Three Persons in One God</u>, writes: "The judgment of any reader of Athanasius' tract *Against the Arians* or Hilary's *On the Trinity* will necessarily be that Catholic preconceptions mark the entire approach to Scripture. The interpretation of every text in the light of the 'analogy of faith' comes through very clearly."[2] In this chapter, the notation in brackets refers to the discourse and its section.

What becomes evident from the beginning is Athanasius' mean-spirited tone; he continuously uses harsh, condemning language, such as "harbingers of Antichrist" [1-1], "in great and grievous error, as neither having studied Scripture, not understanding Christianity at all" [1-1-1], "this in truth is to call even Caiaphas Christian, and to reckon the traitor Judas still among the Apostles" [1-2], "Authors of blasphemy, verily are these foes of God" [1-21], "but as dogs and swine wallow in their own vomit and their own mire, rather invent new expedients for their irreligion" [2-1], "the Ario-maniacs" [3-1], "a heretic is a wicked thing in truth, and in every respect his heart is depraved and irreligious" [3-58], "the devil who is their father" [3-59].

Athanasius rails against the Arian concept that for the Son "There was once when he was not" [1-11], which seems to have been an early declaration by Arius. Athanasius insists that the Son must always be eternal, citing John 1:1, Rev. 1:4, Rom. 9:5 and Rom. 1:20. But a careful reading of these verses says nothing definitive! John's

Gospel's "In the beginning" certainly does not posit existence except at the beginning, and "the Word was God" can be interpreted as "the Word was divine." Revelation cites "grace and peace from him who is and who was and who is to come," but then adds a second person, Jesus Christ. Obviously, the eternal one being referenced is God. Romans 9 references an ambiguous phrase, "to them [the Israelites] belong the patriarchs, and from them, according to the flesh, comes the Messiah, who is over all, God blessed forever," since the last three words can be a blessing on God for what He did. And Romans 1 clearly references "God."

Athanasius inserts his own interpretation when he insists that Arians mean "time" in their statement "there was when he was not," even though the word is not present. Arians believed that the Father preceded the Son (since the Son is begotten by the Father), but do not establish that this happened in time.

In a similar vein, Athanasius objects to the Arian's related demand for an explanation of how the Father could beget the Son if they are co-eternal; thus they should be more like brothers if this is so. Athanasius' argument is specious, resting more on the Son not being created and assuming we should know what eternally begotten might mean [1-14].

For several of his arguments, Athanasius relies on "whoever has seen me has seen the Father" [John 14:9]. This statement, if taken literally, would need to be defined in a full Sabellian sense: the Father is the Son! He further reasons that since Jesus is the image of the Father, he must indeed have the entirety of all the attributes of the Father. This conclusion is invalid; an image is not the same as the object for which it is an image. Furthermore, Athanasius then fails to explain what would follow logically: since man is made in the image of God, he must be God [1-21].

The verses of Philippians 2:9-10 "God highly exalted Him" are addressed in extremely circular reasoning [1-37 to 1-45]. First, Athanasius spends most of the text proclaiming since Jesus is God, he had the exaltation by right—it was not given, but already deserved. In the last section [1-45], he tries to make the point more directly that because Jesus was in the body, so the exaltation was of the body: "the Body being His, and the Word not being external to it, it is natural that when the Body was exalted, He, as man, should, because of the body, be spoken of as exalted." What Athanasius fails to address is how God (who he defines as the Trinity) is now clearly separated between God and Jesus in these verses. The argument, too, is based on a rather flimsy interpretation.

Acts 2:36 is addressed in the Second Discourse, Sections 11-18: "God has made this Jesus, who you crucified, both Lord and Christ." First, Athanasius uses his circular logic to refute the term "made" meaning "created." Remaining consistent with one of his basic premises, he always fights any interpretation that the Son is a created being. But then, in addressing how Jesus became Lord and Christ, he argues that this happened at his incarnation or birth, rejecting the simplest and most scriptural interpretation: that God performed the act of elevating Jesus because of what Jesus did, which is implicitly stated in Philippians:

> ... he humbled himself and became obedient to the point of death—even death on a cross. Therefore God also highly exalted him ... [Phil. 2:8-9]

John 14:1 ["Believe in God, believe also in me"] and other passages (Luke 18:19 ["No one is good but God alone"], Mark 12:29 ["the Lord our God, the Lord is one"], John 6:38 ["for I have come down from heaven, not to do my own will, but of him who sent me"]) which highlight either the "oneness" of God or the separateness between "God" and Jesus are totally glossed in sections 7 – 9 of the Third Discourse. Again, Athanasius reverts to his circular reasoning that because Jesus is God, these phrases must all be interpreted to include him—regardless of the obvious separation that is stated—and makes a mockery of Scriptural interpretation.

The arguments become even stranger as Athanasius addresses passages where Jesus receives power and glory from the Father. Besides the circular arguments, Athanasius reinvents the meaning of "given" to imply that these weren't given at all, but instead, were residing in Jesus' godhead all the time. Thus, "given" means "previously possessed." His main argument in support references Jesus' questions about where Lazarus lay, how many fishes the crowd had before multiplying the loaves, etc. in which Jesus already knew but asked anyway [3-35 to 3-41]. By analogy, when Jesus references being given something, it must mean He already had it!

In the Third Discourse (as well as being sprinkled throughout), Athanasius argues constantly that when Jesus showed any "human" weaknesses, it was because he was in the flesh. When he knows something extraordinary, however, it is because He is God. This obviously leads to contradictions! For it makes Jesus an on-again, off-again deity. In a similar note [3-42 to 3-53], Athanasius claims that because Jesus is human, he doesn't know the time of the end of the world, but that as the Son—God—he does know. But if he knows how the world will end—as God—why wouldn't he also know when? Thus, Athanasius views the "flesh" being capricious in its effects.

In the Fourth Discourse, there's a continuation of two themes. First, since the Son is divine he can't be created (failing to address, of course, any scripture to the contrary, such as "being the first-born of all creation"). In fact, Athanasius seems to be mostly convinced that Jesus' creation is the Arian view. The second theme involves the circular logic. God is ONE; the Son is God; the Son is Wisdom; the Son is the Word. Thus, when we speak of "begotten," we can never mean two, but rather that God's Word and God's Wisdom are not separate, but are totally equal to God. Of course, if we apply that same logic to humans, the words I say are actually a human being—me; the thoughts I think is a human being—me. Therefore, if you hear my words, you have experienced everything that I am.

In fact, Athanasius continuously tries to give the impression that he fully knows the truth about God. For example, he declares that Jesus could not be less than God, since only God could restore fallen man back to communion with himself.[3] But must God be so limited as to not have other ways of doing this, such as sending His divine, subordinate Son? Whatever he makes up, he expounds as the truth, regardless of how illogical or lacking in scriptural verification it might be. Apparently, God must have given an intimate revelation about himself to Athanasius which he didn't feel comfortable doing with Jesus!

"Wherefore God highly exalted Him" and "All power is given to me" are two key scripture references that are addressed [4-6 to 4-7]. Athanasius' reply? They don't apply to Jesus! Instead, they apply (that is, are given) to us through the Son: he writes "as if given to Him, they are given to us" [4-6]. When words have to be warped to impart a particular meaning, based on a presupposition, then any scripture can be made to mean what the "interpreter" desires. This becomes the ultimate in circular reasoning, but it is one of the main disreputable methods of Athanasius!

Athanasius clings to just a few passages and frequently repeats them with his interpretation, as if that makes a valid argument. His two favorites are in John 1:1 and "I and the Father are one." Emphasizing the latter in 4-9, he coins a term "coessentiality" (at least the interpreters do), as if creating a new term will acceptably describe the essence of one God in two persons. Incidentally, based on Athanasius' own logic, this itself must be heretical, since he omits the Holy Spirit! To quote Athanasius with regard to John 1:1: "Moreover the Son, according to John, is not merely 'God' but 'true God;' for according to the same Evangelist, 'And the Word was God;' and the Son said, 'I am the Life." Note Athanasius' expansion of "God" to "true God," even though the meaning of John 1:1 is more that of "divine" rather than "God" in the first place.

In summary, Athanasius avoids most of the disputed scripture, and when he does address a limited selection, the arguments are virtually entirely circular and apologetic (that is, since Jesus is God, then the meaning, however implausible, must be consistent with Jesus being God). He seems to disdain logic. The only reasonable arguments he makes run in favor of a divine status for the Son—but for Athanasius, this implies equality with God. However, that interpretation is not legitimately supported by any of his other arguments. In short, Athanasius has written about 150 pages of "here are a couple passages that support some of what I believe, I extrapolate the rest, ignore the obvious contradictions, warp the meanings of contrary passages to explain them, and describe my opponents with vile epithets."

If anything, Athanasius' discourses reveal the bankruptcy of his argument, and his tirades uncover him as an intolerant egotist. It is hard to believe that these writings are held up as valuable, Christian exposition.

Chapter 24

Historical Conclusion

From this brief historical review, two things can be concluded. First, the early Church often had the idea that Jesus was divine, and so may have called him "God" on occasion. But it had virtually no conception that Jesus was the God, the Supreme Being of the universe, or that the Godhead was a Dyad or a Trinity. They could not fully comprehend what his nature actually was, but they still generally followed what they believed from the writings of the Apostles and their close associates. No "tradition" was handed down by these immediate followers of Jesus which provides support for a broad belief in a co-equal status of Jesus with the Father. If anything, the general assumption was that the Son was subordinate to the Father.

Secondly, The Fourth Century produced a radical change in the Church. Charles Freeman in his insightful book <u>The Closing of the Western Mind</u>, reminds us of the mix with politics, when he quotes a religious leader writing of how those in heaven …

> … in their providence have so designed that good and true principles have been established by the wisdom and deliberation of eminent, wise and upright men. It is wrong to oppose these principles, or desert the ancient religion for some new one, for it is the height of criminality to try and revise doctrines that were settled once and for all by the ancients, and whose position is fixed and acknowledged.[1]

Although this quote could have come from some church leader of the late Fourth or Fifth Century, it actually originated from a Roman emperor, the great Christian persecutor, Diocletian, in A.D. 302 with regard to the pagan gods! Such was the attitude of the Roman emperors that they believed that they were divinely connected. And we see this continued under the umbrage of Constantine, when the Church gained enormous political power—but with a catch. Since this power was always contingent on the emperor's favor, the Church could either oppose the emperor's theology and lose its exalted position, or concur and remain powerful. Historically, the Church followed the latter path, varying its theology depending on the emperor in power, until Theodosius made opposition to the Nicene position extremely costly.

Perhaps originally the establishment of a single doctrine was intended to unify the Church and end the chaos that was occurring between the existing bishoprics. Thus, at one time the Arian view could be seen as a unifying solution, just as the Nicene view was. But ultimately the historical result is this: through Constantine the creed was formulated; with Theodosius, the creed became law. So despite the input of various theologians, the actual establishment of the doctrine should be seen not as the result of an agreement between reasonable bishops, but primarily as an accommodation to imperial authority. In today's views, we would have insisted that a radical change in theological thought would require strong evidence to substantiate the truth of that claim. But we can easily observe that both Constantine and Theodosius were guilty of "jury tampering" in the theological court of the Fourth Century.

What transpired after this imperial backing is revealing. Three major things happened. First, the Church became increasingly intolerant. Pagans, Jews and heretics were persecuted—with the backing of the Empire. Second, doctrine became increasingly faith based. Thus, just as Jesus as co-equal to the Father had little scriptural support, the incorporation of the Holy Spirit as a third co-equal member of the divine Trinity also had little scriptural support, but became dogma anyway. Third, with Jesus being God, other mediators between God and man became necessary. Foremost, the Emperor held such a role. Then Mary was declared the "Mother of God," elevating her to a status of mediator between God and humans. And with the Church declaring itself sovereign in spiritual matters, it displaced Jesus as the center. Jesus had been "personal," but now he was far away, and the Church also assumed a role as mediator between God and His people. All this became doctrine or practice within 75 years. Nearly all these changes were considered divinely revealed through faith. The doctrines became firmly set, and any deviation was considered heresy.

The reliance on faith *sans* reason from then on became a significant source for doctrinal basis. The Cappadocians fell back on the ultimate mystery of things when they were unable to find proof for their claims. Even in the 1200's Thomas Aquinas admitted that natural reason could not explain the Trinity.[2] And the Council of Trent in the 1500's formally declared that the Roman Catholic Church alone could interpret scripture[3], essentially declaring that fideism must dominate.

Following the Roman imperial example, the Church took on a more militant role. The pacifism of Jesus was ignored, and church leaders like Ambrose, bishop of Milan, could write in his work <u>de Fide</u>, that the army was now co-led by Jesus.[4] Thus, the lack of Christian love that followed, with intrigue, defamation, *hubris*, power-grabbing, persecution, and even murder generates even more doubt about the validity of the victorious doctrine. By its fruit you should know it.

This historical revelation is extremely important. Forces outside the Church, no matter how well intentioned, had a major effect in determining a doctrine and a dogma. And it is clear from Athanasius' discourses that the substance of scripture was not fundamental to the Nicene belief. It is further unfortunate that the victors destroyed most of the evidence that the vanquished presented. Perhaps we would have a better idea of how the Arians and subordinationists addressed their arguments, so as to get an even better historical perspective. And the destruction of texts was not limited to Arian writings. Anything considered contradictory to the established dogma would be considered fair game. Thus, any writings by Church Fathers or their sympathizers could have been destroyed if those writings claimed that Jesus was not God. We must realize that we have a very censored view of early Church history, and what survived is highly likely to be biased in favor of the Church's new doctrine.

But ultimately, this history should itself be a witness. If the Nicene doctrine was a product of thoughtful deliberations amongst nonpolitical theologians, arguing the role of scripture in understanding the nature of the Son of God, then strong consideration should be given to its conclusions. Yet, the political culture of the time was powerful. Just as the culture of the British Colonies between 1776 and 1787 led the founders of the United States of America on one hand to state that all men "are endowed by their Creator with certain unalienable rights, among them life, liberty, and the pursuit of happiness," and then on the other hand withhold those rights from Negro slaves and Native Americans, the imperial power of the Fourth Century molded the culture and influenced a great deal of the deliberations and results. This, itself, should provide grave doubts about the doctrine that resulted.

One potential benefit to the Church that the eventual success of the Nicene view created was the centralization of power in the Church that occurred because of the Council of Constantinople. Prior to that time, the regional theological views—as judged by the affected bishops—were dependent on local interpretation. With the Council, the Church essentially centralized itself and ruled what dogma should be. One result was that Christians now must follow whatever the Church dictated. As Herring states: "the history of Christianity might well have taken a very different course had it not been for Athanasius."[5] While Arianism supported individualism; the Nicene theology and formula emphasized an autocratic order strongly flavored with politics.[6] This centralization of the Church may have helped ensure its survival. But it is also likely that the central truths of Christianity, first the redemption of the world by Jesus and second his resurrection—along with God's protection—would have been sufficient for survival.

Incidentally, in the spirit of the Nicene victors, it is important to point out that the creed itself should be viewed as heretical. Later, councils would declare that the Holy Spirit also is to be considered a co-equal and co-eternal person of God. The Nicene Creed omits such statements. Thus, God would have been defined incorrectly. Since the creators of the Creed claimed only two persons in the Godhead, shouldn't they be labeled as heretics, just as Origen was in 553 for his subordinationist views in claiming only one person in the Godhead?

One other development not covered in this book is one of the other early controversies regarding the divine nature of Jesus. This became fully defined at the Council of Chalcedon in 451, which declared that Jesus was both fully divine (God) and fully human. Although this perhaps has bearing on understanding the divine nature of Jesus, its significance in relating the Father to the Son is fairly minimal. Yet it does call into question the Nicene assertion: how can the Son be of identical substance (*homoousia*) as the Father when the Father obviously does not share the human "substance' of the Son?

Part 5

Conclusion

Chapter 25

Conclusion

Throughout the middle centuries of its existence the Church taught that everything revolved around the earth: moon, sun, planets and stars. This held true into the 1600's when the Catholic Church confronted an Italian astronomer, Galileo, who proclaimed that the earth actually revolved around the sun. Since this Church held the geocentric view as if it were doctrine, they threatened Galileo with death if he did not recant his "heretical" beliefs. They cited biblical proofs, such as in the book of Joshua:

> On the day when the LORD gave the Amorites over to the Israelites, Joshua spoke to the LORD; and he said in the sight of Israel,
> "Sun, stand still at Gibeon, and Moon, in the valley of Aijalon." And the sun stood still, and the moon stopped until the nation took vengeance on their enemies.
> Is it not written in the Book of Jashar? The sun stopped in mid-heaven, and did not hurry to set for about a whole day. [Josh. 10:12-13]

Such was the attitude and power of the Church, inherited from the Fourth Century and refined since, that it felt that it could dictate even science as gleaned from a few Bible passages and its "theological reasoning," and enforce those beliefs through persecution. And it wasn't just the Roman Catholic Church that was guilty. Even Martin Luther ridiculed the geocentric idea.[1]

But the Church was wrong in its strongly held belief—a belief that they felt was worthy to kill for.

Too often we humans want to rely on reason to decipher the mystery of God. For example, since the Son was begotten by the Father, and the Father is God, by reason we want to conclude that the Son must also be God in all His fullness. Since God is Love, by reason that love must be perfect so we want to conclude that He must have an equal to love, allowing His love to be complete. Since man is so sinful and very unworthy of God, by reason we may want to conclude that only God Himself can personally redeem us, and furthermore there must be a Purgatory that will purify us and raise us up to a level acceptable to God after we die. Since Jesus is pure and without sin, by reason we may want to conclude that his mother, too, must be pure and without sin.

In a sense, the concept of God as Trinity is only a model, a way for the Church to explain the divinity of Jesus the Son and the divine source of the Holy Spirit. Yet, consider again the model of Geocentricity. The universe was believed to revolve around the earth. Yet scientific observations conflicted with this doctrine. So adjustments were made to the model, and planets were proposed to actually follow smaller orbits within their larger orbits, called epicycles. This resolved the gross observation of retrograde motion. The Copernican model couldn't be right because the doctrine would then be wrong! But then more accurate measurements brought more disagreement, and epicycles within epicycles were proposed, until this drive for greater accuracy resulted in a model that was incomprehensible to most people—including its defenders. Eventually, the Copernican model was accepted. It explained the observations. And it was simple.

The doctrine of the Trinity is analogous. The doctrine is inexplicable, and so its defenders must always fall back on their final defense: "It's a mystery." But like the geocentric doctrine, the doctrine of the Trinity also is inconsistent with the "observations," which arise from the biblical record. Apologists warp the meaning of a few passages to claim scriptural support, and ignore the preponderance of obvious evidence against their doctrine.

Our reason is totally inadequate when it comes to understanding the mind and actions of God. It is a tremendous act of pride for any of us, including the Church, to declare how God must be or how God must act—unless it has been divinely revealed to us. Yet God has revealed something about Himself in the Bible. And these words show the insufficiency and even falseness of the concept of God-as-Trinity, because the Son is revealed as not being God. There is a much better model, a simpler model, and one consistent with the Bible: the subordination of the divine Son to the one true God, His Father.

One of the great mysteries that naturally comes to mind in claiming that the Church is wrong in its fundamental theology about Jesus, is why God would allow his Church to continue so long in error? This is, obviously, an unanswerable question. But there are three other instances when it has happened before. The first involves the Jewish faith. The Jews are the chosen people of God, and in a sense they are the people of His first church. Yet that religion today fails to recognize Jesus as Messiah, a grave theological error. They had the prophecies and the evidence of the fulfillment of those prophecies come into their midst, and yet their religious leaders failed to recognize this and incorporate it as an essential chapter in their faith story. That original "church" failed to see the truth, and many of its members even persecuted those who believed otherwise. That church has continued in that error for nearly 2000 years.

The second major error experienced by the Church faithful occurred in the First Century. The words of Jesus recorded by all three Synoptic Gospels foretell the end of the world and its timing:

> "Truly I tell you, this generation will not pass away until all these things have taken place." [Matt. 24:34, also in Mark 13:30 and Luke 21:32]

This passage poses a great problem for those who interpret the words of the New Testament literally! Did Jesus prophesy wrongly, thereby bringing into question his prophetic ability? Or could an original source have erred, and actually wrote this prophecy in the wrong context, missing that it should have referred to the destruction of Jerusalem? (After all, Jesus also did state that he didn't know the exact time for the end of the world. [Matt. 24:36]) What is evident from many New Testament writings is that this belief was the prevalent view. The day of Christ's coming is considered "near" or "at hand" in Romans 13:11-12, Philippians 4:5, James 5:8, and 1 Peter 4:7, and is written as coming in "a little while" or coming "soon" in Hebrews 10:37 and Revelation 22:7. Furthermore, the *parousia* is hinted at coming soon in Luke 9:27, John 21:22, 1 Cor. 1:7-8, 1 Cor. 7:26, 1 Peter 1:6 and Titus 2:13. How could the Church have made such a fundamental error? This error would deeply affect later generations. With the end being imminent, the early disciples felt it was unnecessary to write the history, for the oral tradition would easily suffice. Thus, the historical writings we do have, the Gospels, were written well after Jesus' death, when recollections could be fogged by the passage of years. Furthermore, the probability is that we would now possess far more "original" work dating from the First Century.

The third manner in which error has permeated the Church is evidenced in our Bible. Bart Ehrman points out that many of the texts that we find in the Bible have been corrupted in some way, usually through transcription errors, but sometimes through deliberate modification of the text. If one of our tenets of faith is that the "original" Bible is the inspired word of God, then why has God allowed the text to become altered? For Ehrman, this has become a roadblock to his belief, for he asks,

For the only reason (I came to think) for God to inspire the Bible would be so that his people would have his actual words; but if he really wanted people to have his actual words, surely he would have miraculously preserved those words, just as he had miraculously inspired them in the first place. Given the circumstances that he didn't preserve the words, the conclusion seemed inescapable to me that he hadn't gone to the trouble of inspiring them.[2]

For most Christians, we see the fundamental truths still come through the words, even if possibly altered. Yes, we may not have the original writings, and we currently have no way to either get those writings or be absolutely certain that we have those writings if we actually do have them. Yet for Christians, the Bible remains the primary source for truth. But which Bible translation has the least error, and which truths are missing? And why has God allowed us to believe the errors that are present for so long? As I've already written, the conclusions of my treatise do not come from single passages, but from both the meaning and the spirit of the entire Bible, which I believe continues to be the inspired word of God as a whole.

One of the earliest heresies springing up in Christianity was Gnosticism. This sect believed that there existed secret knowledge that only a few of the faithful were privy to. This knowledge superseded the known writings, and came via special inspiration. Only with the discovery of various Gnostic texts at Nag Hammadi in 1945 has the depth of Gnostic thought—and diversity—been revealed.[3] It didn't take long for the Church Fathers to vigorously oppose Gnosticism.

Yet what is the tenet of God as a Trinity of three co-equal persons except a statement resulting from the revelation of secret knowledge? It certainly cannot be found in any of the accepted Church Canon. The doctrine of *homoousia*, "identical substance," has no biblical support. Yet we see the arrogance of Athanasius, a vigorous Nicene supporter, declaring his views in *Against the Arians*, sure that his knowledge is superior to those of his Arian opponents, and averring as fact his belief of what divinity is all about. Where did Athanasius get his secret knowledge?

As said at the beginning of this book, theology is a risky enterprise! How can our very limited minds ever approach understanding divinity, deity and the supernatural? In a way, trying to decipher

God's supernatural realm, where time is transcended and there are more physical dimensions than the three that mortal man is familiar with, is more like a scientific issue than a theological one. Yet we have seen how fallible the Church can be when it comes to science. Defining as dogma what cannot be understood even at a simple level seems arrogant, unless Scripture provides an appropriate revelation. Yet the fact is that the Church appears to have overruled what Scripture has revealed. The Church has decided to declare as certain truth what it could never know to be true. Perhaps they need to take to heart what Jesus told the Sadducees:

> Jesus answered them, "You are wrong because you know neither the scriptures nor the power of God." [Matt. 22:29]

Indeed, the Church has violated the admonition of St. Paul. It is clear from Paul's writings that he certainly did not teach a doctrine of the Trinity. And it is similarly clear that the rest of the New Testament authors also did not teach such a doctrine. It was not part of their instruction and could not be one of their fundamental beliefs. So what does it mean for Timothy, and in fact, the rest of the Church, when Paul writes the following?

> I urge you, as I did when I was on my way to Macedonia, to remain in Ephesus so that you may instruct certain people not to teach any different doctrine, and not to occupy themselves with myths and endless genealogies that promote speculations rather than the divine training that is known by faith. [1 Tim. 1:3-4]

And does Paul not ask for steadfastness to the truth of his own teaching?

> So then, brothers and sisters, stand firm and hold fast to the traditions that you were taught by us, either by word of mouth or by our letter. [2 Thes. 2:15]

> I urge you, brothers and sisters, to keep an eye on those who cause dissensions and offenses, in opposition to the teaching that you have learned; avoid them. [Rom. 16:17]

The same admonition can be also found in Colossians 2:6-8, Galatians 1:6-9 and 2 Timothy 1:13-14, so St. Paul has urged at least six times that his followers adhere to what they have been taught, and only what they have been taught. Surely the doctrine of the Trinity, including Jesus being co-equal with the Father, is a doctrine different from what these true authorities knew and taught.

Another important question, and one that is entirely relevant to the Church's defense, is this: does the Holy Spirit guide the Church so that it is enabled to make infallible decisions? Father Raymond Brown addresses this succinctly in regard to the Trinity:

> In discussing how the church moved from the NT to its dogma of the Trinity, some may prefer to speak of "tradition" being the guiding factor. I have no objection provided that "tradition" is not understood in a static way (and indeed provided that it is seen as another name for what I am trying to describe more fluidly). If "tradition" implies that first-century Christianity already understood three coequal but distinct divine Persons and one divine Nature but simply had not developed the precise terminology, I would dissent. Neither the terminology nor the basic ideas had reached clarity in the first century; problems and disputes were required before the clarity came. But, as we can see from the NT, some first-century Christians did have views about the *pre-existent* divinity of Jesus and *personal* characteristics of the Spirit—elements that established a line of development attractive to later church teachers when they finally formulated the Trinitarian dogma. There was a distinct element of the new, but the new in continuity with the old. Precisely because the "Trinitarian" line of development was not the only line of thought detectable in the NT, one must posit the guidance of the Spirit and an intuition of faith as the church came to its decision. The liturgy, the prayer life of the faithful, and the *consensus fidelium* would have all contributed to this intuition. ... in my judgment, even when fixed in a formula, tradition does not stifle further insight derived from a deeper penetration of Scripture.[4]

What Brown implies is that the Church can make dogma out of anything—without biblical basis—as long as it believes that it is inspired, and, supposedly, as long as it does not contradict Scripture. Such have been the Catholic doctrinal teachings of Mary's Immaculate Conception and Assumption, and the infallibility of the Pope when he speaks *ex cathedra*. But foundational to this belief is the *a priori* assumption that the Church is indeed consistently inspired by the Holy Spirit. This obviously becomes a very slippery slope!

But Scripture <u>has</u> revealed truths about Jesus' divine nature and his subordination to God. And ultimately, we need to trust what has been given us through God's *collective* word, the Bible, while being very cautious about clinging to only a few passages, particularly when we are aware that their meaning does not have to be that Jesus is God, and especially when none indicates a co-equal status with God. In fact, one of the premises of this book, that there are different levels of divinity, could be wrong, since no one can truly understand what divinity, deity, or supernatural really mean. The premise is just consistent with Jesus being eternal but not God, and is a way of simply modeling what actually is unknowable.

Parts 2 and 3 have basically been an exposition of what the Bible directly says about the nature of the Son of God. For the most part, I have avoided seeking out different explanations of various verses written by other authors, both pro and con, but have sought out what the meaning of the Greek was when necessary. This was intended to avoid biases in the interpretation of what the Bible does, in fact, say, and try to take more at face value the words that have survived. Again, it is felt that the authors of these words, except perhaps for the book of Revelation, were not typically writing to an elite group who alone could understand the hidden meanings embedded "between the lines." But rather that the authors were writing to a typically unsophisticated and often illiterate audience.

One other very interesting pair of facts was also revealed while I was researching the history of the Church's decision. Although I was aware of various sects' unitarianism, I learned that two of the most brilliant minds in all of history had also taken on the challenge of understanding the nature of Jesus. As has already been written in Chapter 21, the Third Century's premier theologian, Origen, had come to the conclusion that Jesus was not God. But it is fascinating that Sir Isaac Newton also came to that conclusion in the latter half of the Seventeenth Century. Rather than dismiss him as "only" a mathematician or physicist, we need to recognize that this brilliant man put enormous energy into the study of the Scriptures and religious beliefs, perhaps even more than in his mathematical pursuits. He was driven to know the truth. He studied available manuscripts in their original languages, including the writings of the Church Fathers. But to publish his beliefs and reasoning at that time would ensure certain censure and immediate loss of any professional standing, with the likelihood of subsequent physical persecution or execution. Thus, he wrote, but did not publish, and only recent research has uncovered this work.[5] Newton looked to the Scriptures for that truth, and found there neither evidence of a Trinitarian God nor even Jesus being God.

The Bible must be our first source of truth, and the words found there illuminate the true nature of Jesus. To echo Newton—and virtually every other honest author who writes with any ecclesiastic authority—nowhere does it speak of God as a Trinity of three equal persons. And nowhere does it unambiguously call Jesus "God." These are extrapolations based on a few tenuous passages which ignore what the Bible explicitly says in dozens of other places. In fact, the continuous message to be found within the entire Bible is not one of a Trinity, but rather of a single-person God—Yahweh, the Father—who sent His Son—the Messiah—for our redemption. This is what the Bible tells us to believe! Jesus is the <u>Son</u> of God.

> God abides in those who confess that Jesus is the Son of God, and they abide in God. [1 John 4:15]

<u>New Insights are Revealed</u>

When we begin reading the Bible with the altered view that Yahweh is God alone, but shares eternity and power with His divine Son, we benefit in multiple ways. Not only does this show that mankind is more like the Son, but also that the Son's power becomes far more important for us. We should rejoice that we have not only become partnered with Jesus as a man, but that we are now able to join with his divinity in a way that is still incomprehensible to us. We join with Christ as being lower than God but still being able to be <u>in</u> the Father, demonstrated as Jesus prayed to his Father at the Last Supper:

> "I ask not only on behalf of these, but also on behalf of those who will believe in me through their word, that they may all be one. As you Father, are in me and I am in you, may they also be in us, so that the world may believe that you have sent me. The glory that you have given me I have given them, so that they may be one, as we are one, I in them and you in me, that they may be completely one, so that the world may know that you have sent me and have loved them even as you have loved me. Father I desire that those also, whom you have given me, may be with me where I am, to see my glory, which you have given me because you loved me before the foundation of the world." [John 17:20-24]

Some verses take on their obvious meaning, but reveal nuances about Jesus we might not have considered before. Take this previously cited exchange when a rich ruler questions Jesus:

> A certain ruler asked him, "Good Teacher, what must I do to inherit eternal life?" Jesus said to him, "Why do you call me good? No one is good but God alone." [Luke 18:18-19]

This dialogue actually made no sense with the belief that Jesus is God. It is so unlikely that Jesus was just trying to elicit a declaration of belief in his divinity from the young ruler. But accepting the separation between God and His Son now brings a more human face to Jesus, one who had not yet been brought to perfection.

Furthermore, many verses take on new meaning, especially in bringing the focus back onto the Father, but emphasizing Jesus' role in revealing the Father to us. Much of John's Last Supper discourse fits into this altered paradigm. As another example, consider Colossians chapter 3, which is rich in altered meaning:

> So if you have been raised in Christ, seek the things that are above where Christ is, seated at the right hand of God. [Col. 3:1]

Our *spiritual* resurrection, occurring at our conversion in Christ, requires our seeking spiritual growth to follow Jesus, our human example, who has been elevated by God's power. It is not following a God who took human form and could not falter.

> For you have died, and your life is hidden with Christ in God. [Col. 3:3]

Our death to sin now allows us to share God's life beside His Son. It is not a God-the-Son sheltering us.

> And whatever you do, in word or deed, do everything in the name of the Lord Jesus, giving thanks to God the Father through him. [Col. 3:17]

The Son of God is our conduit to God who is to be our true focus. The Son does not get "equal billing." See how the following passage from Second Corinthians reveals a more personal role for Christians in assuming the role that Jesus had:

> From now on, therefore, we regard no one from a human point of view; even though we once knew Christ from a human point of view, we know him no longer in that way. So if anyone is in Christ, there is a new creation; everything old has passed away; see, everything has become new! All this is from God, who reconciled us to himself through Christ, and has given us the ministry of reconciliation; that is, in Christ God was reconciling the world to himself, not counting their trespasses against them, and entrusting the message of reconciliation to us. So we are ambassadors for Christ, since God is making his appeal through us; we entreat you on behalf of Christ, be reconciled to God. For our sake he made him to be sin who knew no sin, so that in him we might become the righteousness of God. [2 Cor. 5:16-21]

The Old Testament becomes more pertinent and personal as well, for there the focus is on one God—Yahweh. Reading the Psalms and properly using His sacred name where the word "LORD" has been substituted can draw one in closer to the relationship God wants, one where we feel more comfortable in calling Him "Abba." We would move from speaking to the impersonal almighty "Lord" God above, to conversing with a genuine person that we know, to even having a childlike talk with "Dad."

As a final example, the words of Jesus from the cross allow us to see God as Jesus saw him in desperate hours:

> "My God, my God, why have you forsaken me?" [Mark 15:34]

> "Father, into your hands I commend my spirit." [Luke 23:46]

Jesus may have felt abandoned and alone at the hour of his death. He expresses a feeling of desperation and confusion. But he also then shows his faith in God, a trust that his Father will take up his spirit—rescue him from spiritual death—and restore his existence. This may easily echo our personal spiritual anxiety at the hour of our own death, and the reassurance through Christ's subsequent resurrection that our trust can be well placed. These are not the words of a dying God confident that his physical death will immediately segue back into a heavenly realm.

I urge the reader to experience—and be awed by—the numerous nuanced changes of meaning when reading the Bible with a Father-to-Son viewpoint.

Suggestions on How We Might View Jesus

Jesus is Messiah. Jesus is the Christ ("Messiah"), whom God sent in fulfillment of His prophesies to the Jewish people. He is the culmination of the Old Covenant and the creator of the New Covenant. As readers of the New Testament, we would also benefit by not calling the Son "Jesus Christ" but rather "Jesus the Christ," to emphasize that role rather then have it sound like a first and last name.

Jesus is Redeemer and Savior. By the actions of Jesus, we have been made acceptable to the Father. By his suffering and passion, he paid the ransom demanded by the Father, freeing us from a death in sin. And by Jesus' supreme sacrifice of his entire life he brought humanity forgiveness of sins and access to the Father. He deserves our honor, gratefulness and praise.

Jesus is Reconciler, Mediator and Intercessor. God has designated Jesus as the only way that we can reach the Father. No other mediator is available or necessary—not the Emperor, not the mother of Jesus, nor any of the Church clergy. Jesus is "the way" to God [John 14:6]. Without Jesus' act of reconciliation, we could not have attained access to God. Now with Jesus' ongoing mediation, we do have access to the Father. But he is even more than reconciler and mediator, for he even takes our side! As intercessor, he pleads for us at God's right hand [Rom. 8:34]. As the comprehensive representative of God, he is also the Truth and the Light.

Jesus is Judge. At the end of the world, everyone will stand before the Son of God to be judged as to whether or not we share his kingdom with his Father [Matt. 25:31-46]. We will not have the excuse that "God really didn't understand me," since Jesus shared our humanity and understands both our strengths and our weaknesses. The basis of his judgment is simple; he will see whether we kept his commandment "Love one another" just as he loved us [John 13:34].

Jesus is Lord. God has presented to his Son the gift of being Lord over all creation. He is king over all earthly kings and lord over all earthly lords. He is also Lord over each of us. Since he is the sole representative of the Father, we must obey and honor Jesus.

Jesus is God's Servant and our Example. Everything Jesus did was in conformance with what God told him to do. He served God perfectly. As a man, he was like us in all ways except sin, so that he experienced virtually everything that a human being could experience. We need to look to him as a paragon of submission, humility, self-giving and love, and strive to follow the example he set. Knowing what lay ahead for him in heaven, he proceeded through his earthly life always with a conviction and commitment to the eternal, providing us with a firm foundation of that very same hope.

Jesus is the Image of God. As far as our human perception is capable, God *appears* to be the same as Jesus. It is as if the Father stays behind Jesus so that we cannot see him in all his glory (which our human senses would not be able to see anyway), and when we look toward God, we can only see Jesus. This is in part why there is a tendency to call Jesus God. For all practical purposes, we cannot perceive the difference. Even our prayers can go through Jesus [1 Cor. 1:2].

Jesus is the Only Begotten Son of God. Begotten before time began—which is an incomprehensible mystery—Jesus shares divinity with the Father. He is heir to all God's gifts—gifts <u>given</u> by the Father. In his deep love, a love that infinitely surpasses the greatest love that an earthly father can have for his own son, God chooses to share the power within his kingdom. And the Son is the primary recipient, being the one who infinitely returns that love and who was totally obedient to the Supreme will.

Jesus is Head of the Church, which is his Body. As believers, we stand together and acknowledge that he is our guide and leader. Jesus commanded:

> "Take, eat; this is my body" [Matt. 26:26]

Very significantly, we are a part of him in a unique spiritual way, and he is not content with the division that his Church experiences [1 Cor. 3:1-15]. Chapter 21 in the book of Revelation declares that a "New Jerusalem" will be the bride of the Lamb. It is likely that the New Jerusalem is his faithful Church, and because we are members of that Church, Jesus will be our bridegroom. What an awesome thought that we can be the spouse of Christ!

Jesus is God's Supreme Gift to Humanity. It is virtually unimaginable that a loving father would offer up his only son to be tortured and then killed for *any* purpose. Yet our God and Father did just that, to fulfill a plan that would bring more love and joy as a further gift to all mankind in a way that we can barely begin to understand. We can almost feel the emotional pain of Mary, Jesus' mother, as she witnessed her son's crucifixion. We cannot imagine the Father's pain who caused it to happen, Who, in a sense, gave up that which was most important to Him.

For most Christians, virtually none of these roles delineated for Jesus is new. What may be most important is the emphasis that Jesus is not God in heaven, but is more like one of us—someone that we perhaps can more easily identify with.

In another way, the change in theology does not make a grand difference in how we are to behave. When we see Jesus, we are still seeing as much of God as we are able as humans. By praying to Jesus as mediator, we are still asking him to exercise a God-like power. We are still to obey the New Testament commandment of loving one another.

Still, all of us, with Jesus Christ included, belong to the Father who is our God. And to the Father belongs everything:

> ... so that God may be glorified in all things through Jesus Christ. To him belong the glory and the power forever and ever. Amen. [1 Peter 4:11]

This same message reverberates throughout the Old Testament as well, such as in Isaiah:

> ... and you shall know that I, the LORD {YHWH}, am your Savior and your Redeemer, the Mighty One of Jacob... but the LORD [YHWH] will be your everlasting light, and your God will be your glory. [Is. 60:16, 19]

Amongst the roles that Jesus had, the central one was to bring to God, his Father, the glory and honor of as many of us humans as possible. The Bible's message seems to be this: to worship the Father, while honoring the Son who redeems and leads us. The Catholic Church had a beautiful prayer that announced this truth:

> *Through Him (Jesus) and in Him and with Him*
> *In the unity of the Holy Spirit,*
> *All glory and honor is yours Almighty Father,*
> *Forever and ever. Amen*

To this end, we should advocate the abolishment of the Nicene Creed, replacing it with something similar to the more ancient Apostles Creed, where twice the expression, "God, the Father Almighty" is used (which again affirms that the original belief was that God was the Father alone). At the very least, the words "God from God, light from light, and true God from true God" should be changed to something like "divine Son from divine Father." Also, the reference to "he descended into hell (or 'to the dead') should be removed, since specific Scriptural support for that statement can only be found in a single book of the New Testament, 1 Peter [verses 3:19-20 and to a more vague extent 4:6].

Summary

Let the diligent reader test these assertions, measuring the Bible's words in the light of a new paradigm. Is faith to be based on what we are told to believe? Or should we rather begin with a more basic faith in the trustworthy collective words of the Bible? Might not our church err by going beyond this? Must we ignore and even deny all those clear and definitive passages just cited? Instead, any who hold the Church's view must truly explain those passages, just as this book has addressed and refuted or deflected the Church's dogma-supporting passages, illustrating that they are mistranslations, alternative translations or involve ambiguous interpretations! It is true that they may support Jesus' divinity, but they do not support an equality with God.

Ultimately, I have found three distinct purposes in writing this book. The first is that I want to bring clarity back to diligent readers of the New Testament who see the many contradictions between their complex Trinitarian doctrine which names Jesus "God" but still has him seated at the subordinate position of being at the right hand of God. Perhaps this clarification will help reconcile those who have rejected Scripture because of the conflict they've encountered between what they wanted to believe and what they were told to believe. Furthermore, I want to clear up the confusion about the nature of God, and bring the focus of our worship back to the

Father. He alone deserves all the glory. And any glory He gives to the Son is returned back to him. Even if we as people give glory to the Son it is passed on to the Father (John 14:13). The Father is the One to whom we should fully turn to in adoration. He is the One we are to love. As Jesus said in quoting Deuteronomy when asked what the greatest commandment was:

> "The first is, 'Hear, O Israel: the Lord our God, the Lord is one; you shall love the Lord your God with all your heart, and with all your soul, and with all your mind, and with all your strength'" [Mark 12:29-30]

A second purpose has always been to defend the truth. The Bible, even with its imperfections, is filled with truth, and only by careful study can this truth be known. We must always be cautious when man-made rules and laws supersede God's own instruction.

A third purpose is to resurrect a proper belief in Monotheism. The idea of three persons in one God is essentially incomprehensible and indefensible. Monotheism of one person in one God is embraceable and consistent with Scripture. When the Christian Church declared God to be a Trinity, they essentially left their monotheistic roots and forever alienated themselves from the Jews. Perhaps Jews could more easily accept Jesus as the Son of God and God's Messiah if they saw him not as competing with God and not as a second god, but as existing and sharing in God's divine life, united with Him as a son is to a father.

Perhaps another hope of this book is to bring Christians together. In a sense, all Christians make up the Body of Christ, the real non-sectarian Church, and I love that Church. Yet there is tragic disagreement and dissension between sects, with so much of that hinging on doctrinal disagreements. If we were to all agree that we really cannot define God and His Son, except insofar as they have been clearly revealed in Scripture, a greater spirit of community could ensue. As one author states with regard to what happened in the Fourth Century:

> In short, the former vibrant, active, free atmosphere has disappeared. Gone, as well, is any flexibility to understand the person of Christ in different ways and still remain within the broader Christian movement. Gone is the sense that these issues are profound mysteries and that the human mind is in the end incapable of comprehending them—so that many

different approaches are needed.[6]

It hurts me to be disobedient to my Church, but it is more important for me to be obedient to God. I have never wanted to hurt the Church. Rather, I want the Church to recognize the truth put forward in the Sacred Scripture. But it appears that this truth is in strong opposition to some of those teachings our Church provides. Furthermore, this truth says that our attention should be on the Father, Yahweh, the Supreme Being, who is our God and deserves our central focus. Let us hope that a new dialogue based on the Bible may emerge and that a new unity of believers occurs, to the glory and honor of God, the Father.

Notes

Bibliography

Scripture Index

Notes

Preface

1. Rodney Stark, <u>Cities of God</u> (2006, HarperCollins, San Francisco), 2.
2. Bruce L. Shelley, <u>Church History in Plain Language</u>, third ed., (2008, Thomas Nelson, Inc.), 83.
3. Raymond E. Brown, <u>Responses to 101 Questions on the Bible</u> (1990, Paulist Press), 23.
4. Ibid., 24.
5. Ibid., 25.
6. William Barclay, <u>The Letters to the Philippians, Colossians, and Thessalonians, Revised Edition</u>, (1975, The Westminster Press), 116.
7. Raymond E. Brown, <u>Biblical Exegesis & Church Doctrine</u> (1985, Paulist Press), 17.
8. Wayne A. Meeks (general editor), <u>The HarperCollins Study Bible; New Revised Standard Version</u>, (1989, HarperCollins Publishers), xxviii.

Part 1

Chapter 1

1. The Athanasian Creed can be found in many sources. The one quoted is from the Marques of Bute's English translation. Though bearing the name of Athanasius of Alexandria, the Creed itself is not believed to have been written by him, although it carries many of his theological thoughts, as well as his condemnatory rhetoric.

Part 2

Chapter 8

1. Raymond E. Brown, <u>Jesus, God and Man: Modern Biblical Reflections</u>, (1967, The Bruce Publishing Company), Chapter 1: *Does the New Testament Call Jesus God?*, 1-38.
2. Edited by Raymond E. Brown, Joseph A. Fitzmeyer & Roland E. Murphy, <u>The Jerome Biblical Commentary</u>, *The New Testament and Topical Articles* (1968, Prentice-Hall), section 63:40, 422.
3. William Barclay, <u>The Gospel of John, Volume 1, Revised Edition</u> (1975, Westminster Press), 39.
4. Andy Gaus, <u>The Unvarnished Gospels</u> (1988, Threshold Books), 185.
5. Gerard S. Sloyan, <u>The Three Persons in One God</u>, (1964, Prentice Hall, Inc.), 17.
6. Gaus, xiv.
7. Brown, et.al., section 66:82, 513-14.
8. Ibid., section 61:11, 384.
9. William Barclay, <u>The Letters to the Philippians, Colossians, and Thessalonians, Revised Edition</u> (1975, Westminster Press), 35.
10. Brown, et.al., section 50:18, 251.
11. Bowman & Komoszewski, <u>Putting Jesus in His Place</u> (2007, Kegel Publications), 84.
12. Barclay, 74.
13. Bowman & Komoszewski; pp. 261-262, 272.

Chapter 9

1. Edited by Gerhard Friedrich, translator and editor Geoffrey W. Bromiley, <u>Theological Dictionary of the New Testament, Vol. VI</u> (1968, Wm. B. Eerdman's Publishing Company, Grand Rapids, Michigan), 763.

Chapter 11

1. William Barclay, <u>The Gospel of John, Volume 1, Revised Edition</u> (1975, Westminster Press), 186.

Chapter 12

1. Bart Ehrman, Misquoting Jesus, the Story Behind Who Changed the Bible and Why (2005, Harper SanFrancisco).
2. Timothy Paul Jones, Misquoting Truth (2007, Intervarsity Press).
3. Ibid., 52, citing *Commentary on Matthew 15.14*, as quoted in Bruce M. Metzger, "Explicit References in the Works of Origen to Variant Readings in New Testament Manuscripts," in *Biblical and Patristic Studies in Memory of Robert Pierce Casey*, ed. J.Neville Birdsall and Robert W.Thomson (Freiburg:Herder, 1968), 78-79.
4. Ibid., 157.
5. Ibid., 113.
6. Ibid., 114.
7. Randall Price, Searching for the Original Bible (2007, Harvest House Publishers), 115-116. An errata addendum states that the original statistical information was produced by Daniel B. Wallace, and taken from the book Reinventing Jesus: What the Da Vinci Code and Other Novel Speculations Don't Tell You, by Komoszewski, Sawyer and Wallace.
8. Jones, 44.
9. Raymond E. Brown, Responses to 101 Questions on the Bible (1990, Paulist Press), 108.
10. Paul L. Maier, Eusebius, the Church History; a New Translation with Commentary (1999, Kregel Publications), 95.

Chapter 15

1. William Barclay, The Letters to the Philippians, Colossians, and Thessalonians, Revised Edition (1975, Westminster Press), 119.

Part 4

Chapter 21

1. Brian Moynahan, <u>The Faith: a History of Christianity</u> (2002, Doubleday), 119.
2. Norbert Brox, <u>A Concise History of the Early Church</u> (1995, Continuum Publishing Co., NY.) 151.
3. J.N.D. Kelly, <u>Early Christian Doctrines</u> (1978, HarperCollins, San Francisco), 91.
4. The four passages cited from Clement are taken from J.B. Lightfoot's <u>The Apostolic Fathers</u> (1974, Baker Book House, Grand Rapids, MI).
5. Kelly, 91.
6. Ibid., 91.
7. Ibid., 92.
8. Ibid., 92-93.
9. Moynahan, 124.
10. The four passages cited from Ignatius are also taken from J.B. Lightfoot.
11. Kelly, 90.
12. Lightfoot, 99.
13. Ibid., 94.
14. Ibid., 93.
15. Ibid., 97.
16. David Chidester, <u>Christianity; a Global History</u> (2000, HarperCollins, NY), 55.
17. Kelly, 98.
18. Ibid., 105.
19. Ibid., 107.
20. Ibid., 107.
21. Maier, Paul L., <u>Eusebius—the Church History; A New Translation with Commentary</u> (1999, Kregel Publications), 201.
22. Kelly, 112.
23. Ibid., 113.
24. Ibid., 115.
25. Gayla Visalli (ed.), <u>After Jesus; the Triumph of Christianity</u> (1992, The Readers Digest), 130.
26. Ibid., 153.
27. Herring, George, <u>Introduction to the History of Christianity</u> (2006, New York University Press), 38.

28. Kelly, 129.
29. Ibid., 129.
30. Gerard S. Sloyan, <u>The Three Persons in One God</u> (1964, Prentice-Hall Inc.), 45.
31. Maier, 350.
32. Ibid., 359.
33. Ibid., 359.

Chapter 22

1. Charles Freeman, <u>A.D. 381</u> (2009, Overlook Press), 48.
2. Norbert Brox, <u>A Concise History of the Early Church</u> (1995, Continuum Publishing Co., NY.), 54.
3. Philip Schaff & Henry Dace, <u>Nicene and Post Nicene Fathers of the Christian Church, Volume IV, St. Athanasius Select Works and Letters</u>, (1892, Parker & Company). The information is taken from their exposition on Athanasius' *Oration Against the Arians*.
4. George Herring, <u>Introduction to the History of Christianity</u> (2006, New York University Press), 58.
5. David L. Dungan, <u>Constantine's Bible</u> (2007, Fortress Press), 112.
6. Richard E. Rubenstein, <u>When Jesus Became God</u> (1999, Harcourt, Inc), 78.
7. Bruce L. Shelley, <u>Church History in Plain Language</u>, third ed. (2008, Thomas Nelson, Inc.), 104.
8. David Chidester, <u>Christianity; a Global History</u> (2000, HarperCollins, NY), 102.
9. Dungan, 118-119.
10. Freeman, 66.
11. Dungan, 119-122.
12. Herring, 61.
13. R.P.C Hanson; <u>The Search for the Christian Doctrine of God</u> (1988, Edinburgh: T. & T. Clark), *the Arian Controversy, 318-381 A.D.*, 344.
14. Bart D. Ehrman, <u>Lost Christianities; the Battle for Scripture and Faiths We Never Knew</u>, (2003, Oxford University Press, Inc.), 248.
15. Brian Moynahan, <u>The Faith: a History of Christianity</u> (2002, Doubleday), 123.
16. Freeman, 88.

17. Herring, 28.
18. Moynahan, 124.
19. Freeman, 99.
20. Moynahan, 152.
21. Freeman, 142.

Chapter 23

1. Schaff, Philip & Dace, Henry, <u>Nicene and Post Nicene Fathers of the Christian Church, Volume IV, St. Athanasius Select Works and Letters</u>, (1892, Parker & Company).
2. Gerard S. Sloyan, <u>The Three Persons in One God</u> (1964, Prentice-Hall Inc.), 67. What Sloyan is quoted as writing is equally true of his own book.
3. Brian Moynahan, <u>The Faith: a History of Christianity</u> (2002, Doubleday), 122.

Chapter 24

1. Charles Freeman, <u>The Closing of the Western Mind</u> (2002, Vintage Books), 79. Freeman is quoting instructions given to Julianus (proconsul of Africa) concerning the Manicheans, and related in S Williams' book <u>Diocletian and the Roman Recovery</u> (London, 1985), 153.
2. Ibid., 191.
3. Ibid., 198. At Trent, the Council declared that a Catholic is required to swear that he accepts only what the Church interprets scripture to mean, and may not interpret it in any other way.
4. Ibid., 177.
5. George Herring, <u>Introduction to the History of Christianity</u> (2006, New York University Press), 62.
6. Herring, 62.

Chapter 25

1. William Barclay, <u>The Gospel of Mark</u> (1956, The St. Andrew Press), 99.
2. Bart Ehrman, <u>Misquoting Jesus, the Story Behind Who Changed the Bible and Why</u>, (2005, Harper SanFrancisco), 211.
3. Bart Ehrman, <u>Lost Christianities; the Battle for Scripture and Faiths We Never Knew</u> (2003, Oxford University Press, Inc.), 113 ff.
4. Raymond Brown, S.S., <u>Biblical Exegesis & Church Doctrine</u> (1985, Paulist Press), 32-33.
5. James Gleick, <u>Isaac Newton</u> (2003, Pantheon Books, NY), 107–113.
6. David L. Dungan, <u>Constantine's Bible</u> (2007, Fortress Press), 123.

Bibliography

Bibles

New American Bible (New Testament / Revised), 1986, Confraternity of Christian Doctrine.

New International Version, 1978, New York International Bible Society.

New Revised Standard Version; The HarperCollins Study Bible, 1989, HarperCollins Publishers.

Other References

Alfs, Matthew, Concepts of Father, Son, and Holy Spirit, 1984, Old Theology Book House, Minneapolis.

Barclay, William, The Gospel of John, Volume 1, Revised Edition, 1975, Westminster Press.

Barclay, William, The Gospel of Mark, 1936, The St. Andrew Press.

Barclay, William, The Letter to the Philippians, Colossians, and Thessalonians, Revised Edition, 1975, Westminster Press.

Bowman, Robert M. Jr., and J. Ed Komoszewski, Putting Jesus in His Place, 2007, Kregel Publications.

Brown, Raymond E., S.S., Biblical Exegesis & Church Doctrine, 1985, Paulist Press.

Brown, Raymond E., Jesus, God and Man: Modern Biblical Reflections, 1967, Bruce Publishing Company, Milwaukee.

Brown, Raymond E., S.S., Responses to 101 Questions on the Bible, 1990, Paulist Press.

Edited by Brown, Raymond E., Joseph A. Fitzmeyer, and Roland E. Murphy, The Jerome Biblical Commentary, 1968, Prentice-Hall.

Brox, Norbert, A Concise History of the Early Church, 1995, Continuum Publishing Co., NY.

Chidester, David, Christianity; a Global History, 2000, HarperCollins.

Dungan, David L., Constantine's Bible: Politics and the Making of the New Testament, 2007, Fortress Press, Minneapolis.

Ehrman, Bart D., Lost Christianities; the Battle for Scripture and Faiths We Never Knew, 2003, Oxford University Press, Inc.

Ehrman, Bart D., Misquoting Jesus, 2005, Harper SanFrancisco.

Freeman, Charles, A.D. 381, 2009, Overlook Press.

Edited by Friedrich, Gerhard; translator and editor Geoffrey W. Bromiley, Theological Dictionary of the New Testament, Vol. VI; Πε – P, 1968, Wm. B. Eerdman's Publishing Company, Grand Rapids, Michigan.

Gaus, Andy, The Unvarnished Gospels, 1988, Threshold Books.

Gleick, James, Isaac Newton, 2003, Pantheon Press, NY.

Hanson, R.P.C., The Search for the Christian Doctrine of God, 1988, Edinburgh: T. & T. Clark.

Herring, George, Introduction to the History of Christianity, 2006, New York University Press.

Jones, Timothy Paul, Misquoting Truth, 2007, Intervarsity Press.

Kelly, J.N.D., Early Christian Doctrines, 1978, HarperCollins, NY.

Latourette, Kenneth S., A History of Christianity, 1953, Harper & Brothers.

Lightfoot, J.B., The Apostolic Fathers, 1974, Baker Book House.

Maier, Paul L., *Eusebius, the Church History; a New Translation with Commentary*, 1999, Kregel Publications.

Moynahan, Brian, *The Faith: a History of Christianity*, 2002, Doubleday.

Price, Randall, *Searching for the Original Bible*, 2007, Harvest House Publishers.

Rubenstein, Richard E., *When Jesus Became God*, 1999, Harcourt, Inc.

Schaff, Philip and Henry Dace, *Nicene and Post Nicene Fathers of the Christian Church, Volume IV, St. Athanasius Select Works and Letters*, 1892, Parker & Company.

Shelley, Bruce L., *Church History in Plain Language*, third ed., 2008, Thomas Nelson, Inc.

Sloyan, Gerard S., *The Three Persons in One God*, 1964, Prentice-Hall, Inc.

Stark, Rodney, *Cities of God*, 2006, HarperCollins, San Francisco.

Edited by Visalli, Gayla, *After Jesus; the Triumph of Christianity*, 1992, The Readers Digest.

Scripture Index

An asterisk denotes a passage supporting that Jesus is not God. Double asterisks are particularly strong passages in this regard.

Old Testament

Genesis
1:26	31, 130
1:26-27	21
2:2	62
2:21-22	21
3:22	31
6:2	31
28:10-17	116
35:1	116
35:9*	116

Exodus
3:14*	31, 31, 128
4:22	134
20:2*	31
20:2-4	101
24:9-10	77
24:9-11	116
33:11	77, 117
33:20	77, 117

Deuteronomy
4:15-18	101
6:4*	31
32:4	154
32:43	90

Joshua
10:12-13	209

2 Samuel
22:2, 32, 47	154

1 Kings
3:5	77
3:12	141
9:1-2	78
11:9	117
17:17-23	142
18:36-38	142
22:19	77, 117

Job
4:9	152

Psalms
2:6-7*	32
18:31*	31
22:10*	36
24:10	153
33:6	152
45:6*	75
82:1	104
82:6-7	105
89:27	134
118:22	64
136:3	152

Proverbs
8:22	182
8:22-23	134
8:27, 30	134

Isaiah
6:1, 5	78, 117
7:14	84
9:6	84
11:4	152
42:1-7*	62
42:8	153
43:14	153
44:6	153

Isaiah
48:11	153
49:1-7	62
50:4-9*	62
52:13-53:12	62
53:10*	52
53:12*	52
55:9	9
60:16, 19	221
61:1-3*	62

Daniel
7:9	32, 153
7:13-14*	32

Amos
9:1	78

Micah
5:2	133
5:2-4*	35

New Testament

Matthew
1:22-23	84
2:6	35
2:11	89, 149
3:16-17	97
3:17*	39
4:7*	36, 47
4:10*	47, 90
6:9*	100
6:9-13	40
8:2	55, 89
8:29*	65, 99
9:3	142
9:5	142
9:8	143
9:18	89
10:40*	43
11:25*	35
11:27*	51
12:8	143
12:48-50	41
14:33*	88, 149
15:24*	19, 43
15:25	89
16:15-17	137
16:16*	61, 89
17:1-7	145
17:5*	39
17:25-26*	146
18:26	89
18:32	55
19:16-17*	106
20:19	49
20:20	89
20:21, 23*	53
21:12 ff	115
21:33-45*	63
21:42*	64
22:20	66
22:29	213
22:43-45*	38, 141
23:8, 10*	63
24:34	115, 211
24:36	211
25:31-46	219
26:26	60, 220
26:39,42,44	44
26:63-64*	39, 52
27:38,39,44	114
28:6*	48
28:9	88
28:16	113, 115
28:16-17	88, 149
28:17	51, 78
28:18-19*	111
28:19	14, 112, 113, 117

Mark		Luke	
1:9-11	97	1:31, 32, 35*	39
1:11*	39	1:32*	51, 98
1:24*	98	1:33	85
1:24-25*	65	1:35*	98, 140
2:4-12	143	1:76*	96
2:27-28	143	2:40*	46
3:5	114	2:49	44
3:11*	40	2:52	46
5:6	89	3:21-22	97
5:7*	65, 98	3:22*	39
8:29*	61	4:8*	47, 90
8:38-9:1*	116	4:12*	36, 47
9:2-8	145	4:13	103
9:7*	39, 145	4:18-19	61
9:19	114	4:34*	98
9:23	114	4:34-35*	65
10:14	114	4:41*	39, 65
10:17-18*	106	4:43*	43
10:35-40*	53	5:18-26	143
10:45*	43	6:5	143
11:15 ff	115	6:12*	35
12:1-12*	63	6:35-36	96
12:10	64	7:6	55
12:16	66	8:28*	65, 98, 146
12:29*	199	8:39	146
12:29-30	223	9:20*	61
12:36-37	38, 141	9:22*	49
13:30	115, 211	9:27	211
14:30	114	9:28-36	145
14:36	44	9:35*	39
14:61-62*	15	9:48*	44
14:62	53	10:16*	44
14:68	115	10:21*	35
15:27-32	114	10:22*	51
15:34*	36, 218	12:41-42	55
16:6*	49	18:18-19	217
16:9-20	108	18:19*	199
16:19*	53	19:28 ff	115

Luke
19:44	10, 82
20:9-19*	63
20:17	64
20:24	66
20:42-44	38, 141
21:32	115, 211
22:19	161
22:28-29*	52
22:42	44, 102
22:43-44	108
22:69*	53
22:70*	39
23:34	108
23:39-43	114
23:46*	218
24:50	115
24:50-52	113
24:51-53	88, 89, 150

John
1:1	16, 17, 33, 37, 65, 70, 71, 72, 79, 95, 138, 161, 197, 200, 201
1:1-3	130
1:14	65, 130, 139
1:15	128
1:18	77, 110, 116, 139, 146
1:26-27	129
1:30	128
2:13 ff	115
2:19-22	50
3:13	159
3:14-17	159
3:16*	46
3:17*	43
3:31-35	129
3:34*	43
3:35*	51
4:25-26*	93
5:16-18	79, 105
5:17	63
5:18	145
5:19*	51, 105
5:20-29	106
5:21-23*	149
5:22*	52, 160
5:30*	51
5:44*	35
6:27*	46
6:29*	42
6:35	93
6:38	129, 199
6:38-39	160
6:39*	51
6:41	93
6:44*	43
6:46*	145, 146
6:48	93
6:51-55	144
6:53-54	160
6:57*	43
7:28-29*	43
7:33*	43
7:41	74
7:53-8:11	108
8:12	93, 153, 160
8:19	145
8:23	145
8:24	93
8:26*	43
8:28*	51, 93
8:29*	43
8:38	145
8:40*	46
8:42**	42, 43
8:48	74
8:54**	35

John

8:54-55	57
8:54-58	128
8:58	93
9:4*	43
9:5	93
9:9	93
9:35-41	87
10:7	93
10:11	93
10:14	93
10:14-15	118
10:17-18*	50
10:30	146
10:31-33	80, 104
10:34-36*	79, 104
10:36	105
11:16	73
11:21-22*	47
11:25	93
11:42*	43
12:44-45*	81
12:45	43, 80, 146, 162
12:49*	43
13:3**	51
13:13	55
13:16**	62
13:20*	43
13:34	160, 219
14:1*	35, 199
14:6	2, 142, 219
14:6-7	176
14:7	81
14:9	81, 146, 162, 198
14:10	63, 81
14:13	223
14:23	97
14:28**	51, 62
14:31*	41
15:1-11*	52
15:5*	142
15:16*	51
15:21*	43
16:5*	43
16:27-28*	43
17:1-3	57
17:2*	51
17:3**	33, 35, 42, 120, 159
17:5	129
17:8*	43
17:18*	43
17:20-24	216
17:21*	43
17:23*	43
17:24*	54, 129
17:25*	43
18:5	93
18:8	93
18:28	115
18:36	130
19:14	115
20:17**	37, 120
20:21*	43
20:23	74, 143
20:25	73
20:28	70, 72, 139
20:31**	74
21:22	211

Acts

1:4	113, 115
1:5	116
1:24-25	99
2:24*	48
2:32	49
2:32-33*	54
2:32, 33, 36	15
2:36**	56, 62, 148, 151, 199

Acts
2:38	112
3:13*	54, 62
3:14-15	131
3:15*	49
4:5-6	64
4:10*	49
4:11*	64
5:30	49
5:30-31*	56
5:42	61
7:47-48	95
7:55-56*	54
7:59-60	99
8:14-16	112
9:20*	40, 96
10:1-48	19
10:40*	49
10:48	112
11:16	116
13:16	19
13:30*	49
13:33*	49
13:37*	49
13:46-48	19
16:17	96
17:11	2
17:31*	49
19:5	112
20:21*	47
20:28*	109

Romans
1:4*	40
1:7*	32, 45
1:8*	100
1:9*	47
1:20	197
3:23-25*	44, 59
4:24*	49
5:1*	46
5:10*	60
6:3	112
6:4*	49
6:9*	49
7:4	49
8:3*	43
8:11*	49
8:15-17**	41, 42
8:29*	41, 134, 147
8:32*	44
8:34*	54, 219
9:5	82, 83, 197
9:33	154
10:9*	49, 148
13:11-12	211
15:6**	34
16:17	213
16:27	46

1 Corinthians
1:2	100, 220
1:3*	45
1:7-8	211
1:9*	46
1:11-13	112
1:23-24	135
1:24*	66
1:30*	66
2:8	153
2:9	20
3:1-15	220
3:23*	37, 68
6:14*	49
7:26	211
8:5	21
8:6**	33, 85, 121
10:2, 4	154
11:3**	37, 67
11:24	161
12:4-7	97, 111

1 Corinthians
12:13	112
15:4*	48
15:15*	49
15:20-22*	134
15:22-24	33, 85
15:22-28**	68, 121
15:27	153
15:28*	15, 126
15:35-55	127
15:47-49	132
15:49	42
15:50-52	127
15:57*	46

2 Corinthians
1:2*	45
1:3**	34
1:19*	40
3:4*	46
3:18	126
4:4*	66
4:14*	49
5:15*	49
5:16-21	218
5:18*	46
5:18-19	60
11:31**	34
13:13	46, 97, 111

Galatians
1:1*	49
1:3*	45
1:6-9	213
1:15	46
2:20*	40
3:19-20	63
3:27	112
4:4*	43

Ephesians
1:2*	45
1:3	34
1:3-4	133
1:17**	34
1:20*	54
1:20-23**	56
2:13-18	97
2:16*	60
2:19-22*	64
2:18	111
3:14-16, 21	99
3:21*	46
4:4-6**	33, 85, 120
5:2*	47, 59
5:5*	46
5:20*	46
5:25	40
6:23*	46

Philippians
1:2*	45
2:5-6	76, 138
2:5-11*	155
2:6	10, 16, 81
2:8	44, 102
2:8-9	199
2:9-10	198
2:9-11	15, 56, 149
4:5	211
4:6	99

Colossians
1:3*	34
1:15*	66, 133, 134
1:15-17	131
1:15-17, 19	138
1:20-21*	60
2:6-8	213
2:9	140
2:12*	49

243

Colossians
3:1*	54, 217
3:3	217
3:17*	47, 217

1 Thessalonians
1:1*	45
1:2	45
1:3*	45
3:11*	45
3:14*	45

2 Thessalonians
1:1*	45
1:2*	45
1:12*	45
2:8	152
2:15	213
2:16*	45

1 Timothy
1:1*	46
1:2*	45
1:3-4	213
1:16-17**	83
2:5**	33, 63, 86, 120
3:16	109, 110
6:13	46
6:13-16**	135

2 Timothy
1:2*	45
1:8-10	132
1:13-14	213
2:8	49
4:1*	46

Titus
1:4*	45
2:13	82, 139, 211
2:14	153

Philemon
3*	45

Hebrews
1:1-2	41
1:1-4*	157
1:5*	135
1:5-6	90, 150
1:6	157
1:8	135
1:8-9*	70, 75
2:9*	132, 157
2:10-11*	158
2:14-15	158
2:17-18	158
3:3	132
3:6	132
4:4	62
4:12-13	66
4:15*	102, 158
5:1-10*	59
5:7*	49
5:8*	44
6:19-20*	59
8:1*	54
8:1-2*	69, 158
8:6*	63, 159
9:15*	63
9:24**	37, 59, 69, 159
9:28	69
10:5, 7*	44
10:37	211
12:1-2*	157
12:24*	63
13:20*	49

James
1:1*	37, 45
1:27*	45
5:8	211

1 Peter

1:2*	46
1:3**	34
1:6	211
1:20	133
1:21*	49
2:5*	46
2:6*	64
3:18*	49
3:19-20	222
3:21-22**	37, 54
4:6	222
4:7	211
4:11*	221

2 Peter

1:1-2	84
1:2*	46
1:17*	52

1 John

1:1-2	130
1:1-3	140
1:5	153
2:1*	63
3:2	20, 127
4:9-10*	43
4:14*	44
4:15*	40, 216
5:5*	97
5:7	14
5:7-8	108, 109
5:9	24
5:20**	38

2 John

3*	45

Jude

1*	46
4	83
25*	37

Revelation

1:4	198
1:6**	34
1:14	153
1:17	153
2:28*	51
3:12**	34
3:14	131
4:10-11	92
5:11-14	150
5:14	92
7:10	46
7:10-12*	92
11:15*	46
11:16	92
12:10*	46
14:7	92
15:2-4*	91
19:4	92
19:10	91
19:16	152
21:9	40
21:22*	46, 92
21:23	46
22:1*	46, 92
22:3*	46, 92
22:7	211
22:8-9	91

www.ingramcontent.com/pod-product-compliance
Lightning Source LLC
LaVergne TN
LVHW021809060526
838201LV00058B/3295